Communications in Computer and Information Science   701

Commenced Publication in 2007
Founding and Former Series Editors:
Alfredo Cuzzocrea, Dominik Ślęzak, and Xiaokang Yang

More information about this series at http://www.springer.com/series/7899

Maristella Agosti · Marco Bertini
Stefano Ferilli · Simone Marinai
Nicola Orio (Eds.)

Digital Libraries and Multimedia Archives

12th Italian Research Conference on Digital Libraries, IRCDL 2016
Florence, Italy, February 4–5, 2016
Revised Selected Papers

 Springer

Editors
Maristella Agosti
Dipartimento di Ingegneria
 dell'Informazione
Università degli Studi di Padova
Padua
Italy

Marco Bertini
Dipartimento di Ingegneria
 dell'Informazione
Università degli Studi di Firenze
Florence
Italy

Stefano Ferilli
Dipartimento di Informatica
Università degli Studi di Bari
Bari
Italy

Simone Marinai
Dipartimento di Ingegneria
 dell'Informazione
Università degli Studi di Firenze
Florence
Italy

Nicola Orio
Dipartimento dei Beni Culturali
Università degli Studi di Padova
Padua
Italy

ISSN 1865-0929 ISSN 1865-0937 (electronic)
Communications in Computer and Information Science
ISBN 978-3-319-56299-5 ISBN 978-3-319-56300-8 (eBook)
DOI 10.1007/978-3-319-56300-8

Library of Congress Control Number: 2017937300

Printed on acid-free paper

This Springer imprint is published by Springer Nature
The registered company is Springer International Publishing AG
The registered company address is: Gewerbestrasse 11, 6330 Cham, Switzerland

Preface

Since 2005 the Italian Research Conference on Digital Libraries (IRCDL) has been providing a great opportunity for researchers in the field of digital libraries to present and discuss their current research activities and to envision together further developments. The IRCDL conferences were launched and initially sponsored by DELOS, an EU FP6 Network of Excellence on Digital Libraries, together with the Department of Information Engineering of the University of Padua. Over the years IRCDL has become a self-sustainable event that is supported by the Italian digital libraries community.

The IRCDL 2016 edition, in line with the conference series tradition, was committed to preserving the emphasis on the multidisciplinary nature of the research on digital libraries that has been characterizing the conference over the years. This multidisciplinary nature ranges from computer science to humanities in the broader sense, including research areas such as archival and library information sciences, information management systems, semantic technologies, information retrieval, and new knowledge environments. This is a continued challenge for the DL field and there is the need to continue contributing toward improving the cooperation between the many communities that share common objectives.

IRCDL 2016 hit its target and once more provided the opportunity to explore new ideas, techniques, and tools, and to exchange experiences also from on-going projects. This volume contains the revised accepted papers selected, on the basis of reviewers' comments, from those presented at the 12th Italian Research Conference on Digital Libraries (IRCDL 2016). The conference was organized by the Department of Information Engineering of the University of Florence, Italy, during February 4–5, 2016. The conference was held at the Murate Complex, using the facilities provided by the NEMECH (New Media for Cultural Heritage) Center of Competence established by the Tuscany Region and the University of Florence; the NEMECH Centre promotes the transfer of know-how of research from the university laboratories to the places where cultural goods are exposed and benefited.

The Program Committee comprised 21 members, including representatives of the most active Italian research groups on digital libraries. The Program Committee accepted 70% of the papers presented at the conference for inclusion in this volume, which contains expanded versions of the conference papers. These papers were reviewed again and the results of the final selection are the papers appearing in these proceedings. The topics covered and that reflect the interests of the community are:

– Formal methods
– Long-term preservation
– Metadata creation, management, and curation
– Multimedia

– Ontologies and linked data
– Quality and evaluation
– System interoperability

Here we would like to thank those institutions and individuals who made this conference possible: the committees members, the Department of Information Engineering of the University of Florence, the NEMECH Center of Competence, and the MICC Center of Excellence in the area of new media.

December 2016

Maristella Agosti
Marco Bertini
Stefano Ferilli
Simone Marinai
Nicola Orio

Organization

IRCDL 2016 was organized by the Department of Information Engineering and the Media Integration and Communication Center (MICC) of the University of Florence.

Executive Committee

General Chairs

Simone Marinai	University of Florence, Italy
Marco Bertini	University of Florence, Italy

Honorary Chairs

Maristella Agosti	University of Padua, Italy
Costantino Thanos	ISTI CNR Pisa, Italy

Program Chairs

Stefano Ferilli	University of Bari, Italy
Nicola Orio	University of Padua, Italy

Steering Committee

Maristella Agosti	University of Padua, Italy
Tiziana Catarci	Sapienza University of Rome, Italy
Alberto Del Bimbo	University of Florence, Italy
Floriana Esposito	University of Bari Aldo Moro, Italy
Carlo Tasso	University of Udine, Italy
Costantino Thanos	ISTI CNR Pisa, Italy

Program Committee

Andrew Bagdanov	University of Florence
Stefano Berretti	University of Florence
Rosa Caffo	President of the MICHAEL Culture AISBL
Diego Calvanese	Free University of Bozen-Bolzano
Vittore Casarosa	ISTI CNR Pisa, Italy
Michelangelo Ceci	University of Bari, Italy
Fabio Ciotti	University of Roma Tor Vergata, Italy
Rita Cucchiara	University of Modena and Reggio Emilia, Italy
Nicola Ferro	University of Padua, Italy

Costantino Grana	University of Modena and Reggio Emilia, Italy
Maria Guercio	Sapienza University, Italy
Séamus Lawless	Trinity College Dublin, Ireland
Donato Malerba	University of Bari, Italy
Paolo Manghi	ISTI CNR Pisa, Italy
Antonella Poggi	Sapienza University, Italy
David Rizo Valero	University of Alicante, Spain
Marco Schaerf	Sapienza University, Italy
Gianmaria Silvello	University of Padua, Italy
Anna Maria Tammaro	President at Open Edition Italia
Francesca Tomasi	University of Bologna, Italy
Paul Weston	University of Pavia, Italy

Sponsoring Institutions

University of Florence
MICC Center of Excellence

Contents

Practices

The *Archivio dei Possessori* of the Biblioteca Nazionale Marciana.
A Provenance Database   3
   Orsola Braides and Elisabetta Sciarra

An IT Support for an Exhibition of Illuminated Manuscripts   16
   Chiara Ponchia

Motivating and Involving Users Through Gamification: A Proposal   20
   Andrea Micheletti

Digital Scholarship Innovation and Digital Libraries: A Survey in Italy   31
   Anna Maria Tammaro

Multimedia

Hermeneutic Implications of Cultural Encoding: A Reflection on Audio
Recordings and Interactive Installation Art   47
   Federica Bressan, Sergio Canazza, Tim Vets, and Marc Leman

Searching and Classifying Affinities in a Web Music Collection   59
   Nicola Orio

Searching and Exploring Data in a Software Architecture for Film-Induced
Tourism   71
   Sandro Savino and Nicola Orio

Semantics

An Ontology to Make the DELOS Reference Model and the 5S Model
Interoperable   85
   Maristella Agosti, Nicola Ferro, and Gianmaria Silvello

Realizing a Scalable and History-Aware Literature Broker Service
for OpenAIRE   92
   *Paolo Manghi, Claudio Atzori, Alessia Bardi, Sandro La Bruzzo,
   and Michele Artini*

Stratifying Semantic Data for Citation and Trust:
An Introduction to RDFDF 104
    Dario De Nart, Dante Degl'Innocenti, Marco Peressotti,
    and Carlo Tasso

Formal Components of Narratives 112
    Valentina Bartalesi and Carlo Meghini

Evaluation

Proposal for an Evaluation Framework for Compliance Checkers
for Long-Term Digital Preservation 125
    Nicola Ferro

Towards Sentiment and Emotion Analysis of User Feedback
for Digital Libraries. 137
    Stefano Ferilli, Berardina De Carolis, Domenico Redavid,
    and Floriana Esposito

Layout

Layout Analysis and Content Classification in Digitized Books. 153
    Andrea Corbelli, Lorenzo Baraldi, Fabrizio Balducci,
    Costantino Grana, and Rita Cucchiara

A Study on the Classification of Layout Components for Newspapers 166
    Stefano Ferilli, Floriana Esposito, and Domenico Redavid

Author Index 179

Practices

The *Archivio dei Possessori* of the Biblioteca Nazionale Marciana. A Provenance Database

Orsola Braides and Elisabetta Sciarra[✉]

Biblioteca Nazionale Marciana, Venice, Italy
orsola.braides@beniculturali.it,
elisabetta.sciarra@beniculturali.it

Abstract. In November 2014, the Biblioteca Nazionale Marciana launched a provenance database on the Library's website.

The *Archivio dei possessori* is a project collecting data and photographic records of data referring to the owners of the Library's printed books and manuscripts: bookplates, stamps, ownership and readers' notes, and binding marks. The project – together with other similar projects implemented by Italian and international libraries – aims at reconstructing the origin of the library's rare collections and retracing the history of previous ownership of every single item.

Keywords: Owners' archive · Provenance · Biblioteca Nazionale Marciana

1 Introduction[1]

In November 2014, the Biblioteca Nazionale Marciana launched a provenance database on the Library's website (called Archivio dei Possessori – hereafter AP: http://marciana.venezia.sbn.it/la-biblioteca/cataloghi/archivio-possessori).

The AP is a project collecting data and photographic records of data referring to the owners of the Library's printed books and manuscripts: bookplates, stamps, ownership and readers' notes, and binding marks. The project – together with others implemented by Italian and international libraries – aims at reconstructing the history of the Library's holdings and of every single item. It is part of a broader project supported by the Marciana focusing on the history of its holdings and collections, as well as on single exemplars, and is linked to the cataloguing of ancient printed books in SBN (Servizio Bibliotecario Nazionale), with particular attention being paid to single items, to the cataloguing of manuscripts in NBM (Nuova Biblioteca Manoscritta) and to involvement in the international MEI project (Material Evidence in Incunabula), which aims to reconstruct the history of book circulation in the 15th century through material evidence found in books.

The software was designed from the outset to integrate data from several libraries. Indeed, the Biblioteca Universitaria di Padova has just begun to insert its own data in the AP, and the Fondazione Giorgio Cini in Venice has recently adhered to the project.

---

[1] Paragraph no. 2 is by Orsola Braides; paragraph no. 3 is by Elisabetta Sciarra. Paragraph no. 1 (Introduction) was written by both. All the links to the records and web pages were last consulted on 26th April 2016.

© Springer International Publishing AG 2017
M. Agosti et al. (Eds.): IRCDL 2016, CCIS 701, pp. 3–15, 2017.
DOI: 10.1007/978-3-319-56300-8_1

Today, the AP includes around 850 records, provided with more than 2,500 free access images and is constantly expanding. It catalogues identified and unidentified owners, in order to facilitate recognition. Although data can be simply consulted by browsing, it is also possible to query the system starting with ownership marks, the owner's name and shelfmark. Every record indicates one (or more than one) shelfmark and each is linked to its online cataloguing description. Thus, AP consultation is complementary to catalogue consultation. The AP is supplied with a brief "User's Guide" [1], where common-use abbreviations are also indicated.

2 Provenance Archive Structure

The Marciana bibliographical descriptions, available on the local OPAC – Polo VEA [2] – always record notes related to the items, with specific attention paid to owners and provenance. In the SBN cataloguing system the data related to the owners are exclusively available on the local OPAC, but in the current version of Sebina software in use on Polo VEA they do not appear in the UNIMARC record (UNIversal Machine Readable Cataloguing) [3], where owners and notes containing provenance information are tagged as 317 and Name (Author) is tagged as 702 or 712, depending on "Type" (personal or corporate body names).

A new version of the software – Sebina (3.1) – will be launched shortly for the local OPAC, which supplies the UNIMARC mapping of the owners, in order to enable data search and retrieval. Moreover, this update will provide access to the AP from the OPAC system through a link, whereas for now only the reverse is possible.

Therefore, the AP has been designed to support and complement the online library catalogue. After a period of testing (July–October 2014), it was inserted on the Library's official website in November 2014. At first, it contained 160 records, but by the beginning of 2015 the records had already reached 280 and nowadays they number 850.

The need to create a simple, functional, low-cost database, which includes at the same time detailed descriptions, has led to the creation of a system divided into a small number of fields: owners (personal or corporate body names), type of ownership marks, library and related shelfmark, supported by a series of images.

Querying the AP directly from the Library's website has enabled the development of an easily consultable system, in coordination with Bazzmann srl Venice. Like the Library's website, the AP system is based on Drupal version 7, which assigns a unique code to all data inserted by the librarians in order to facilitate data storage management. A unique code is serially assigned to every item managed by the system: Users/Librarians, Nodes (including images in the owners' records), and taxonomy (connecting "terms" among nodes, such as owners and corresponding shelfmark).

Each item is given its own code, having a different denomination – UID (User Identifier) for librarians, NID (Node Identifier) for nodes and TID (Term Identifier) for taxonomies.

In the same way that users normally consult an online catalogue – without necessarily knowing the main entry – in the *AP* system the access point to the owner's name (main entry) is linked to several added entries, including those available on the items and those derived from external sources, catalogues, and bibliographies. A textual note (Description) is linked to the univocally identified owners, enabling access to external links. What is especially significant for the reconstruction of the history of Marciana and its rare holdings are the "Non identificati" (Unidentified) owners (with single TID), when identity is unknown. The *AP* enables the aggregation and retrieval of items characterized by identical ownership marks, even if they have not been identified under an owner's name. The choice of dealing with Unidentified owners derives from problems arising in the case of a similar SBN entry such as the "unidentified printers' device", which has a single entry linked to several editions, which cannot be catalogued under printers as they are printers' devices, while in the *AP* they may be catalogued under type of ownership mark – Unidentified stamps, Unidentified binding marks etc. – and under image correspondence.

Persons and corporate body names are in authorized form according to Italian Cataloguing Rules (REICAT) [4] and are linked to as many added entries as possible (Fig. 1).

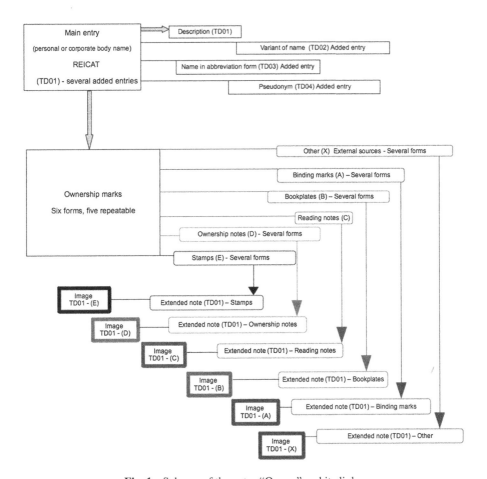

Fig. 1. Schema of the entry "Owner" and its links.

On the basis of this system an "Owner Index" has been designed, which automatically records all entries for the owners. During the creation of a new entry, the option of advanced research for existing entries is available, so as to enable recognition of previously recorded entries.

Considering a constant increase of entries – with 650 main entries, there are more than 450 added entries – if a record is unavailable, the system provides a negative answer. Likewise, when a new entry is being recorded the system checks all available entries so as to avoid creating duplicates.

The "Description" field displays bio-bibliographic data relating to owners. Where owners are unrecorded an indication of the century is provided if possible. We have chosen to create a "free-text field", where librarians can provide links to external sources, in order to provide as much historical and biographical information as possible. Each record is given a sequence number automatically generated by the system, also readable by users, which if deleted or merged is no longer considered by the system.

The field "Ownership marks" is linked to the main entry; this field also includes temporary custody (not only ownership). The field Ownership marks has been divided into six headings, or five plus one that cannot be included under any of the other headings. The headings are as follows:

Other: None of the headings mentioned below, as data is derived from external sources to the book, such as handwritten or printed catalogues;

Binding marks: These include coat of arms, initials, printed names, and representations linked to specific owners;

Bookplates *(ex libris)*: Small labels that bear woodcuts, engravings, and photomechanical prints serially produced and glued onto the volumes, usually on front pastedown, in order to indicate ownership. This heading includes all *ex libris*, as well as *ex dono*, whether armorial or artistic;

Reading notes: Marginalia, annotations, corrections, and drawings;

Ownership notes: Initials, cryptograms, signatures, handwritten annotations (i.e. "Ex libris d.ni…"), hand-drawn, illuminated coats of arms;

Stamps: All kinds of stamps, with no distinction between armorial, and artistic or official stamps, unlike for the *ex libris*.

The only forms of attestation of ownership that can be repeated several times in the same form and whose measurements are recorded, are A–B, D–E (see Fig. 1). Therefore, this system allows librarians to combine together a specific owner (TID01) with six different types of ownership marks, in turn represented in different forms, which is to say that an owner (TID01) can have several bookplates, and thus separate records will be associated to them.

The management of Unidentified owners is especially important in order to study the history of the Library's holdings, as these owners are treated individually according to the ownership marks found in the copies. Thus there are: Unidentified (TID6375) stamps; Unidentified (TID6375) ownership marks; Unidentified (TID6375) reading notes etc., each of them available with one or more images and its own serial number, to allow the maintenance of record data linked to the entry of an already identified owner, in case of recognition (Fig. 2).

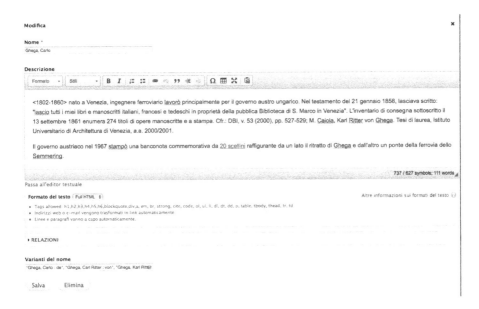

Fig. 2. "Owner" Carlo Ghega [5].

Thus, when creating a record the owner is linked to only one mark of ownership at a time, an extended note referring to such ownership mark, the Library and corresponding shelfmark, and at least one image related to the mark.

The "Extended note", which also includes a "Summary" that is only accessible to librarians – especially useful to condense a series of shelfmarks where there are long notes and multiple references, for example – displays the library code, the shelfmark (not in the standardized form of the online catalogue as this is recorded in the specific field, but in the form of historical catalogues or in the one by which it is known through the bibliography), the exact location of the ownership mark (binding, book spine, leaves etc.) and its complete transcription (Fig. 3). The data may be supplemented by extensive notes with links to external sources. The same field also records external contributions such as Institutions that have consented to the publication of images related to identical ownership mark evidence in their copies, or else scholars that have been responsible for identifying material evidence.

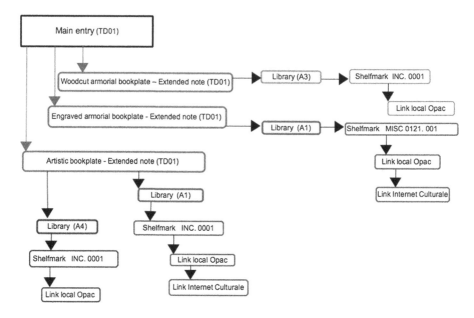

Fig. 3. Example of the schema of "owner" entry, with a type of ownership mark in three different forms, found in three different libraries.

The descriptive record of an owner immediately shows the type of ownership mark linked (Fig. 4).

Fig. 4. Extended note of the owner Carlo Ghega.

The "owner" entry always displays its own TID; this entry can be modified and such a procedure is implied in all the records associated to the same entry.

The "Library and Shelfmark" field lists all the libraries taking part in the *AP* project, therefore each shelfmark is uniquely linked to the library that describes it, as the system filters the selection of existing shelfmarks based on the relevant library. Therefore, records of identical shelfmarks for several libraries – i.e. INC. for incunabula – may exist without creating mistakes. The shelfmark is linked to the URL of the bibliographic description in the local OPAC, as the data of the copies are recorded only in the local OPAC and not in the national OPAC SBN. In cases where the items have been reproduced in digital format, in the local OPAC description corresponding to the data of the digitized exemplar there is a link to the "Internet Culturale" portal. Thus, from the *AP* the user can pass to the local OPAC and from there to the "Internet Culturale" portal to view the whole copy.

As regards Shelfmarks, like the Owners' entries, a consultation Index has been created, from where librarians can select the already existing entries. The system checks the existence of other shelfmarks that may be duplicated in each library when a new shelfmark record is created.

At least one image is linked to each owner, which is the image that is immediately visible to the user carrying out a search. Subsequently, a whole series of other images can be added. The Title of every image is recorded according to the same characteristics as for the Extended note: library code, shelfmark and exact location of ownership mark (Fig. 5).

Fig. 5. Image gallery

Finally, a general list of the records, indicating all data referring to compilers, creations and revisions, shelfmarks and libraries, can be exported into Excel format.

3 Initial Results

The types of ownership marks referring to a single owner can vary, but they all provide different clues to the history of the holdings. A case in point is Cardinal Bessarion's (1403–1472) founding collection housed in the Marciana; his ownership marks on the incunabula (the Cardinal's less famous collection of volumes), are all now collected in *AP* [6]. Only in one case has ownership been attested, thanks to marginal notes on an incunabulum made by Bessarion himself, although this inscription is considered to be of dubious origin [7]. In other cases, his ownership is testified by handwritten notes in two languages, Greek and Latin – the so-called *loci* – which also record the shelfmark in his own library [8]. Although the inventories of Bessarion's library have been published and its transfer to Venice has been thoroughly researched, the transcription of Greek-Latin *loci* on the manuscripts has not yet been completed, nor has a systematic study of the physical structure of the library when it was still in Rome been carried out. A significant number of Bessarion's incunabula are richly illuminated, also with the Cardinal's coat of arms [9] and in two cases with his portrait. Again, there is currently insufficient precise information to indicate the number and nature of the manuscripts bearing his own coat of arms, nor how the various illuminators' commissions, which could be studied through the comparison of images, provide clues to the constant expansion of his collection (Fig. 6).

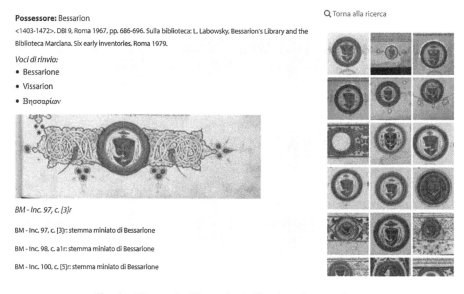

Possessore: Bessarion

<1403-1472>. DBI 9, Roma 1967, pp. 686-696. Sulla biblioteca: L. Labowsky, Bessarion's Library and the Biblioteca Marciana. Six early inventories, Roma 1979.

Voci di rinvio:
- Bessarione
- Vissarion
- Βησσαρίων

Q Torna alla ricerca

BM - Inc. 97, c. [3]r

BM - Inc. 97, c. [3]r: stemma miniato di Bessarione

BM - Inc. 98, c. a1r: stemma miniato di Bessarione

BM - Inc. 100, c. [5]r: stemma miniato di Bessarione

Fig. 6. AP record of Bessarion's illuminated coats of arms.

From the outset identification has been achieved thanks to the possibility of viewing images, and in several cases it has even been possible to link books whose provenance is still uncertain, but which have identical ownership marks.

For example, among the unidentified stamps, an unknown oval stamp [10] seems to have a specific meaning – not necessarily indicating provenance – when it appears on opera librettos in the Marciana, but it can also be found in several copies housed in the Biblioteca Nazionale Braidense, the Fondazione Giorgio Cini in Venice and in the Biblioteca Nazionale Centrale in Rome. If we take the example of the libretto of *Le nozze disturbate*, printed in Venice by Modesto Fenzo in 1766 [11][2], it is seen that the copies in the Fondazione Giorgio Cini, in the Biblioteca Nazionale Centrale in Rome and in the Biblioteca Nazionale Braidense in Milan all bear the same stamp on page 71. Since the stamp also appears on several items of the same edition, it is likely that its use may be attributed to selling practices or to events surrounding publication, rather than to a specific provenance.

What are just as interesting, above all for historical-textual implications, are the dense collation and reading annotations, mostly in Greek, written by an anonymous reader [12] in the margins of two printed editions by Apollonius of Rhodes (Biblioteca Nazionale Marciana, Aldine 510) [13] and Theocritus (Biblioteca Nazionale Marciana, 67 D 187) [14]. The author of the handwritten annotations has not yet been identified, but most likely it must have been a Greek or Italian humanist, who could write in Greek and was interested in the Classics. Highlighting this hand will enable scholars to identify it elsewhere in the future (Fig. 7).

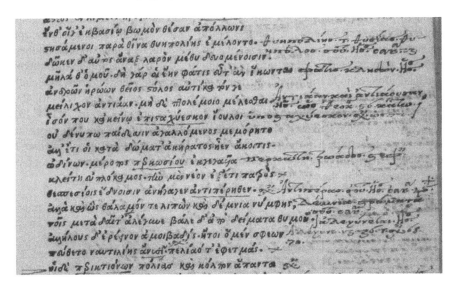

Fig. 7. Biblioteca Nazionale Marciana, Aldine 510, f. c6r, detail.

---

[2] It is available in SBN Music under BID MUS0320672, linked to the copies in the Biblioteca Nazionale Braidense in Milan (digitized copy), in the Fondazione Giorgio Cini in Venice (digitized copy) and in the Biblioteca Nazionale Marciana; it is also available in the SBN Early printed book under BID BVEE060946, linked to the item in the Biblioteca Nazionale Centrale in Rome (digitized copy).

Numerous annotators – previously considered anonymous – have already been identified [15]. The project catalogues both manuscripts and printed books, and the *AP* is a means of enhancing the collections of autographs owned by the Library and spread across its collections. That is why the *AP* can be also used as a collection of autographs of scholars, above all Italian. A case in point is an autograph letter (Marc. It. XI, 207 [=4071]) from Aldus Manutius (1450–1515) held in the Marciana, but also a printed book with glosses in which Manutius made annotations in the margin in Greek and Latin [16, 17]. To him we can also attribute a single note of correction in Aldine 132, f. a8v [18] (Fig. 8).

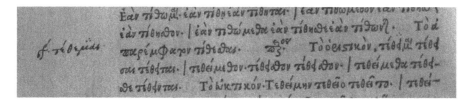

Fig. 8. Biblioteca Nazionale Marciana, Aldine 132, f. a8v, gloss by Aldus Manutius.

The *AP* has already discovered private collections of books which have long been considered lost. For example, not only does the Marciana house several autograph manuscripts by Marin Sanudo the Younger (1466–1536), as well as other manuscripts belonging to him, but it also holds at least one printed book belonging to him; all these documents were donated by Girolamo Contarini [19, 20]. Up to that time printed books which had belonged to Marin Sanudo had only been traced to other libraries, especially the Biblioteca Colombina in Seville and other European collections [21–30], but strangely enough not in the Marciana, where the holding of origin, acquired in 1843 [31, 32] has yet to be explored thoroughly. The finding of this first printed book suggests that there may be others. If the wording "Est Marini Sanudi Lionardi Filij" were not enough, Sanudo's identity is supported by the comparison with one of the numerous autograph manuscripts housed in the Marciana (It. VI, 277 [=5806]) (Fig. 9).

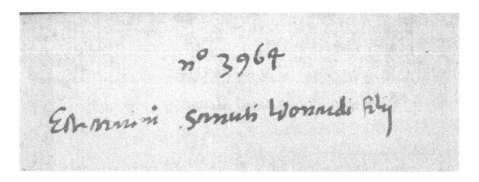

Fig. 9. Biblioteca Nazionale Marciana, Misc. 379.3, f. [I]r, ownership note by Marin Sanudo.

The project has also resulted in a revision of acquired data of even those holdings whose history and events had been considered well-researched. Such is the case of Apostolo Zeno's library (1668–1750). He donated his own private collection to the library of the Observant Dominicans of the Zattere (Gesuati), writing a will in 1747 and implementing it in 1750 before his death, when more than 200 crates full of books were taken to the conventual library. Subsequently, due to the suppression of religious institutes, the whole Dominican library was stripped and the books were dispersed, largely ending up in the Marciana, Zeno's books included [33]. These are marked with a woodcut bookplate, with many variants [34]. Most of Zeno's books were marked with two handwritten cryptographic annotations, one "&" [35] and a "rhombus" [36]; there is also another one that is less documented [37]. Finally, Zeno's Miscellaneous books were famous for a handwritten index on the book spines and the shelfmark in Zeno's library, together with a further index added on the upper flyleaves [38]. Although incomplete, the catalogue of this vast private collection is housed in the Marciana, Marc. It. XI, 289–293 (= 7273–7278).

The presence of cryptographic notes and of the bookplates had long been considered as a sign of provenance of Zeno's library. The fact that both have also been found in books printed after his death has led scholars to reinterpret the sources concerning the history of his library.

Apostolo Zeno's bequest to the Collegio del Santissimo Rosario would have been implemented only if the library had been kept separate from the one already existing in the convent, if the friars had compiled a new catalogue and had not sold the duplicates. Thus, Andrea Corner, Zeno's step-brother, sued the Dominicans because he wanted the library back; his sons carried on the legal case until 1770. The legal proceedings are still partially available in printed format [39]. To defend themselves from Corner's accusations of selling the duplicates and not keeping the library separate, the friars wrote a large number of memoirs, thoroughly documenting the whole question (Marc. It. X, 55 [=6531]). Thus, in the manuscript housed in the Marciana, on f. 23v it is written: "*Allora fu che, per evitare ogni qualunque minima confusione tra questi nuovi libri, e quelli del Sig.r Apostolo, si pensò di marcare i libri zeniani, uno per uno niun accettuato con un viglietto contenente il nome e cognome del gran benefattore* Apostoli Zeni" (It was then, to avoid even the least confusion among these new books, and those owned by Mr Apostolo, we thought of marking the volumes by Zeno, one by one, with a piece of paper containing the name and surname of the great benefactor *Apostoli Zeni*); the bookplate was therefore inserted by the Dominicans of the Collegio del Santissimo Rosario, after they received Zeno's library, in order to clearly distinguish his books from the other collections. It is likely that some books not belonging to Zeno were marked by mistake, or others that were acquired with the money raised from the duplicates sold, as happened in other conventual libraries. We can also attribute to the Dominicans the manuscript cryptograms that distinguish Zeno's copies: the "&" is in fact attested in the same Marc. It. X, 55 (=6531) [40].

The above-mentioned handwritten catalogue of Zeno's collection remains the most reliable, albeit incomplete source, and should be consulted more often in order to determine provenance.

The Biblioteca Nazionale Marciana welcomes records by researchers who wish to contribute to the *AP*. Indeed, in 2015 it published two records concerning handwritten annotations made by Francesco Petrarca and Giovanni Boccaccio that were identified by Marco Cursi in the manuscript Marc. Gr. IX, 29 (=1007).

References

1. http://marciana.venezia.sbn.it/la-biblioteca/cataloghi/archivio-dei-possessori/guida-alluso
2. http://polovea.sebina.it/SebinaOpac/Opac
3. Hopkinson, A.: UNIMARC Manual: Authorities Format. 3rd edn., pp. 326–328, 538–539. K.G. Saur, München (2009)
4. Regole italiane di catalogazione: REICAT. ICCU, Roma (2009)
5. http://marciana.venezia.sbn.it/immagini-possessori/688-ghega-carlo
6. Labowsky, L.: Bessarion's Library and the Biblioteca Marciana. Six Early Inventories, Roma (1979)
7. Bessarionis cardinalis Sabini & patriarche Constantinopolitani Capitula libri primi aduersus calumniatorem Platonis incipiunt feliciter, [Roma], Conradus suueynheym: Arnoldus pannartzque magistri Rome impresserunt talia multa simul. Petrus cum fratre Francisco Maximus ambo huic operi aptatam contribuere domum, [post 1469] (Biblioteca Nazionale Marciana, Inc. 219)
8. http://marciana.venezia.sbn.it/immagini-possessori/107-bessarion
9. http://marciana.venezia.sbn.it/immagini-possessori/106-bessarion
10. http://marciana.venezia.sbn.it/immagini-possessori/94-non-identificati
11. Le nozze disturbate, dramma giocoso per musica del signor Gaetano Martinelli romano da rappresentarsi nel Teatro Giustiniani di San Moisè il carnovale dell'anno 1766, in Venezia, appresso Modesto Fenzo (1766)
12. http://marciana.venezia.sbn.it/immagini-possessori/376-non-identificati
13. Apolloniou tou rodiou Argonautika, meta tōn palaiōn te, kai panu ōphelimon scholiōn. Apollonij rhodij Argonautica, antiquis una, & optimis cum commentarijs, Venetiis, in aedibus Aldi, et Andreae soceri, mense Aprili 1521
14. Tade enestin, entē garou sē biblō. Theokritou eidyllia, hex kai triakonta. Tou autou epigrammata ennea kai deka, [Roma], analōmasi … Kornēliou Benignou … pronō de kai dexiotēti, Zachariou kalliergou tou krētos, Ianuariou (1516)
15. Sciarra, E., Livres imprimés annotés: notes de propriété, notes de lecture, notes d'étude dans la base de données des possesseurs de la Biblioteca Nazionale Marciana, in: Le changement dans les écritures et les manuscrits du Moyen Age et de la Renaissance (jusqu'à 1550 environ), Berlin, 16 au 19 septembre 2015 [being printed]
16. Aldi Manucii Bassianatis Romani Institutiones grammaticae, Impressae Venetiis summa diligentia, septimo Idus Martias (1493)
17. Venier, M.: Nota Manuziana. Lettere Italiane **56**(4), 618–653 (2004)
18. In hoc uolumine hæc insunt. Theodori introductiuæ grammatices libri quatuor. Eiusdem de mensibus opusculum sanequampulchtum [sic]. Apollonii grammatici de constructione libri quatuor. Herodianus de numeris, Impressum Venetiis, in ædibus Aldi Romani, octauo Calendas Ianuarias (1495) (Biblioteca Nazionale Marciana, Aldine 132)
19. http://marciana.venezia.sbn.it/immagini-possessori/7-contarini-girolamo
20. http://marciana.venezia.sbn.it/immagini-possessori/538-sanudo-marino
21. Crescini, V.: Marin Sanudo precursore del Melzi. Giornale storico della letteratura italiana **5**, 181–185 (1885)

22. Wagner, K.: Sulla sorte di alcuni codici manoscritti appartenuti a Marin Sanudo. La Bibliofilia **73**, 247–262 (1971)
23. Wagner, K.: Altre notizie sulla sorte dei libri di Marin Sanudo. La Bibliofilia **74**, 185–190 (1972)
24. Wagner, K.: Nuove notizie a proposito dei libri di Marin Sanudo. La Bibliofilia **83**, 129–131 (1991)
25. Padoan, G.: La raccolta di testi teatrali di Marin Sanudo. Italia medioevale e umanistica **13**, 181–203 (1970) (after in id., Momenti del Rinascimento Veneto. Antenore, Padova, 68–93 (1978))
26. Caracciolo Aricò, A.: Marin Sanudo il giovane: le opere e lo stile, Studi veneziani n.s. **55**, 351–390 (2008)
27. Harris, N.: Marin Sanudo Forerunner of Melzi. La Bibliofilia **95**, 1–37, 101–145 (1993), **96**, 15–42 (1994)
28. Contò, A.: Ancora sui libri di Marin Sanudo. La Bibliofilia **96**, 195–199 (1994)
29. Caracciolo Aricò, A.: Inattesi incontri di una visita alla biblioteca di Marin Sanudo il Giovane. In: Pelusi, S., A. Scarsella, A. (a cura di) Humanistica Marciana. Saggi offerti a Marino Zorzi. Biblion, Milano, 79–91 (2008)
30. Caracciolo Aricò, A.: Il terzo visitatore nella biblioteca di Marin Sanudo il giovane e nelle sue camere. Studi veneziani n.s. **62**, 375–418 (2011)
31. Wiel, T.: I codici musicali Contariniani del secolo XVII nella R. Biblioteca di San Marco in Venezia. F. Ongania, coi tipi de' Fratelli Visentini, Venezia (1888)
32. Bibliotheca universa Hieronymi Contareni Marciae anno 1843 testamento legata. In: Valentinelli, G., Codices MSS. latini. Bibliotheca manuscripta ad S. Marci venetiarum. ex Typographia commercii, Venetiis, 163–169 (1868)
33. Zorzi, M.: La Libreria di San Marco: libri, lettori, società nella Venezia dei Dogi. Mondadori, Milano, 367–368 (1987)
34. http://marciana.venezia.sbn.it/immagini-possessori/5-zeno-apostolo
35. http://marciana.venezia.sbn.it/immagini-possessori/4-zeno-apostolo
36. http://marciana.venezia.sbn.it/immagini-possessori/9-zeno-apostolo
37. http://marciana.venezia.sbn.it/immagini-possessori/394-zeno-apostolo
38. http://marciana.venezia.sbn.it/immagini-possessori/209-zeno-apostolo
39. Per li rr. pp. Domenicani Osservanti delle Zattere (1770) (Biblioteca Nazionale Marciana, Marc. It. X, 55 [= 6531])
40. Barzazi, A.: Dallo scambio al commercio del libro. Case religiose e mercato librario a Venezia nel Settecento. Atti dell'Istituto veneto di scienze, lettere ed arti, Cl. di scienze morali, lettere ed arti **156**, 42–44 (1997–1998)

An IT Support for an Exhibition of Illuminated Manuscripts

Chiara Ponchia[✉]

Department of Cultural Heritage, University of Padua, Padua, Italy
chiara.ponchia@unipd.it

Abstract. The paper reports on a project which envisages the employ of IPSA, an originally high-specialized digital archive and web environment purposely developed for professional researchers in History of Art and History of Illumination, to enrich and complete visitors experience in a forthcoming exhibition of illuminated manuscripts.

Keywords: IPSA digital archive · Illuminated manuscripts · User engagement

1 Introduction

IPSA (*Imaginum Patavinae Scientiae Archivum*) is a digital archive of illuminated codices which includes both astrological and botanical manuscripts produced mainly, but not exclusively, in the Veneto region and Northern Italy during the XIV and XV centuries[1]. It was initially designed for a specialist public of scholars and researchers [1] with specific interest in manuscripts and illuminations.

Due to involvement in the CULTURA project[2], it was decided to open IPSA to other categories of users, such as non-domain professional researchers, students and the general public. To accomplish this difficult task, it was essential to draw a precise profile of the different types of user and to study new ways of requirements elicitation: therefore different kinds of interactions with the final users were designed, such as trials with groups of undergraduate students and master students and interviews with domain and non-domain professional researchers [2, 3]. At the same time IPSA had been progressively changed according to the collected user requirements, and as a result it became more intuitive and user-friendly and it can now be used for other purposes than those for which it was designed.

Currently, the research team of the University of Padua which contributed to CULTURA is planning to furtherly extend IPSA possibilities as a tool for scientific knowledge dissemination and to use it in a forthcoming exhibition of illuminated manuscripts to be held in Padua in the spring of 2017.

---

[1] http://www.ipsa-project.org/.
[2] http://www.cultura-strep.eu/.

© Springer International Publishing AG 2017
M. Agosti et al. (Eds.): IRCDL 2016, CCIS 701, pp. 16–19, 2017.
DOI: 10.1007/978-3-319-56300-8_2

2   Changing IPSA for Non-professional Users

IPSA was created purposely for professional researchers of History of Art and History of Illumination to allow them to study and compare the illuminated images held in the archive: it was therefore originally conceived as a high-specialist tool.

It should be underlined that IPSA is not only a digital archive, but also a web-application that enables users to work with images in different ways. In History of Art disclosing new relationships between images brings about further knowledge on a specific artistic period, on a painter or an illuminator, and so on: as a consequence, according to this specific user requirement in IPSA professional researchers are provided with tools that allow to link images and to annotate them [4]. Such a specialist tool turned out to be difficult to use by non-professional users, such as students and members of the general public, and overall the frequent interactions with these user categories highlighted the necessity of working on simplification. In fact these types of users generally do not have particular interest in illuminations or manuscripts but they can find fascinating to browse a beautiful collection if the experience is made easier.

Thus changes and improvements to the system aimed at smoothing users' interaction with IPSA. For example, in the original IPSA professional researchers, accustomed to the complexity of illuminated manuscripts which sometimes can hold hundreds of illuminations, when consulting a manuscript catalogue file were shown a wall with the thumbnails of all the illuminations. This was perceived as confusing by non-professional users, so the list of images of a manuscript evolved from a simple wall of all images, very heavy to render and to explore, to a partial wall of twenty images, much faster to render. Browsing the images was made ever easier by a drop-down menu from where users can select the *folio* of the illumination they want to see (Fig. 1).

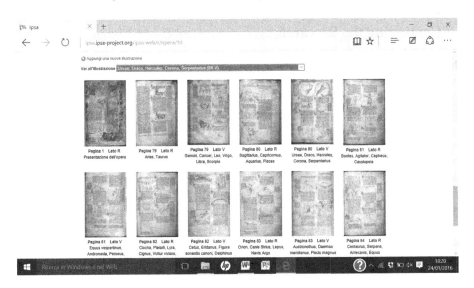

Fig. 1. Wall of images in the new IPSA version

3   Preparing an Exhibition

In the context of the project *Word and Image in the Padua University Library manuscripts*, funded by the University of Padua through a post-doctoral research grant, an exhibition of illuminated manuscripts is currently being organized for the spring of 2017.

The project aims at continuing and completing the research work started with the exhibition *Splendore nella regola. Codici miniati da monasteri e conventi nella Biblioteca Universitaria di Padova* (2011), which presented the results of a study on twenty-four manuscripts held in the Padua University Library [5]. Considering the positive outcomes of this experience, the research is now being extended to those manuscripts that weren't included in the previous exhibition, with the objective to achieve a complete catalogue of the illuminated manuscripts of the Library and to present them to the citizenry.

The research will focus on a *corpus* of approximately thirty manuscripts, from the XIII to the XVI century, not sumptuous but with a wide range of different decorations and illuminations which testify their various provenances. The *corpus* includes liturgical and religious books –e.g. the *Sermones* by Saint Leo Magnus or the *Summa de casibus conscentiae* by Bartholomaues de San Concordio - but also books for studying, such as the *Codex repetitae praelectionis* by Justinan or the *Expositio super libros Aristotelis de generatione et corruptione* by Paolo Veneto. Illuminations can be very different as well: beautiful French gothic illuminations, XIV century Bolognese illuminations, Renaissance decorated pages with the typical ornamental pattern of the *bianchi girari*, etc. These manuscripts testify to the great flow of books in Padua in the Middle Ages and in the Renaissance connected to the presence of national and international students attending the University and the schools in the local convents.

4   Continuing the Research

The exhibition will be a valuable chance to further evaluate IPSA as a tool for scientific knowledge dissemination and to collect useful data for new investigations.

In fact, one of the main limits of illuminated manuscripts exhibition is the impossibility to show all the illuminations of the manuscripts: usually manuscripts are opened on their most beautiful illuminated pages, but the others, although equally interesting, remain hidden. Facing this problem not only requires difficult decisions to select the best opening page of each manuscript, but it also gives the visitors the wrong perception that manuscripts are like small paintings, while they are completely different objects, a treasure that it is possible to appreciate only leafing through the pages and discovering their many illuminations, decorated initials and other kinds of embellishments.

To this respect, IPSA will be a precious tool to complete visitors' experience: all the manuscripts in the exhibition will be digitized and a new instance of IPSA will be created to collect all the digitized images and their metadata (description of the manuscript, description of its illuminations, date, provenance, calligrapher, illuminator, etc.). Thus visitors, via a computer terminal located in the exhibition, will be able to see all the illuminations hidden in the manuscripts they just saw and to easily get information on them. Visitors' interaction with IPSA will be possibly made more involving through the development of engaging systems for presenting the content, such as narrative and serious games. Afterwards, visitors will be asked to fill in a satisfaction questionnaire, in order to obtain new data for further improvements to IPSA.

Acknowledgements. The author would like to thank Professor Maristella Agosti and Professor Federica Toniolo for their support and the useful discussions on many aspects related to the project.

The work reported has been partially supported by the CULTURA project as part of the Seventh Framework Programme of the European Commission, Area "Digital Libraries and Digital Preservation" (ICT-2009.4.1), grant agreement no. 269973.

References

1. Agosti, M., Benfante, L., Orio, N.: IPSA: a digital archive of herbals to support scientific research. In: Sembok, T.M.T., Zaman, H.B., Chen, H., Urs, S.R., Myaeng, S.-H. (eds.) ICADL 2003. LNCS, vol. 2911, pp. 253–264. Springer, Heidelberg (2003). doi: 10.1007/978-3-540-24594-0_24
2. Ponchia, C.: Engaging the user: elaboration and execution of trials with a database of illuminated images. In: Agosti, M., Esposito, F., Ferilli, S., Ferro, N. (eds.) IRCDL 2012. CCIS, vol. 354, pp. 207–215. Springer, Heidelberg (2013). doi:10.1007/978-3-642-35834-0_21
3. Agosti, M., Benfante, L., Manfioletti, M., Orio, N., Ponchia, C.: Issues to be addressed for transforming a digital library application for experts into one for final users. In: Ioannides, M., Fritsch, D., Leissner, J., David, R., Remondino, F., Caffo, R. (eds.) Proceedings of 4th International Conference - Progress in Cultural Heritage Preservation (Euromed 2012), Brentwood, UK, pp. 89–94 (2012)
4. Agosti, M., Ferro, F., Orio, N.: Annotating illuminated manuscripts: an effective tool for research and education. In: Marlino, M., Summer, T., Shipman, F. (eds.) Proceedings of 5th ACM/IEEE-CS Joint Conference on Digital Libraries (JCDL 2005), pp. 121–130. ACM Press, New York (2005)
5. Toniolo, F., Gnan, P. (eds.): Splendore nella regola. Codici miniati da monasteri e conventi nella Biblioteca Universitaria di Padova. Biblioteca Universitaria di Padova, Padua (2011)

Motivating and Involving Users Through Gamification: A Proposal

Andrea Micheletti[✉]

Department of Cultural Heritage, University of Padua,
Piazza Capitaniato 7, 35139 Padua, Italy
andrea.micheletti@unipd.it

Abstract. This contribution addresses the problem of motivating users to collaboratively enrich a digital collection of multimedia items. The first part of the paper provides some insight on the motivations which drive people to actively participate in social networks. It pays particular attention to the narcissistic act of exhibitionism aimed at social recognition. It then briefly reviews the state of the art on gamification, which plays an important role in improving user involvement. In the final part, it introduces a project that aims at enriching a digital collection on fashion, by letting the users play a question/answer game. It also includes a brief illustration of the expected results and the planned methods to gather data.

Keywords: Crowdsourcing · Gamification · Reputation · Consensus

1 Introduction

Self-assertion is a life-long process that does not seem to end with adulthood and maturity. Emulation and imitation are facets of this process and are related to the concept of meme, introduced by Richard Dawkins in his 1976 book "The Selfish Gene" as: the minimal unit of information, which allows cultural transmission from generation to generation through imitation. Imitation corresponds to an information transfer from the external environment to our brain and, in the special case of emulation of a cultural model, satisfies a number of additional needs: looking more self-confident, being accepted by the group of peers, elaborating a personal style and in general affirming and reproducing identity models. Facebook seems answer these needs, giving a spotlight to anyone who was hiding in the anonymous backyards of existence. The need to assert our identity and to consolidate our status through consensus is shared by real and digital life. For instance, just before buying a new dress or posting a new comment on Facebook we probably ask ourselves the same questions: "What will others think about me?" and "Are the things I am going to buy/say in line with my reputation?". Although this parallelism can be extended to most real life activities, consumption plays a central role in the way our identity is put under stress. As Marina Bianchi noted in her preface to Scitovsky [26]: consumption

© Springer International Publishing AG 2017
M. Agosti et al. (Eds.): IRCDL 2016, CCIS 701, pp. 20–30, 2017.
DOI: 10.1007/978-3-319-56300-8_3

is a complex task, which encompasses the way of life, the time-use and energy, investment in knowledge and information, ability to relate to others and the meaning of one's identity. In the case of fashion consumption, people express a number of specific needs: affirmation of identity, the desire to emulate and feel a sense of belonging, demonstration of competences and, more in general, public consensus. Similar needs motivate participation in any social network, with the difference that the network represents both the ends and the means, depending whether it is used as a channel to transmit information or as an information source. The prototype system presented in this paper starts from these premises and tries to merge them in a social network about fashion using a gamified question and answer approach. Before introducing the system, the paper presents a theoretical background on identification, identity and consensus with the aim of showing that these general concepts can motivate other projects in which users willingly share their knowledge in order to enrich a multimedia collection. Projects such as Wikipedia or Open Street Maps have demonstrated that a large number of non-experts can, under certain conditions, be as effective and precise as a small group of experts [24,28]. Although this particular project is about fashion, most of the idea can be applied to any other thematic collection, such as the ones hosted by digital libraries.

2 Identification and Projection

In its earliest days, when the Internet offered a small range of file transfer and communication services that were used by a relatively homogeneous population of early adopters, human-computer interaction researchers tended to treat both services and users monolithically. They implicitly assumed that all Internet use had similar effects on most users [15,16]. However as Internet services became richer and users more heterogeneous, researchers began to ask whether different types of Internet use, (e.g. communication with family and friends, meeting new people, and finding information) had different effects on those, varying in demographics and social resources [4,18]. Social network sites and research on their impact have reached a similar inflection point. Social network sites are designed to connect people with friends, family, and other strong ties, as well as to efficiently keep in touch with a larger set of acquaintances and new ties. Therefore, they have strong potential to influence users' social capital and the psychological well-being that often flows from social capital [7,9]. Social capital corresponds to the actual or potential resources which are linked to a durable network of more or less institutionalized relationships of mutual acquaintance or recognition [5]. It is the benefit derived from one's position in a social network, the number and type of ties one maintains, and the resources those ties themselves possess [29]. Investment in social capital seems to be one of the drives of our actions, both in the real and virtual life [3]. A direct consequence is the birth of an inflated social self, which tries to expand to the new territory of social networks [10]. This paradigm shift represented a huge opportunity for those who understood that consumption, of goods and culture, does not stop at the financial level.

Consumption is an act of identity, which may express either genuineness or forgery but cannot be limited to a monetary transaction [10].

2.1 Identity

The connection between brand and consumer is strengthened by the psychological and social meanings that the consumer ascribes to the brand. We are involved in a relationship with the vinyl, the toothpaste, the scarf we buy [19]. Brands build our identity rather than produce our goods. The transformation from simple factory name to identity builder has been described by Naomi Klein [19]. In XIX Century, the first large-scale advertising campaigns in US aimed at selling goods, not ideals. Marketing just had to inform consumers about the benefits they could gain through purchases. Brand names were displayed on goods, but they had little influence on consumers' choices. With the Ford factory and mass production of basically identical goods, advertising needed to transform from a source of information into a means of persuasion, promotion and valorization. Brand identity played a central role in this shift [19] and consumption evolved from a way to express richness and success to a way to express (true or false) identity [10].

2.2 Group Identity and Consensus

Two additional concepts are required to better define the concept of belonging: role and identification. Roles regulate interactions among individuals [3] and provide rules for structures, encounters and collisions [23]. They are the scripts, followed by all individuals, made of social expectations, actions, manners based on our position in a society. Depending on the meaning we give to our behaviour as consumers, we play different roles, which can confirm or negate the representation of ourselves that we are giving. Roles change through time. For instance, expressions like "being fashionable" that were popular some years ago have been replaced by expressions like "being a fashion addict", and the same idea of "fashion" is replaced for the younger generation with the idea of "fad" (i.e. a short-lived craze for a particular look) [10]. In each role they play, consumers are not alone. From being confined inside the family boundaries, consumption and sharing is becoming a collective behaviour [10]. In the Web 2.0 era, consumption is increasingly detached from an actual purchase and more and more associated with identity aspects, for instance belonging to a brand community. This identification with a group, based on sharing just for the pleasure of it with no hidden agenda, is one major aspect of new digital media also because digital objects (i.e. recordings in a music digital library) can be replicated an infinite number of times without losing quality. Moreover, sharing with the group both what we have and what we know is becoming a pleasure without the expectation of reciprocity, an openness based on the selfless approach [10]. This sense of belonging, which is also shared by online communities and has been called emotion community, is balanced by an opposite drive: consumption and participation as a narcissistic act of exhibitionism in order to be socially recognized [10]. Social consensus can be obtained in two ways. First, by promoting our image through the construction of a forged identity, based on shallow and external aspects, that can be quickly created thought advertising actions [12]. Second, by promoting our reputation through the construction of an authentic identity; reputation takes time to be built although it can be quickly lost [13] and it is based on behaviour and actions [11]. The creation of consensus in the fashion field has been compared to a game, where players cooperate and compete with the goal of promoting their image and increase their reputation depending on their consumption, their style, their ability to forecast tendencies and so on [20].

3   Users Engagement

Game dynamics are shared by other fields, obviously sports but also social networks. It seems that videogames train us to wait for rewards for each action we do, to look for even illogical achievements. According to Bernard Suits [27]: "playing a game is the voluntary attempt to overcome unnecessary obstacles". The starting point is that reality is trivial in its linearity, while games challenge us to tackle a number of goals in a parallel world. Games can be classified depending on the number of players (from single player to massive multiplayer), on the required hardware (from bats and balls to computers and portable devices), on the environment (from outdoor to game rooms and personal rooms) and on the required time (from a few minutes for each play to several hours to complete a complex game).

3.1   Gamification

Gamification is defined as the use of game elements and game design techniques in non-game contexts [30]. Its goal is to transform boring and repetitive activities into something more fun and engaging as games usually are. Points, badges and leaderboards are part of the process, but fun and engagement require the design of a coherent game experience [22]. Gamification is becoming very popular. It is envisaged that, only in the US, the investment in gamification systems will exceed 2.5 billion dollars [21] with an increasing interest also in the Italian market [2]. The number of games increases as well. According to AESVI [1] half of the European population between 16 and 29 and about one third of the population between 30 and 49 had played a videogame at least once in the previous six months. Consumption has been promoted through gamification for many years through trans-toying [14,25], which the transformation of daily use products into puppets, animals and board games [6]. Another technique is advergaming, for instance the "3D Vince Carter" game launched by Nike, where real games are used to promote visits to the brand's website or to make the public more product aware [8]. Going towards these directions, fashion catalogues have been enriched by colouring books, paper figures to cut out QR codes linked to interactive web sites. Moreover, products have been created from videogames characters and, at the same time, testimonials and logos become characters of new videogames [17].

4 A Social Network for Fashion

In the light of the above mentioned considerations, I decided to venture into the design and development of a social platform about fashion with the collaboration of a computer engineer and a database expert. The project is still in an early development stage and it is based on the idea to build a platform comprising elements typical of social games, social networks, online communities and question/answer sites. The aim of the project is to spread the knowledge about celebrities' outfits to a wide public in a simple, intuitive and entertaining way. The aim is also to provide the users with a powerful tool to find and share their

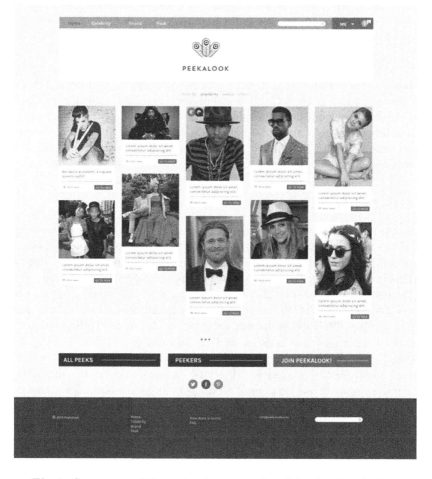

Fig. 1. Cover page of the under development social network web site.

knowledge about valid cheap alternatives to the original outfits. The home page of the social network, also called "cover page", is shown in Fig. 1. The website is composed of different kinds of pages, the most important being the "celebrity page" and the "brand page" (the latter shown in Fig. 2). Both pages can be created and maintained directly by users and are composed of:

- A picture depicting the celebrity or the logo of the brand.
- A brief description or biography.
- The most popular/recent threads of discussion about the brand or celebrity.
- Links to similar or related brands and celebrities.

The main kind of page in the website is however the "peek page" (Fig. 3), which is the name the project uses to address the discussion page.

To create a new thread (and a new peek) the user has to upload a photo of a celebrity and then ask the community for information about the outfit of said celebrity. This is where the social game begins, with users trying to give the best answers. Users can classify their answers into of these three categories:

- **This one:** the answer links to the exact brand which produced the garment.
- **Alike:** the answer links to a brand producing a similar and often cheaper alternative to the exact one.
- **Just Comment:** the answer was made just to participate in a discussion.

By giving either a "this one" or an "alike" answer, users enter a social game which challenges them to prove their knowledge about brands and fashion in general and helps to increase the enjoyment of the users' experience. Voting is the second part of the game, and every answer can be voted by other users who choose the best or most pertinent one, while casting out the incorrect information. The voting process has two aims: on the one hand, it elects and rewards the users who gave the best answers, extending their engagement; on the other hand, it validates the answers so that only useful and correct knowledge emerges.

4.1 Exporting the Experience

At its core the project is essentially based on its own digital library. This library, as we already discussed earlier, is composed of two main entities: celebrity and brand. Much like what happens in other structured libraries, these two entities are filled in by the authors. What is then the contribution users can give to the system? The main problem with most libraries is that, while they are fully structured, they still miss some forms of refined cataloguing or unconventional links between the entries they contain. This occurs because the amount of work needed to make such cataloguing is simply prohibitive for the small communities who create and manage the data. So, would it be possible to have a big number of users do the job for us? The internal structure of the project is specifically conceived to allow users to discuss similarities between items of the database and create links that can be used to get better analysis of the correlations between data. When we strip the structure of the project, which is depicted

Fig. 2. A brand's dedicated page.

in Fig. 4, from its particular nomenclature we can see that it can be applied to any similar project like libraries of music, books, documents. Users ask questions about entries in the library and get answers from other users who create associations with other entries based on similarities or other appropriate criteria. The answers are then reviewed through votes cast by the community. It is even possible to consider the opportunity to allow the best users, emerging from the voting scheme, to insert new items into the collection. This entire process is enveloped in a gamified frame which involves the users and encourages them to actively participate in the cataloguing process. This is beneficial for the library

Fig. 3. Example of a peek page.

in two different ways: it distributes the workload of the cataloguing amongst the entire community and it provides the analysts with genuine and often unbiased information.

4.2   Expected Results and Evaluation Methods

The project presented is still in a prototypical phase and for this reason there is no available data yet to analyze. However successful examples of the application of gamification and the feedback gathered from a small selected base of users who had a brief experience with the prototype suggest that the proposed idea can be expected to produce significant results.

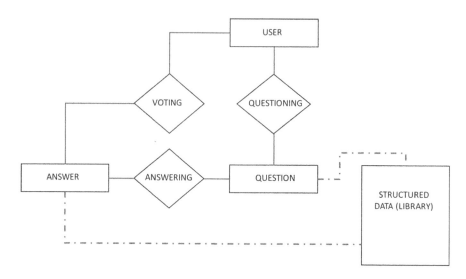

Fig. 4. Excerpt of the E-R schema for the underline database.

- To improve user engagement: by implementing an achievement and reward system we appeal to the need to be socially recognized by exhibiting one's competence in a given field. This should both increase user engagement and enjoyment and motivate them to participate in the cataloguing process even without monetary payment.
- To refine and expand the extent of the current forms of cataloguing: we expect to be able to channel the knowledge users have to obtain a deeper, wider and more refined cataloguing of the data. Users may also provide some unconventional cataloguing criteria, developing new interesting links between items included in our libraries. This would especially apply to cultural fields like music, fashion, films etc.

To evaluate the actual results in an empirical way we plan to use two different approaches. On one side we will be analyzing statistical data directly from the portal and the database. This will give us a quantitative measurement of the number of users who actively participate in the cataloguing process and the number of produced classifications. On the other, we will administer questionnaires to evaluate user engagement and enjoyment, gathering their feedback in order to compare it to non gamified systems.

Acknowledgements. The author wishes to thank Dario Urbani, from the Department of Information Engineering of the University of Padua, for his contribution in developing the system and his useful insights on how to interpret the results.

References

1. AESVI: Video gamers in Europe (2010). http://www.aesvi.it/cms/view.php?dir_pk=902&cms_pk=1171. Accessed 13 Jan 2017
2. ANES: Marketing trends, le tendenze degli investimenti marketing delle aziende italiane (2012). http://anes.it/upload/file/ANESMonitor/ANES_Monitor_MarketingTrends_2012.pdf. Accessed 13 Jan 2017
3. Berger, P.L., Luckmann, T.: La realtà come costruzione sociale. Il Mulino (1966)
4. Bessière, K., Kiesler, S., Kraut, R., Boneva, B.S.: Effectes of internet use and social resources on changes in depression. Inf. Commun. Soc. **11**(1), 47–70 (2008)
5. Bourdieu, P.: The forms of capital. In: Richardson, J., (ed.) Handbook of Theory and Research for the Sociology of Education, pp. 241–258. Greenwood Press, New York (1986)
6. Buganè, G.: Ufficio marketing & comunicazione. Principi, attività e casi di marketing strategico e operativo. Hopeli (2006)
7. Burke, M., Marlow, C., Lento, T.M.: Social network activity and social well-being. In: Proceedings of the 28th International Conference on Human Factors in Computing Systems, CHI 2010, Atlanta, Georgia, USA, 10–15 April 2010, pp. 1909–1912 (2010)
8. Eberlein, K.: La considerazione dell'infanzia nella nostra società: quando bambino fa rima con consumo (2014)
9. Ellison, N.B., Steinfield, C., Lampe, C.: Connection strategies: social capital implications of facebook-enabled communication practices. New Media Soc. **13**(6), 873–892 (2011)
10. Fabris, G.: La società post-crescita. Consumi e stili di vita. EGEA (2010)
11. Frombrun, C., Rindova, V.: Constructing competitive advantage. Strateg. Manag. J
12. Gregory, J.R., Wiechmann, J.G.: Branding Across Borders: A Guide to Global Brand Marketing. McGraw-Hill Professional, New York (2002)
13. Invernizzi, G.: L'individuazione dell'assetto strategico dell'azienda. McGraw-Hill (2004)
14. Ironico, S.: Come i bambini diventano consumatori. Editori Laterza (2014)
15. Katz, J.E., Aspden, P.: A nation of strangers? Commun. ACM **40**(12), 81–86 (1997)
16. Kraut, R., Patterson, M., Lundmark, V., Kiesler, S., Mukopadhyay, T., Scherlis, W.: Internet paradox: a social technology that reduces social involvement and psychological well-being. Am. Psychol. **53**(9), 1017–1031 (1998)
17. Maestri, A., Polsinelli, P., Sassoon, J.: Giochi da prendere sul serio. Gamification, storytelling e game design per progetti innovativi. Franco Angeli (2016)
18. McKenna, K., Bargh, J.: Coming out in the age of the internet: Identity "demarginalization" through virtual group participation. J. Pers. Soc. Psychol. **75**(3), 681–694 (1998). Annual Meeting of the Society-for-Experimental-Social-Psychology, Toronto, Canada, Oct, 1997
19. Naomi, K.: No logo. BUR Biblioteca Univ. Rizzoli (2012)
20. Pedroni, M.: Coolhunting. Genesi di una pratica professionale eretica. Franco Angeli (2010)
21. Research, M.: Gamified engagement (2012). http://m2research.com/Gamification.htm. Accessed 13 Jan 2017
22. Roganti, P.: Gamification Semplice: Game design applicato in contesti non ludici (2014)
23. Romania, V.: Le cornici dell'interazione. La comunicazione interpersonale nei contesti della vita quotidiana. Liguori (2008)

24. Savage, N.: Gaining wisdom from crowds. Commun. ACM **55**(3), 13–15 (2012)
25. Schor, J.: Nati per comprare. Salviamo i nostri figli, ostaggi della pubblicità. Apogeo (2005)
26. Scitovsky, T.: The Joyless Economy: The Psychology of Human Satisfaction. OUP, USA (1976)
27. Suits, B.: The Grasshopper: Games Life and Utopia. Broadview Pr, Calgary (2014)
28. Surowiecki, J.: The Wisdom of Crowds. Anchor, New York (2005)
29. Weber, M.: Economia e società. Comunità. Donzelli (2005)
30. Werbach, K., Hunter, D.: For the Win: How Game Thinking Can Revolutionize Your Business. Wharton Digital Press, Philadelphia (2012)

Digital Scholarship Innovation and Digital Libraries: A Survey in Italy

Anna Maria Tammaro[(✉)]

UNIPR CoLab Centre, University of Parma, Parma, Italy
`annamaria.tammaro@unipr.it`

Abstract. A profound change is happening in the world of scholarly communication, where the object of scientific communication is no longer a linear text, although digital, but a networked digital object-centered that consists of text, data, images, videos, blogs. This is stimulating the innovation of scholarly communication workflow also called "Digital scholarship". This change is likely to deeply modify the nature and the role of digital libraries and their relationship with the national research platforms (CRIS), thematic data center and other stakeholders. The paper presents the findings of a survey about the needs and practices of scholars in Italy, as part of the international Project 101 Innovations in Scholarly Communication. The impact of digital scholarship on digital libraries has to be understood and the digital libraries' mission could be that of how different knowledge representations could be combined, queried, stored and re-used, in virtual collaborative spaces.

Keywords: Digital scholarship · Open science · Digital libraries

1 Introduction

A profound change is happening in the world of scholarly communication, where the object of scientific communication is no longer a linear text, although digital, but an object-centric network, consisting of text, data, images, videos, blogs, etc.

"Digital scholarship" is the term defining the innovation of scholarly communication and it is invoked by those advocating for open access to scholarly knowledge such as. Charles Bailey's Digital Scholarship[1] [2] as well as those promoting collaborative research methodologies in the research lifecycle. Science has entered a "fourth paradigm" that is more collaborative, more computational, and more data intensive [5, 6] than the previous experimental, theoretical, and computational paradigms. This emerging scientific paradigm is often referred to as Open Science, e-science or e-research [5, 6].

This change is likely to deeply modify the nature and the role of the digital libraries and its relationship with the national academic research platforms (such as CRIS Current Research Information System), publishers and/or thematic data center. This paper advocates that connectivity is the technological foundation of digital scholarship and argues that the characteristics of modern science are data-centric, multidisciplinary, open,

---

[1] http://digital-scholarship.org.

M. Agosti et al. (Eds.): IRCDL 2016, CCIS 701, pp. 31–43, 2017.
DOI: 10.1007/978-3-319-56300-8_4

network-centric and heavily dependent on internet technologies. A Digital Library that supports scholars should be composed of interconnected discipline-specific data spaces, to enable more effective scholarly communication, to include, for example, enhanced papers and books, better links to data, the publication of software tools, mathematical models, protocols and workflows, and facilitating research collaboration by means of social media channels. The main functionality of a digital library as "knowledge and learning" infrastructure should have the ability to effectively and efficiently support a linking environment, openness, resource sharing and collaboration.

1.1 Background

Issued in 2011, the Future of Research Communication and e-Scholarship [4] group is a community of scholars, librarians, archivists, publishers and research funders. The group published a Manifesto[2] offering a comprehensive vision of post-Gutenbergian scholarly communication. It forecasts:

> "a future in which scientific information and scholarly communication more generally become part of a global, universal and explicit network of knowledge can be explicitly represented, along with supporting data, software, workflows, multimedia, external commentary and information about provenance. In this world of networked knowledge objects, it would be clear how the entities and discourse components are related to each other, including relationships to previous scholarship".

The Manifesto also outlines six key problems that prevent scholarly communication from achieving its full potential:

- how scholarship is evaluated;
- current copyright constraints;
- the financial aspects of scholarly publishing;
- the mechanisms for assessing the quality and value of researchers;
- how scholarly data, information, and knowledge are (or could be) represented;
- how readers, users, authors, editors and computers can interact with these representations;
- and how different knowledge representations could be combined, queried, stored and reused.

Force11 is collaborating with the Digital Library Federation DLF to provide their unique perspectives in scholarly communication. Understanding the new workflow of the scholars is important for digital libraries that want to support the innovation of **digital scholarship.**

An online complement to the Force11 Manifesto, the European Web site "101 Innovations in Scholarly Communication - the Changing Research Workflow"[3], has been prepared by Jeroen Bosman and Bianca Kramer[4], both from Utrecht University Library in the Netherlands [3]. The website and the infographic with the same name visualize

---

[2] https://www.force11.org/about/manifesto.

[3] http://dx.doi.org/10.6084/m9.figshare.1286826.

[4] Bosman is the subject librarian in the Geosciences Library branch; Kramer, in the Life sciences and medicine branch.

how innovation is taking place across the research cycle, according to 6 phases of the research workflow:

- collection of data & literature,
- analysis,
- writing,
- publishing & archiving,
- outreach,
- and assessment.

Using this map, Bosman and Kramer have created some typical workflow examples that show how existing innovative tools and platforms could have been used for different approaches: traditional, modern, innovative, experimental research workflows.

For example, a traditional workflow would use Web of Science, SPSS, Endnote 7 and Microsoft Word, Nature, ResearcherID, and Journal Citation Reports at each stage, respectively. However, modern, innovative workflows would use different tools such as Google Scholar, Google Books, Figshare, and Altmetrics. Furthermore, the most important developments in the six research workflow phases are discussed by Bosman and Kramer in the visualization. Some of the developments include:

- *Trends*: Increased use of social discovery tools and scholarly social media
- *Expectations*: More use of "publish first, judge later" and more open and post-publication peer review
- *Opportunities*: Using repositories for institutional visibility
- *Technology* is disrupting scholarly research and communications with trends like the increased use of social recommendations and circumvention of traditional publishers.

This overview of the Bosman and Kramer infographic evidences the current processes of innovation, disruption, diffusion, consolidation, competition and success of digital scholarship, including Altmetrics and other tools for research assessment.

2   New Opportunities for Digital Libraries

Digital libraries are designed to improve the methods of collecting, storing, and organizing information in digital forms and to make information available for searching, retrieval, and dissemination via communication networks. They cover information creation, access, sharing and reuse, and archiving and preservation for information and data. Libraries have always been at the intersection of research, publishing, career advancement and technical advancement within the academy. Often they act however as intermediary, instead of gaining insight into patrons' research practices, and to be embedded in the research cycle in a "proactive" way.

Bosman and Kramer [3] have also evidenced the current and expected services that digital libraries can offer to digital scholars, distributed in the workflow of the research: preparation, discovery, analysis, writing, publication, outreach, assessment. In this workflow, digital libraries can do more than the present intermediary role in discovery services. The authors have classified the innovative and traditional digital libraries services in four classes:

1. Advice: this includes commenting and review tools, systematic reviews, biblio-metric analyses, annotation tools, collaboration writing tools, journal selection, checking copyr, authors ID, researcher profiles, altmetrics monitoring, peer review models, citation analysis.
2. Infrastructure: it includes access mechanism, collaboration platforms, providing a repository, Open Access journal incubator, Open Access fund.
3. Spaces: such as meeting spaces, collaborative work environment.
4. Training: traditional and altmetrics advice and tutorials, search strategy and techniques, discovery tools, selecting evaluating sources, reference management, researchers profile.

How are digital libraries reacting to the different behaviour of scholars? Some examples of digital libraries supporting digital scholarship include: support to publishing activities, research data curation, open data publication, semantic technologies, support to research evaluation.

Many digital libraries have also turned towards advancing new models and platforms for knowledge dissemination either in conjunction with or in addition to their local university presses [10]. Library Publishing Coalition [8][5] is an independent, community-led membership association to support an evolving, distributed range of library publishing practices and to further the interests of libraries involved in publishing activities on their campuses.

Some examples di digital libraries supporting digital scholarship include: publishing activities, research data curation, opening catalogue data using semantic technologies. The principal transformations in digital libraries are now being enabled by advanced linking and semantic technologies. SHARE consortium of university libraries coordinated by the University of Naples is involved in linked open data publishing together with university presses tools. Linked Open Data in libraries, archives and museums (LODLAM[6]) [9] continues to be a fast growing area of organizational and technological change, having a major impact on the way digital libraries are transforming themselves adapting to new seeking behaviour of faculty and opening the services to new typologies of research, discovery and access tools (Fig. 1).

Research Data Management (RDM) is now part of the research process, and aims to make the research process as efficient as possible, with two objectives: to support the University community's visibility of scholarship and to extend the University's research results outreach, in the context of the third mission. Research data curation is important for institutions as well as for researchers. RDM roles exist in almost every university today and many digital libraries are supporting the changing scenario of the research data management. In the U.S. and Canada, individual large academic research libraries often lead these activities [1]. In 2014, the Scholarly Communication and Research Infrastructures Steering Committee of LIBER in Europe published 11 case studies on Research Data Management[7] [7].

---

[5] http://www.librarypublishing.org.

[6] The LODLAM acronym was coined in the fall of 2010 by Jon Voss http://lodlam.net/about/.

[7] http://libereurope.eu/committees/scholarly-research/research-data-management-case-studies/.

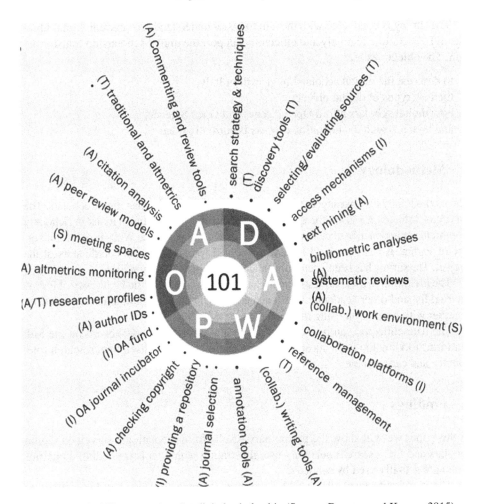

Fig. 1. Digital library services for digital scholarship (Source: Bosman and Kramer 2015)

2.1 Aims and Objectives

The paper supports the vision of the digital library as a virtual research space, that would enable scalable and innovative research of scholars, within digital collections and using innovative tools. Very much intended as a conversation starter, the paper is presenting the first findings of a survey investigating how digital scholarship is evolving in Italy. The survey is a follow up of a Workshop held in Parma in 2013, trying to understand the transformation of digital scholarship.

The survey is conducted with the aim to better understand how current digital libraries in Italy could effectively and efficiently support the digital scholarship transformation. The objectives are:

- to describe the digital scholarship growth in Italy,
- the new types of digital objects,
- how digital scholars afford Open Access and Open Science,
- and how research data curation process is currently done.

3   Methodology

The methodology has investigated the needs and workflows of Italian digital scholars. The survey of scholars has used the questionnaire prepared by 101 Innovations in Scholarly Communication which has been translated into Italian and put on the Website of the University of Parma. It has been used a customized URL prepared by the coordinators of the Project. The survey has been open from January 2016 until February 2016.

The invitation to fill the questionnaire has been distributed to the University of Parma internal list and other academic lists (such as AIUCD Digital Humanities Association) together with promotion using the social media tools.

The data collected can be explored through a user-friendly dashboard on the Silk platform[8] to view the full data sets as charts, and filtering on discipline, research role, country and career stage.

4   Findings

In this paper we will show the preliminary results from the national survey on digital scholars and the research tools they use, illustrating which tools (including altmetrics tools) are actually used by scholars.

The worldwide respondents to Kramer and Bosman Project "101 Innovations in Scholarly Communication" were 22.663. The Italian scholars responding to the questionnaire were 525, covering all disciplines as illustrated by the Fig. 2: Areas of the Italian respondents.

Results have been grouped according to the level of innovation of the processes compared to the traditional organization; innovation is defined by Bosman and Kramer [3] in this way:

Actually change 'the way it's Always Been done' - e.g. user-driven, different business models, changes in the sequence of research activities, shifting stakeholder roles".

4.1   Open Science in Italy

The "openness" paradigm is definitely the most important challenge for the transformation of scholarly communication, involving not only open ways of publication but also

---

[8]   http://dashboard101innovations.silk.co/.

Discipline(s)

- ⬤ Social Sciences & Economics
- ⬤ Medicine
- ⬤ Life Sciences
- ⬤ Arts & Humanities
- ⬤ Engineering & Technology
- ⬤ Physical Sciences
- ⬤ Law

Fig. 2. Areas of the Italian respondents

changing the traditional flow of research and involving various actors with different responsibilities from traditional organization.

Results show (Fig. 3) that there is a positive attitude of Italian scholars towards the Open Access (72%) and the Open Science (77%). However the most used type of publication (Fig. 4) continues to be the journal article in academic journals, with peer review and impact factor, while Open Access journals (Gold and Green road) remain a minority experience. The preferred publishing channels depend on disciplinary differences, with IEE the favorite channel, ACM and ACS for the Areas of Science and Technology. The humanistic Area continues to prefer books as typology of publication, with the favorite channels of publication indicated in Casalini Digital and the University Press (Fig. 4).

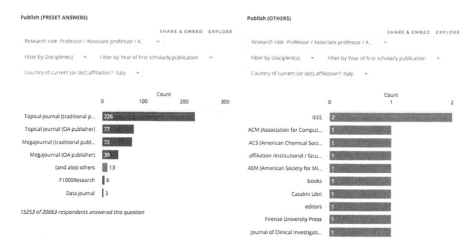

Fig. 4. Preferred typologies of publication

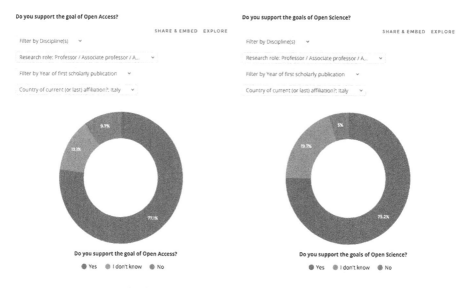

Fig. 3. Open Access and Open Science attitude

Interestingly, the open cycle of scholarly communication has already had an impact on Italians scholars for sharing and collaborating with research results and for the ways of storage that are used. For archiving research publications the preference is for institutional repositories and Department website (Fig. 5), together with ResearchGate, Academia.edu, Dropbox, etc.

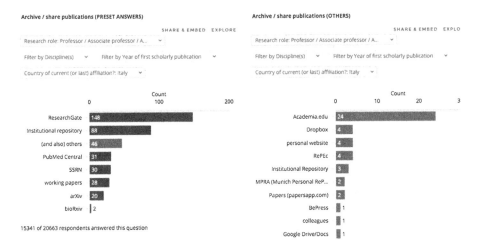

Fig. 5. Archiving preferences

For data and code sharing (Fig. 6), all respondents use non-institutional platforms, with preferences ranging from Github and Fligshare to include Academia.edu, Research-Gate, Dropbox and Google Drive. The only exception is the preference for the Department website as institutional infrastructure.

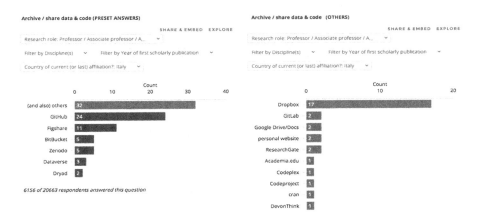

Fig. 6. Sharing research data and code

4.2 Discovery and Access Tools

For research and access to publications, Italian scholars now have several possibilities. It is surprising to note that the first search is done in Google Scholar, followed by other tools such as Scopus and Web of Science. The library catalog is one of the last source: the Italian scholars listed Worldcat-OCLC, which the Italian academic libraries are participating to (Fig. 7). Instead, the access behavior to the identified academic literature still continue to prefer the library, through access to licensed digital resources. In some cases scholars even prefer to pay publishers for the needed item (Fig. 8). Other access tools include Google books and other specific bibliographical tools of the discipline, together with the preference of direct contact with author by mail or in presence.

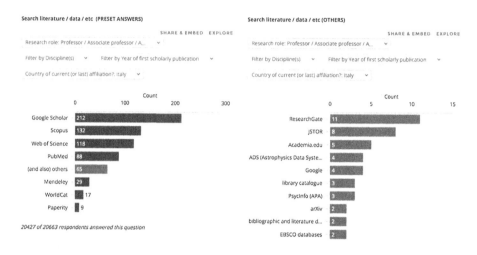

Fig. 7. Preferred discovery tools

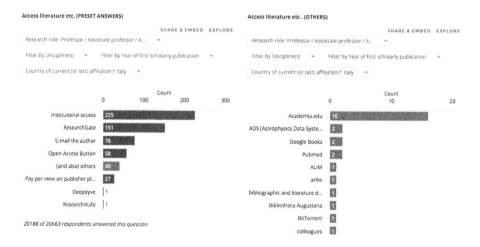

Fig. 8. Preferred access tools

4.3 Dissemination and Outreach

The infrastructure for the dissemination of the research results, seems to depend almost totally from the three academics favorite social media: Blog, Twitter, and Wikipedia (Fig. 9). The personal Web site and the site of the Department continue to be the only preferred institutional channels for this activity.

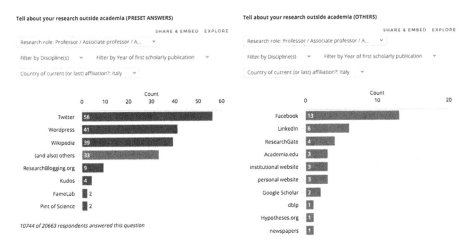

Fig. 9. Preferred dissemination tools

5   Discussion

Trying to reply to the research objectives of the survey, the survey has given evidence:

- to describe the digital scholarship growth in Italy,
- the new types of digital objects,
- how digital scholars afford Open Access and Open Science,
- and how research data curation process is currently done.

5.1   Digital Scholarship Growth

The findings have given a picture of the transformation of the scholarly communication in Italy, adapting to the Open Science paradigm, with clear trends very similar to the international innovation workflow. Evaluation of research results however is not changing and this is an organizational challenge in Italy.

5.2   New Types of Digital Objects

Journals article and books remain the preferred typology of publications respectively in Science and Technology and in Humanities sectors. There are however also new channels of collaboration and dissemination such as Blog, Research Data repositories, personal and departmental website, academic social media.

Disciplinar, contextual and individual differences need to be further researched.

5.3 Research Data Curation Process

The infrastructure weakness for archiving and sharing research data seems evident, due to the digital libraries absence. Digital libraries will need a strong re-organization for participating to the new scholarly communication process.

5.4 Copyright Issue

The Open Access and Open science movement does not seem to have much opposition among Italians scholars who participated in the survey, while it seems that there is a positive attitude for sharing research results, now carried out through tools like ResearchGate and Academia.edu.

6 Conclusions

In conclusion, digital libraries are now absent from the digital scholarship workflow.

The digital libraries' mission could be that of how different knowledge representations could be combined, queried, stored and re-used, in virtual collaborative spaces. From a more traditional concept of library they have to transform toward the vision of digital libraries integrated in the research workflow. The digital library concept could be that of virtual collaborative spaces, where different knowledge representations could be combined, queried, stored and re-used.

Digital libraries have very many opportunities to participate in the transformation of scientific communication, and above all can bring added value to the communication of science and improve the impact of the research results obtained in their institutions. Further study could investigate the many opportunities of digital libraries to participate "proactively" in the transformation of scientific communication, and bringing added value to the scholarly communication, improving the impact of the research results achieved in their institutions.

References

1. Association of Research Libraries: E-science and data support services: a study of ARL member institutions Association of Research Libraries, Washington, DC (2010). http://www.arl.org/storage/documents/publications/escience-report-2010.pdf
2. Bailey, C.: Digital Scholarship Blog. http://digital-scholarship.org
3. Bosman, J., Kramer, B.: 101 Innovations in Scholarly Communication - the Changing Research Workflow (2015). https://figshare.com/articles/101_Innovations_in_Scholarly_Communication_the_Changing_Research_Workflow/1286826
4. Future of Research Communication and e-Scholarship (FORCE 11) (2011). https://www.force11.org/about/manifesto
5. Hey, T., Tansley, S., Tolle, K.: The Fourth Paradigm: Data-Intensive Scientific Discovery. Microsoft Corporation, Redmond (2009a). http://research.microsoft.com/en-us/collaboration/fourthparadigm/4th_paradigm_book_complete_lr.pdf

6. Hey, T., Tansley, S., Tolle, K.: Jim Gray on eScience: a transformed scientific method. In: Hey, T., Tansley, S., Tolle, K. (eds.) The Fourth Paradigm: Data-Intensive Scientific Discovery, pp. xix–xxxiii. Microsoft Corporation, Redmond (2009b). http://research.microsoft.com/en-us/collaboration/fourthparadigm/4th_paradigm_book_complete_lr.pdf
7. LIBER Scholarly Communication and Research Infrastructures Steering Committee: 11 case studies on Research Data Management (2014). http://libereurope.eu/committees/scholarly-research/research-data-management-case-studies/
8. Library Publishing Coalition (LPC). http://www.librarypublishing.org
9. LODLAM. http://lodlam.net/about/
10. Okerson, A., Holzman, A.: The Once and Future Publishing Library. Council on Library and Information Resources (2015). http://www.clir.org/pubs/reports/pub166/Pub166-pdf

Multimedia

Hermeneutic Implications of Cultural Encoding: A Reflection on Audio Recordings and Interactive Installation Art

Federica Bressan[1(✉)], Sergio Canazza[2], Tim Vets[1], and Marc Leman[1]

[1] IPEM - Department of Musicology,
Ghent University, Ghent, Belgium
`bressanf@dei.unipd.it,`
`{tim.vets,marc.leman}@ugent.be`
[2] Department of Information Engineering,
University of Padova, Padua, Italy
`canazza@dei.unipd.it`

Abstract. This article proposes a reflection on what the emerging discipline of digital philology means to the encoding, preservation and access of multimedia cultural material. In particular, it focuses on audio recordings and interactive multimedia installations. It describes a general setup required for the re-mediation of audio recordings that supports a *philologically informed* methodology for long-term preservation, and it points out some of the major challenges posed by interactive art in long-term preservation. This article extends the discussion started at the IRCDL in 2013, in the light of the authors' activity during this time.

Keywords: Digital philology · Digital humanities · Audio documents · Interactive multimedia installation art

1 Introduction

Digital libraries are defined by dedicated and often sophisticated storage, retrieval and management systems. But most importantly they provide their users with trustworthy content. Trustworthiness applies both to the *accuracy* of the data and to the *reliability* of the content, i.e. to its (cultural) *meaning* within a specific context or community. The services offered by digital libraries are only effective if the content they manage meets the requirements of integrity, consistency and reliability (a term related to the much more complex concept of *authenticity*). This article proposes a reflection on what the emerging discipline of *digital philology* means in the *preparation* of cultural digital material aimed at digital libraries. In particular, this article evolves the discussion on digital philology started at IRCDL in 2013, in the light of the authors' activity in the field of the digital humanities during this time.

© Springer International Publishing AG 2017
M. Agosti et al. (Eds.): IRCDL 2016, CCIS 701, pp. 47–58, 2017.
DOI: 10.1007/978-3-319-56300-8_5

1.1 Cultural Encoding

The way in which inscriptions are photographed and text corpora are transcribed and encoded, as well as the way in which a sound recording is re-mediated[1], "is crucial for the way in which these research objects will be studied in the future" [1, p. 11]. In other words, the digital representation of data (the bit stream) and the organization and presentation of the data (the *cultural interfaces* [2]) are not neutral with respect to the final perception that users have of the 'real' or 'original' object, which may often not be available for comparison. In addition, the relationship between the digital objects and the real objects they allegedly represent "is not only very complex, it also develops over time" [1, p. 10]. In order to ensure that the electronic sources, that scholars and the general public are getting more and more accustomed to refer to for their research and personal interest, meet the requirements of *authoritativeness, accuracy and reliability* (see Sect. 2), it is necessary to define what makes a digital document authoritative, accurate and reliable. This definition implies the understanding of what the document means in its cultural context and it is therefore not limited to technical questions that only computer scientists and engineers should be in charge of. "Digital philology" is the multidisciplinary research field that addresses this problems. While philology ("without adjectives" [3, p. 65]) has a long tradition, the reflections about *digital* philology are very recent, and so is the academic production about it. There is much work to be done in order to provide new methodological and operative tools to scholars whose aim is to author *electronic editions* based on digital sources. The shift that the electronic medium introduces in how texts are coded and accessed goes beyond their presentation, affecting the *perception of the content.*

The existing scientific literature about digital philology is mainly limited to written texts[2]: making a parallel in the audio domain, any recording of the same event can be considered as a *variant copy* of the "original" event, thus being the equivalent of a manuscript for textual criticism. It remains to be defined what the *text* can be for a multimedia interactive artwork where the aesthetic experience (the "effect") is only achieved in a dynamic process and with the combination of physical and virtual elements that may change their micro- and macro-relations over time.

Unlike the field of text encoding, analysis and philology, where a longer tradition provides ascertained references to scholars and researchers, the field of audio documents long-term preservation is relatively new and it lacks a similar background of knowledge and experience. Audio documents have gained the status of documentary sources only recently, and it is not uncommon to find

---

[1] Re-mediation is the process of transferring the [acoustic] information from a medium onto another medium.

[2] To overcome this gap, some of the authors have organised the First International Workshop on Digital Philology for the Preservation of Sound Archives (IPPSA) on the 17th of September 2015 near Padova in Italy. The Workshop aims to be a place for discussion on the present and future trends in digital philology: http://csc.dei.unipd.it/ippsa/index.html.

that texts and icons are still considered "first class" sources while sound recordings are considered "second class" sources for scholarly studies. Unless certain criteria to ensure that digital audio (and other multimedia) can be considered *authoritative, accurate and reliable* sources [4], this trend may be hard to get rid of in the future.

Besides the on-going multiplication of digitized documents, the number of born digital documents is also increasing, making the definition of procedures for storage and cataloguing even more urgent because a "physical original" is never available for comparison. The hybrid nature of multimedia installations imposes the consideration of a grey zone between analogue, digitized and born digital documents, i.e. cultural material where meaning is found in the integration of physical and virtual elements.

This article is organized as follows: Sect. 2 explores the concept of digital philology, with specific connections with traditional philology and textual criticism. Section 3 discusses some concepts involved in the preparation of the cultural digital materials. Section 3.2 instantiates these concepts in the preservation of audio documents and introduces some challenges posed by interactive installation art.

2   Digital Philology

"Where lies the truth – or where lie the truths – about philology?" [5, p. 3]

The philological activity of text comparison goes back to Antiquity: one of the means to compare texts was to present them in parallel columns. For example, Origen's third-century *Hexapla* presented six versions of the Old Testament (including the Hebrew text, a transliteration of the Hebrew in Greek characters, and four Greek translations) in parallel alignment [6]. The comparison, a core activity in the philological analysis, is implicitly based on a notion of "text". According to philology, any text is a variant copy of an archetypal text, which the philologist is trying to reconstruct. Before even mentioning sound and music, let us consider how the adjective "digital" is associated to the term "philology". First of all, the simple fact that a text is represented in electronic format and examined on a computer screen rather than a paper book does not justify the expression "digital philology". Just as an electronic reproduction of Leonardo's Mona Lisa is not "digital art". The medium is certainly not neutral, and we are addressing this issue in a few lines, but the adjective "digital" next to philology needs to have a greater impact on the concepts and the methods of philology. It is, in fact, a new research field, stemming out of the combination of two disciplines: philology and computer science. Computer science brings to the table its approach, some of its concepts and methodologies – not only technology. From its part, philology is changed in its own concepts and methods thanks to the encounter with computer science. "Going beyond, discovering the new frontiers of philology, does not depend on the computer. It depends on us, the scholars" – said Marcos Marìn in 2001, when apparently "many people [were] still looking at computers as enemies of the intellectual activity that has characterized the approach to texts from the beginning. We are not convincing them by saying that we get more accurate accounts of words, or thousands of examples. What is different is not the quantity, it is the new insights, the new questions that we can ask." [7]

The advantages that computer science offers "traditional" philology (or probably we could start saying *non-digital* philology) are twofold:

1. technological tools (for quantitative analyses and for sharing *corpora* through a network);
2. methods and concepts that stem from a theoretical reflection.

From the point of view of how deeply computer science modifies philology by contributing to it, two distinct steps can also be distinguished:

1. preparation of the working materials;
2. support to textual criticism (assisted or [semi]automated analyses).

Often the expression "digital philology" refers to the "effort of reproducing texts on paper in electronic format as faithfully as possible" (point 1), but the output of this operation is in fact "the *starting point* of the philologist's work" [3, p. 68]. Although it is desirable that the second step is also accomplished (point 2), this first and preliminary step is crucial because the *trans-coding* of the text may lose some information and/or introduce errors and artefacts. While the digitization of a text can happen in multiple ways (direct acquisition by means of scanner device, or text encoding by means of formal languages, often based on tags such as XML), audio is generally digitized by extracting the signal from the source medium and by memorizing it onto another medium (usually a redundant array of independent disks). Innovative methods to store audio recordings are based on *optical systems* such as PoG (Photos of GHOSTS: Photos of Grooves and HOles, Supporting Tracks Separation) [8]. These systems may not only bring about new approaches in the workflow of preservation, but could (and should) trigger new reflections on the meaning of re-mediation itself. Regardless of the source medium and of the digitization technique, it should be clear that *re-mediation* and [cultural] *trans-coding* are never neutral operations.

3   Preparation of the Working Materials

> "Even an image capture and editing, which may at first sight be a rather straight-forward and 'objective' procedure [...] require intellectual, critical choices, interpretation, and manipulation." [9]

In order to plan and to perform the *trans-coding*, it is necessary to have a *model* of the object/document. The definition of the model is where computer science and philology may have communication problems, because "humanities generally show terminological ambiguity due to the heterogeneous and elusive object of study", while computer science deals by definition with the "processing of data (encoded information) expressed in non-ambiguous languages" [10, p. 48]. Creating a model of the object to be digitized means to analyze it and to select what relevant features will represent it. And as a reminder of the multidisciplinary approach that should characterize any work in this field, it is important to keep in mind that the creation of the model is not required exclusively for the sake of the computer: it should rather be seen as an "important space for analysis and for the formalization of the knowledge about the subject of the study" [10, p. 53].

The definition of the model is a "crucial" part of the preliminary activities (see [1, p. 11] quoted in Sect. 1): any further analysis will manipulate the electronic representations of the original physical objects. Gigliozzi [10] suggests that a model already underlies any written text (a code for graphic symbols, syntax, narrativity, language, . . .), and that it can be useful to reflect on what features make it effectively represent the message (information) intended by the author. Starting the transition to the audio domain, the notion of "text" is among the first to be defined. Is any recording of an acoustic event or electronic composition a witness of the archetypical sound? Is there anything such as an archetypical sound at all? In the authors' methodology (see Sect. 3.2, and [11,12] for more exhaustive explanations) every audio document is considered a "master" recording in the sense that it bears witness of the acoustic event in a unique way, due to the manipulation and conditions that the document has been subject to through the years, including the mere ageing of the carrier. Without attempting to say that an archetypical sound exists, the authors see each recording as the equivalent of the written "text" according to philology.

Considering that the equivalent of textual criticism is performed by musicologists, linguists and experts other than computer scientists, the author's work finishes when the equivalent of the *diplomatic editions* (defined in the next lines) are ready. The process of preservation goes from the diagnosis of the physical document to the preparation of the digitized document for access (resources and interfaces). The documents for access may have been re-organized during the cataloguing, in function of the contents: the type of object that is produced directly from the digitization is called "preservation copy" and is by definition the equivalent of the diplomatic edition (see [13]). According to the definition of diplomatic edition, the eventual mistakes or imperfections of the physical document are maintained in the digital copy, because they provide information about the author's creative process (e.g., erased words), about the history of transmission of the document, and about the ageing of the document (from dog-eared pages to patches of mould). The implication is that *no restoration is allowed in the audio of the preservation copy* (such as noise removal or speech enhancement).

The details of the model always have to be documented and publicly accessible. Anyone who accesses the digital resources has the right to access this information. Resources that "do not declare their objective and their limits, nor the procedures employed, nor the quality of the data to which the procedures have been applied, are *low-profile* products." [10, p. 120] According to the same source, a low-profile product is one that "uses the potential of computer technology without reflection" [10, p. 121].

The expected output does not only consist of the digital set of preservation copies, but also of the audio resources, analyzed and catalogued by an experts team, ready for access from the final users. The entire process represents the preliminary step to the real philologist's work, as mentioned a few paragraphs earlier. Preservation (which also includes the concept of *restitution*, because data that is stored not to be used again in the future is a waste of time and resources) consist in the preparation of the working materials (the preservation copies). A valid critical edition must base on diplomatic editions [10, p. 122] that meet the requirements of authoritativeness, accuracy and reliability. These three need to be "a primary concern in long-term preservation [... With physical documents,] trustworthiness was all wrapped up in the concept of authenticity so that an authentic document was also reliable and accurate. This is no longer true." [4] Authenticity needs to be re-defined for electronic documents, because they can not "be preserved as [...] unchanged resources: we have only the ability to reproduce them" [14] and (un)intentional modifications introduced at some point of the files manipulation may be very difficult to backtrack. "Authenticity cannot be recognized as given, once and for ever, within a digital environment", and it can only be "approached asymptotically" [15].

According to InterPARES 3[3], authenticity refers to "the trustworthiness of a record that is what it purports to be, untampered with and uncorrupted: it must be based on its identity and integrity, and on the reliability of the records system in which it resides. Reliability is the trustworthiness of a record as a statement of fact: it must be based on the competence of its author, its completeness, and the controls on its creation. Accuracy is the correctness and precision of a record's content: it must be based on the above, and on the controls on content recording and transmission" [4].

3.1   Support to Textual Criticism

"Virtually all parameters in the process [...] require intellectual, critical choices, interpretation, and manipulation." [9]

What could be the digital equivalent of text comparison in the audio field? Traditionally, musicologists are trained in the study of musical scores. Only a few who specialized in the Twentieth century repertoire consider audio recordings a relevant documentary source for their studies – although the score (when existing) has always a powerful gravitational attraction. How can recordings on different tapes be effectively compared? Is it easier to do so with digital files? What are the sound parameters that are relevant and meaningful to a musicologist? Are there any? The list may go on, and it is clear that open issues in this field are definitely not only of technological nature. Answering these questions

---

[3] International Research on Permanent Authentic Records in Electronic Systems (InterPARES) 3 Project: http://www.interpares.org/ip3/ip3_index.cfm, last visit December 14th, 2015.

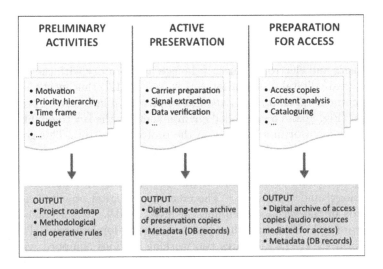

PRELIMINARY ACTIVITIES	ACTIVE PRESERVATION	PREPARATION FOR ACCESS
• Motivation • Priority hierarchy • Time frame • Budget • ...	• Carrier preparation • Signal extraction • Data verification • ...	• Access copies • Content analysis • Cataloguing • ...
↓	↓	↓
OUTPUT • Project roadmap • Methodological and operative rules	OUTPUT • Digital long-term archive of preservation copies • Metadata (DB records)	OUTPUT • Digital archive of access copies (audio resources mediated for access) • Metadata (DB records)

Fig. 1. The scheme summarizes the main steps involved in the process of preservation of audio documents according to the methodology adopted at the Centro di Sonologia Computazionale in Padova.

is the only way to enable the development of truly innovative methods and tools to assist or automate the musicologists' work, and interesting answers can only be found in a truly inter-disciplinary approach.

"In postulating a typology of Electronic Philology, we must take into account the *data*, the *procedures*, and the *results*." [7, p. 16] The majority of computational analysis of texts are quantitative (e.g. word count), therefore the lowest extent in which the computer can serve the philologist is by providing him/her with a great amount of data and by extracting other data from it. Any list of words, sorted in any order, can be a good example. Features such as the file duration or the signal average amplitude could be the audio equivalents.

These first, basic, useful results constitute a set from which secondary results can be obtained. In particular, secondary results can be *selected* from primary, using complex information retrieval systems and rich query languages that have been developed to exploit huge textual resources. An example is the list of selected words obtained from a whole list of words. Selecting all files with a maximum peak over −3 dB could be the audio equivalent. Finally, tertiary results are obtained from the selected (secondary), following an exact pattern. Human interpretation is crucial. And example for texts: using a concordance or an index to build a dictionary, or the results of the *collatio* to prepare a critical edition [7, p. 16].

3.2 Towards a *Philologically Informed* Methodology for Preservation

IPEM at Ghent University and the Centro di Sonologia Computazionale (CSC) in Padova have been active in the field of experimental music since the 1960s and

1970s, and both own a fine collection of audio tapes with finished works, sketches, samples and interviews. Along the decades, the CSC has developed research in audio preservation and restoration, building on a strong scientific background in sound synthesis and electronic music. It houses a laboratory with the equipment required to create digital preservation copies (see [11,12]) that meet the requirements of *accuracy, reliability and authenticity* presented in Sect. 3. A protocol for re-mediation (Fig. 1) and a controlled environment are the key to quality control along the workflow (for more details on the protocol see [16]). This goal is also achieved thanks to original open-source software developed on purpose at the CSC [12], as well as with the multidisciplinary approach that distinguishes the methodology for audio preservation of the CSC (mainly information engineering, music[ology] and chemistry). "The creation of digital objects has to meet the standards of the various disciplines involved, and [...] is a crucial part of humanities research. It is more than just preparation for research." [1, p. 11].

The laboratory at CSC features two working stations equipped with Apple desktop machines. The main station is dedicated to the analog-to-digital transfers (A/D) and uses an A/D-D/A Converter (PRISM ADA-8XR) that supports 96 kHz/24 bit audio quality. Audio and video (Fig. 3) are acquired on separate machines, and the entire re-mediation system is connected for safety to uninterruptible power supplies (UPS). A professional STUDER A-810 with stereo heads is used to read most tapes 1/4 in. wide. Digitized audio is exported in a non-compressed open format and stored on three different locations; the metadata is automatically ingested into the database by a software developed by the authors [12]. The same software completes the preservation copy by processing the remaining data (checksums, images, video, etc.).

The laboratory also features a photographical working station for the production of the contextual information (photographical documentation of the source carrier). It was designed for short and frequent photographical sessions, maximizing the quality of the picture with the minimum effort to (i) adjust the positioning of the camera and its parameters for each session; and to (ii) transfer the new files to the desktop working station without dismantling the photographical setting nor moving too many things around. The functionality of the photographical working station was first based on the requirements reported by the Istituto Centrale per il Catalogo e la Documentazione (ICCD) and by the Italian Ministry of Culture in [17].

For the physical recovery of magnetic tapes, a precision incubator is used (Memmert INP 400). Thermal treatment, performed with the incubator, consists in applying consistent heat to the tapes over a specified period of time; it is aimed at reverting the effects of the so-called Soft Binder Syndrome - Sticky Shed Syndrome (SBS-SSS) [18]. Among the effects of this condition are sticking, squealing, and abnormal shedding of the magnetic coating. It should be noted that not all tapes are suitable for thermal treatment. In order to find alternate recovery methods, chemical analyses and experiments are currently being performed by the CSC in collaboration with the Department of Industrial Engineering – chemical sector, of the University of Padova [13].

(a)   (b)

Fig. 2. The BilliArT experimental setup at IPEM at Ghent University, Belgium, in December 2015. The dark room aims to re-create the atmosphere of a billiard hall, at the same time favouring the detection of the special reflective balls by the motion capture system. The trajectories of the balls are processed in real-time by a software patch (Pure Data) and create a jazz-inspired sound composition.

The IPEM laboratory in Belgium represents the ideal environment to carry out research on how people engage with artistic installation and to observe their modes of interaction with technological systems. On-going research at IPEM involves bio-sensors and motion capture systems, allowing for quantitative measurements of parameters (mainly related to body movements and gestures) that relate to the aesthetic experience of interaction. The creation of "preservation (or archive) copies" of multimedia interactive installations requires the definition of paradigms and concepts to deal with the complexity of the technology involved in art making, as well as a deeper understanding of how interaction really happens and how it becomes a meaningful (aesthetic) experience for people. In order to get this understanding, the authors re-installed an artwork called BilliArT that was first presented in a public fair in Ghent in 2013 [19]. The installation is a dynamic system in which generative music and visual textures emerge from the interaction of the participants with a standard carom billiard table (Fig. 2). The importance of the experiment carried out at IPEM (December 2015, data analysis currently in process) transcends the specific results obtained form the data analysis[4], because it is the first attempt to introduce a systematic approach into the field of installation art preservation. This field is basically unexplored and the role of academia is of paramount important in organizing and guiding the research activities. The complexity of multimedia interactive art amplifies the risks of falsifying the [documentation about the] original work, because the methods and the techniques to capture the experience have not been formalized yet. A reflection around the trustworthiness of the archival documentation for multimedia interactive installations can definitely benefit from what has been said about audio recordings, and in turn can contribute to devise better preservation models and strategies for non-artistic complex systems such as robots for

---

[4] The experiment took place in December 2015 and some subjects were still expected to participate as this article was being written.

Fig. 3. Test for video shooting. On the left, a correct setting of the camera: each frame is clear and the text is readable. On the right, a wrong setting of the camera. The aim is to detect physical defects of the tape (due to aging or joints) that may correspond to a specific noise in the audio signal. Audio is directly recorded from a secondary line-out of the STUDER A-810.

automatic music expressive performance [20] and other computer-based systems involved in scientific research.

3.3   A Searchable Collection of Interactive Multimedia Installations

Current cataloguing standards provide that documents are classified by homogeneous types and, accordingly, that multimedia works are dismembered and their components grouped by category. Multimedia installations come as a *multidimensional* "assembly of artefacts" [21], i.e. they consist in the combination of several partial documents, mainly sonic/musical and visual documents representing intangible contents with a cultural and/or social signification. The documentary unity must be (temporarily) violated for cataloguing, and subsequently restored to re-create the aesthetic experience as a whole. This approach leads to a variety of information systems using different formats for data storage, and the low or absent *interoperability* among repositories makes the reconstruction of the documentary unity a problematic or impossible task.

The collaboration between the IPEM center at Ghent University and the CSC in Padova aims to provide a breakthrough solution for the problem of describing, classifying and preserving interactive multimedia installations. A complete overview of the state of the art in the extra-academic field of preservation (mainly led by large museums across the world) is beyond the scope of this article. There is a number of critical points in the current preservation practices, especially in the long-term and from the viewpoint of digital philology. One critical point that is being overlooked is the lack of a searchable database of interactive multimedia installations. In a world where searching texts, images and music by keyword (or occasionally by content) is a given fact, the impossibility to browse collections of interactive multimedia installations by characterising features (degree and mode of interaction, type of sensors involved, etc.) seems anachronistic. The on-going research at IPEM and CSC aims to define what these features may be, in order to achieve a formalization that will bring about a whole new way of grouping, approaching and studying interactive multimedia installations.

4   Conclusions

Much research conducted in the field of computer science is *preparatory* to other scientific fields, such as (ethno-)musicology, linguistics and anthropology, mainly with methods and tools (e.g., information retrieval, signal processing, data compression). In the field of musical cultural heritage and digital libraries, computer science is instrumental in performing the re-mediation of the audio documents and in managing the digital data produced during the re-mediation. Even more crucial is the help of computer science in modelling interactive multimedia installation art for archiving and preservation, since the complexity of these artworks challenges the existing approach applied in cataloguing systems. Most importantly, the role of academia is key in systematizing and organizing the research in the future of this field.

This article has proposed a reflection around the emerging discipline of digital philology. Traditional philology can contribute to the field of the digital humanities with concepts (e.g. authorship) and activities (e.g. textual criticism). This article has tried to point out that the challenges in this field are not only of technical and technological nature, a quite common misunderstanding especially in the non-academic world. The role of academia in leading the cultural shift needed to formalize and systematize the future of research in this field will never be stressed enough. Our cultural heritage is at stake, and the threat of those who only want to make a profit out of it is real.

References

1. van Peursen, W.: Text comparison and digital creativity: an introduction. In: Text Comparison and Digital Creativity - The Production of Presence and Meaning in Digital Text Scholarship. Scholarly Communication, vol. 1, pp. 1–28. Brill (2010)
2. Manovich, L.: The Language of New Media. MIT Press, Cambridge (2001)
3. Leonardi, L.: Filologia elettronica tra conservazione e ricostruzione. Arti Spazi Scritture. In: Digital Philology and Medieval Texts. Pacini Editore, Ospedaletto, Pisa, Italy, pp. 65–75 (2007)
4. Duranti, L.: Interpares3 - team Canada final report. Technical report, University of British Columbia, March 2012
5. Ziolkowski, J.: What is philology: introduction. Comp. Lit. Stud. **27**(1), 1–12 (1990)
6. Bressan, F., Canazza, S.: Digital philology in audio long-term preservation: a multidisciplinary project on experimental music. In: Proceedings of the 10th Italian Research Conference on Digital Libraries (IRCDL 2014). Procedia - Computer Sciences, vol. 38, pp. 48–51. Elsevier (2014)
7. Marcos Marín, F.A.: Where is electronic philology going? The present and future of a discipline. In: Fiormonte, D., Usher, J. (eds.) Proceedings of the First Seminar on Computers, Literature and Philology, pp. 11–22. University of Oxford, Edinburgh (2001)
8. Canazza, S., Dattolo, A.: Listening the photos. In: Proceedings of the 25th ACM Symposium On Applied Computing - Multimedia and Visualization Track, Sierre, Switzerland, vol. 3, pp. 1941–1945, 22–26 March 2010

9. Dahlström, M.: Critical editing and critical digitisation. In: Text Comparison and Digital Creativity - The Production of Presence and Meaning in Digital Text Scholarship. Scholarly Communication, vol. 1, pp. 79–98. Brill (2010)

10. Gigliozzi, G.: Introduzione all'uso del computer negli studi letterari. Bruno Mondadori, Milan (2003)

11. IASA-TC 04: Guidelines on the production and preservation of digital objects. IASA Technical Committee (2004)

12. Bressan, F., Canazza, S.: A systemic approach to the preservation of audio documents: methodology and software tools. J. Electr. Comput. Eng. **2013**, 21 (2013). Article ID 489515

13. Bressan, F., Canazza, S., Rodà, A., Bertani, R., Fontana, F.: Pavarotti sings again: a multidisciplinary approach to active preservation of the audio collection at the Arena di Verona. J. New Music Res. **42**(4), 364–380 (2013)

14. CASPAR Consortium: Report on OAIS - access model. Technical report, Centre national de la recherche scientifique (CNRS) and Université de Technologie de Compiègne (UTC), February 2008

15. Factor, M., Henis, E., Naor, D., Rabinovici-Cohen, S., Reshef, P., Ronen, S., Michetti, G., Guercio, M.: Authenticity and provenance in long term digital preservation: modeling and implementation in preservation aware storage. In: First Workshop on the Theory and Practice of Provenance, San Francisco, 23 February 2009

16. Bressan, F., Canazza, S., Bertani, R., Rodà, A., Fontana, F.: The safeguard of audio collections: a computer science based approach to quality control in the archive of the Arena di Verona. Adv. Multimedia **2013**, 14 (2013). Article ID 276354

17. Galasso, R., Giffi, E.: La documentazione fotografica delle schede di catalogo - metodologie e tecniche di ripresa. Technical report, Istituto Centrale per il Catalogo e la Documentazione (ICCD) - Ministero per i Beni e le Attività Culturali (1998)

18. Hess, R.: Tape degradation factors and challenges in predicting tape life. ARSC J. **39**(2), 240–274 (2008)

19. Saenen, I.P., Bock, S., Abdou, E., Lambert, P., Walle, R., Vets, T., Lesaffre, M., Demey, M., Leman, M.: BilliARt - AR carom billiards. In: Stephanidis, C. (ed.) HCI 2014. CCIS, vol. 434, pp. 636–641. Springer, Cham (2014). doi:10.1007/978-3-319-07857-1_112

20. Bressan, F.: The preservation and restoration of systems for automatic music performance. In: Canazza, S., Rodà, A. (eds.) Proceedings of the 1st International Workshop on Computer and Robotic Systems for Automatic Music Performance (SAMP 2014) in Conjunction with the 13th International Conference on Intelligent Autonomous Systems (IAS), Venezia, Italy, pp. 1–8, 19 July 2014

21. Bowers, J., Bannon, L., Fraser, M., Hindmarsh, J., Benford, S., Heath, C., Taxén, G., Ciolfi, L.: From the disappearing computer to living exhibitions: shaping interactivity in museum settings. In: Streitz, N., Kameas, A., Mavrommati, I. (eds.) The Disappearing Computer. LNCS, vol. 4500, pp. 30–49. Springer, Heidelberg (2007). doi:10.1007/978-3-540-72727-9_2

Searching and Classifying Affinities in a Web Music Collection

Nicola Orio[✉]

Department of Cultural Heritage, University of Padua, Padua, Italy
nicola.orio@unipd.it

Abstract. Online music libraries available on the Web contain a large amount of audio content that is usually the result of digitization of analogue recordings or the direct acquisition of digital sources. The acquisition process is carried out by several persons and may last a number of years, thus it is likely that the same or similar audio content is present in different versions. This paper describes a number of possible similarities, which are called *affinities*, and presents a methodology to detect the kind of affinity from the automatic analysis and matching of the audio content.

1 Introduction

The automatic detection of duplicates and near duplicates of textual documents has become an important research trend after the development of the Web [3]. In fact the same textual information may be contained, with minor modifications, in several web pages maintained by different organizations or individuals. One of the reasons why there exists a large number of near duplicate pages can be tracked back to a general tendency on the Web to underestimate the importante of copyright. And in fact, near duplicate identification has also important applications in patent analysis and in plagiarism detection [6].

With the increasing availability of multimedia content on the Web and in cloud services duplicate detection is gaining relevance also for media other than text, in particular to help managing large video collections [9] and to improve image retrieval tasks [2]. Most of these approaches are based on the concept of *fingerprinting* as a way to reduce the very high dimensionality of the problem. The basic idea of fingerprinting is that multimedia objects can be represented by a compact array of features, with a size orders of magnitude smaller than the original object, allowing feature indexing and in general faster processing. Moreover, a robust fingerprinting algorithm is able to extract features that are mostly related to human perception, in order to identify duplicates of a given multimedia object even when some post-processing has been applied.

The approach can be applied also to the music domain, and in fact acoustic fingerprinting is a well-known technique commercially exploited for music identification, which is at the basis of *Shazam!*, one of the most popular music services on the Internet [14], and of many others systems, such as the *MusicID* software patented by Gracenote [4] and the *AudioID* software used by MusicBrainz [8] based on an application of computer vision [7].

© Springer International Publishing AG 2017
M. Agosti et al. (Eds.): IRCDL 2016, CCIS 701, pp. 59–70, 2017.
DOI: 10.1007/978-3-319-56300-8_6

However, detection of duplicates and near duplicates has been relatively less investigated in the case of music perhaps considering it a marginal problem in comparison with audio identification. A focus on remixing, which is one of the reasons why music near duplicates exist, has been given in [1] where Locality Sensitive Hashing has been applied as an alternative to audio fingerprinting. An interesting approach [12] proposes to model the processing operators that possibly create music duplicates and near duplicates.

Although it does not apply to the test collection used in this work, in many cases near duplicates are created ad-hoc to dodge digital rights management software and publish copyrighted material on the web [10]. Yet, in the music domain most of duplicates and near duplicates exist as a natural process of artistic creation, which is intrinsically based on resemblance and differentiation with existing music, often using already published tracks as the basis to create new music. This paper focuses on this latter problem, the detection and classification of *affinities* between music tracks in a music digital library that is the basis for an online web service of music delivery.

2   Affinities in a Music Collection

The goal of the project described in this paper is to improve the access of large music collections, as the one available from music web services, by detecting variants of the stored songs and by classifying the kind of variant. The results can be applied both to large web collections, where digital objects can be provided by the end users and thus there is basically no control on the inclusion of new files in the existing collection, and to audio digital libraries, where management can be improved by the detection of content similarities. The objectives, for both domains, can be summarized as follows:

1. Duplicate removal helps saving storage space; although the increasing number of cloud services reduced its cost, storage is still a relevant cost for institutions.
2. Near duplicate detection can highlight inconsistencies in metadata information, which is the typical case when content is uploaded by the end users; moreover, detection can be carried out while new content is uploaded thus, in case near duplicates are already present, the use can be suggest with suitable metadata.
3. It has been shown that metadata insertion is an error prone process even in the case of digitization campaigns for music digital libraries [11], because usually digitization is carried out as a separate process in respect to metadata creation; the identification of near duplicates can be used to discover the presence of errors in the cataloguing process.
4. The content-based music search engine of the digital library should be aware of the presence of duplicate material; similarity matches tend to cluster around duplicates of a given track, possibly hiding additional relevant tracks.
5. The presence of subtle differences between tracks may be of interest for musicologists, musicians and eventually for the simple music fans; alternate takes of a given composition or different live versions of a studio recording are likely to be presents in the collection and be both relevant for the final user.
6. Music composition is increasingly a collaborative process, where the final product is often the result of manipulation of existing material that is remixed, looped, sampled, and so on; the possibility to track this process, which goes beyond the mere

identification of the new track, can improve music enjoyment and partially guarantee correct attribution to different authors.

This paper presents a research carried out in collaboration with the staff of a music digital library which is the basis of a web service for online music broadcast and delivery. The methods have been developed to address the real needs of the music experts who created and manage the music collection. Although it addresses the specific needs of a single web service, it is expected that the methodology can be extended also to other similar collections and, possibly, to social networks where content is directly provided by end users.

3 The Test Collection

The music collection used to train the model and run the tests contains more than 350,000 audio tracks in MP3 format for an estimate global duration of about 20,000 h. The collection has been created in more than ten years by a group of music experts, starting from commercially available CDs that have been individually bought and converted in MP3 format. Descriptive metadata are managed by a DBMS while audio tracks are maintained by an external storage. For this experiment, the owner of the collection granted access to a limited amount of cataloguing information — basically title, authors and main performer — and full access to the MP3 content. The collection focuses on pop and rock genres, with less than 10% of the tracks belonging to classical, jazz and other repertoires. Clearly the used collection is orders of magnitude smaller that the one of popular web services, such as Spotify of Last.fm, but we considered it large enough to obtain significant results.

Since popular songs are likely to be included in different CD editions — first release, remastering, best of, compilations — a certain redundancy was expected with a number of duplicates inside the collection. These can be, as it has been shown by the initial results, *exact duplicates* when the same audio source was present in different CDs, and *near duplicates* when different takes of the same song have been published or when remastering heavily affected the audio content. Because of the long time span required to create the collection, a number of different tools has been used for MP3 ripping, resulting in a different quality of the lossy compression and thus in audible differences between songs, that thus become near duplicates a well. It has also to be considered that a number of different persons was involved in the cataloguing process, with potential inconsistencies in the metadata creation that make metadata not completely reliable.

Being used as the source material for the creation of the soundtrack of TV programs of a major Italian broadcaster, the collection contains also the result of post-processing of the original tracks. Hence the collection includes also what can be called *far duplicates*. In this context, far duplicates are considered two tracks that share a consistent part of audio content like in the case of remixing of song with additional instruments, loops used as the basis of new songs, mashups using more than one audio source and different montages of the same audio material. We define all the kind of duplicates — exact, near and far — with the general term *affinities*. The typology of affinity thus depends on a number of factors: the amount of audio material that is shared between two songs, the acoustic differences of the same source due to post-processing and re-mixing, the presence of different editing.

All the tracks in the collection were already fingerprinted because an audio identification engine was already in place as the result of a previous project. The audio fingerprinting engine aims at identifying the usage of the audio tracks inside TV broadcasts in order to manage legal rights of authors, editors, performers and labels. The existing fingerprints, which are described in the next section, were computed in order to identify also very short music excerpts also in the presence of additional signals, mainly speech and environmental noise (e.g. clapping, car engines, crowd cheering, and so on). The computation of the 350,000 audio fingerprints required approximately two months on a octa-core machine with processors at 1.6 GHz. This relatively long computation time is comparable to the one required to compute grab music from an audio CD or to download/upload the files.

4   Detection of Affinities

Given the size of the audio collection, a pairwise comparison of all the tracks was impracticable. Even on the fast octa-core machine available for the experiments, the existing audio fingerprinting engine would have completed the identification of affinities within all the songs in an estimated time of about three months. For this reason we decided to divide the procedure in two steps.

4.1   First Step: Pruning Candidate Affinities

A common approach to audio fingerprinting consists of summarizing with a sequence of integer numbers the audio content of short overlapping parts of the audio signal. A complete song is thus transformed in a sequence of integers, with the characteristic that similar audio excerpts are represented by the same integer. Thus, we can view this approach as audio hashing where collisions between buckets happen when the original audio excerpts are perceptually similar. A general approach exploits Locality Sensitive Hashing to create a set of hash function that guarantees at least a collision in case of similar audio content [13]. The fingerprints used in this work were computed following a simpler approach, proposed in [5], which uses a single hashing function computed from the frequency representation of the signal.

Given an audio track t^k sampled at the common CD rate of 44.1 kHz, we divide it in frames of about 0.1 s and compute their Fast Fourier Transform. Hash values are computed according to the distribution of the signal energy in a number of spectral bands. Thus the original track t^k can be represented by a sequence of time ordered hash values

$$l^k = \left(h_1^k, h_2^k, \cdots, h_L^k \right) \qquad \text{with} \qquad h \in \mathbb{N}$$

where L depends on the length of the audio track and in an even more compact way as a set of unordered hash values

$$s^k = \left\{ h^k_1, \cdots, h^k_D \right\} \quad \text{with} \quad h \in \mathbb{N} \quad \text{and} \quad h^k_i \neq h^k_j \; \forall \; i \neq j$$

where D is the number of distinct hash values.

A first approximation of the affinity between two tracks t^h and t^k can thus be computed as the percentage of hash values they have in common, that is

$$af\left(t^h, t^k\right) = \frac{\left\| s^h \cap s^k \right\|}{min(\left\| s^h \right\|, \left\| s^k \right\|)}$$

where the normalizing factor guarantees that the maximum affinity value is 1 when a track is completely contained into the other (or the two tracks are identical).

The results of the first step are summarized in Table 1. The analysis showed that the collection contained 1057 exact duplicates (0.3% of the whole collection), at least from the point of view of the audio content because the actual size and content of the files may slightly differ. Although this has not been tested extensively, it is likely that almost all of these pairs can be identified with simple hashing techniques such as MD5. Another 104 pairs overlapped by more than 90% of their audio fingerprints. Since this high overlap is likely to be related to the use of different lossy compression software applied to the same CD track (according to the collection managers three different software were used along the years), this result seems to show that the fingerprinting technique is quite robust to lossy compression. These 1161 song pairs have been directly reported to the collection administrators in order to have one of the two files removed without additional manual checking. These files have not been used in subsequent analyses. It is interesting to note that in many cases the two songs of a pair were catalogued with different titles, which explains the double acquisition of the same material. Thus the analysis had a major impact on metadata correction, while the effect on MP3 cleanup was not particularly relevant in terms of storage reduction. The selection of the correct title in case of inconsistencies was carried out by a pool of experts.

Table 1. Amount of common fingerprints between song pairs in the collection.

Overlap	# song pairs	% song pairs
Complete ($af = 1$)	1057	0.3%
High ($af > 0.9$)	104	0.03%
Partial ($af > 0.5$)	712	0.2%
Low ($af > 0.25$)	2098	0.6%
Minimal ($af > 0.1$)	1041	0.3%
Total	5012	1.43%

Yet, the first step aimed at pointing out near and far candidates, to be checked in the second step of the analysis. There were 712 song pairs that overlapped for more than a half of their audio content while the largest group of song pairs (2098) had an overlap between one quarter and a half of their content. Finally, a group of 1041 song pairs had an overlap between one tenth and one quarter. We decided not to consider in further analyses song pairs with an overlap smaller than one tenth. The choice of the thresholds was made according to the collection managers, in order to prioritize the process of manually investigating the identified affinities. The choice of ignoring overlaps smaller than 10% was another requirement in order to let the human intervention affordable and reduced the number of false positives basically to zero. A second experiment on affinity detection will be organized in the future in order to deal also with the remaining song pairs and to investigate in more details how false positives can impact the overall process of tracking affinities. False negatives were not measured with this collection. Yet, in a previous experiment carried out with a selection of 1000 songs the number of erroneous detection was about 6.3%.

After the first step we obtained a total of 3851 song pairs to inspect in more detail during the second step of the analysis. Having reduced consistently the size of the problem, the second step can focus on effectiveness without having to deal with scalability issues.

4.2 Second Step: Pairwise Match Between Affinities

The output of the first step is a list of song pairs annotated with their affinity value as an overall measure of the shared audio content. The second step aims at refining the computation of affinities with a more descriptive representation of the similarities between songs. For this reason we represent each track as a sequence of time ordered hash values and, for the sake of clarity, we assume that a generic song pair is always in the form $p = \{l^1, l^2\}$ where the length N of $l^1 = (h^1_1, \cdots, h^1_N)$ is always shorter or equal to the length M of $l^2 = (h^2_1, \cdots, h^2_M)$, thus in all subsequent equations we assume $N < M$.

According to [5] it is possible to compute hash values in order to define a similarity function between them. For instance, if hash values are in binary form the similarity $d\left(h^1_i, h^2_j\right)$ can be set inversely proportional to the hamming distance between h^1_i and h^2_j (which can be easily normalized in the interval [0,1]). It is then possible to compute, for any short time interval in l^2, the best matching time interval in l^1, according to equations

$$m_j\left(l^1, l^2\right) = \max_i \sum_{k=1}^{N} d\left(h^1_{i+k}, h^2_{j+k}\right)$$

$$p_j\left(l^1, l^2\right) = \arg\max_i \sum_{k=1}^{N} d\left(h^1_{i+k}, h^2_{j+k}\right)$$

where m_j is the similarity value of the best match between the two tracks around time position j of l^2 and p_j is the corresponding time position in l^1. The plot of these two functions can give interesting insight if paired with a manual inspection of the corresponding audio tracks.

For instance, Fig. 1 shows an example on how exact duplicates are represented, in order to have a better understanding of the results presented in the subsequent figures. The top graphs depict the trend of m_j and the bottom graphs depict p_j. For all the graphs, the x-axis represents time of the longer track l^2, in seconds. The y-axis in the m_j (top) graphs represents the value, in log scale, of the best match between the two tracks, while the y-axis in the p_j (bottom) graphs represents the time position, in seconds, of the best match on the shorter track. Thus two identical tracks have the top graph consistently equal to zero and the bottom graph coincident to the bisect of the first quadrant (in order to save space on the page, the aspect ratio of the bottom graphs has been compressed along the y-axis). Two typologies of near duplicates are shown in Figs. 2 and 3. In particular, Fig. 2(a) represents the effect of heavy audio remastering of the same original material. While the two tracks are perfectly aligned (bottom) the value of the best match m_j (top) reveals the result of post-production which, in this particular case, is almost negligible at the beginning of the tracks becoming more relevant towards the end. Figure 2(b) represents the effect of a lighter remastering, which affects consistently the value of the best match m_j (top). Another case of near duplicates is encountered when the two tracks slightly differ in the orchestration. For instance, in Fig. 3(a) the two songs are almost identical apart from three short excerpts towards the end of the song, where one of the takes has a choir doubling the main voice. Similarly, Fig. 3(b) shows differences in two longer parts, which correspond to two choruses where a clearly audible synthesizer has been added in the orchestration. In all these cases the linear monotonic trend of p_j is a good evidence of a near-duplicate, while the trend of m_j may help discriminate between remastering and alternative takes.

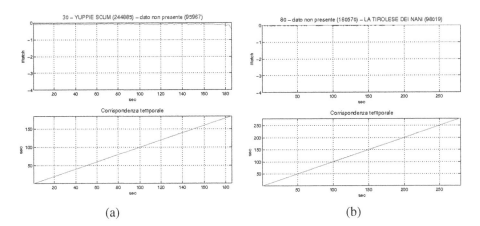

(a)   (b)

Fig. 1. Exact duplicates: result of (a) and (b) ripping with different lossy compression software of the same PCM audio source.

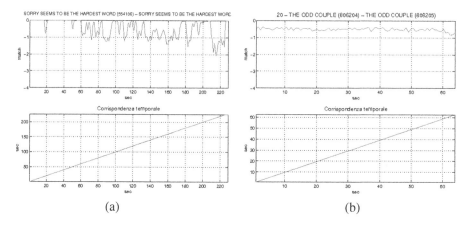

Fig. 2. Near duplicates: effect of heavy (a) and light (b) remastering of the same audio source.

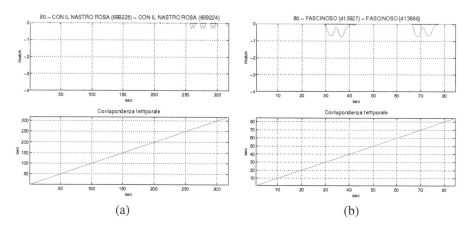

Fig. 3. Near duplicates: different takes of the same song, with (a) additional choir in three short parts at the end and (b) additional synthesizer in two long parts.

Clearly, the choice of whether maintaining or not both tracks depends on the usages of the music collection. For the purpose of musicological analyses the two tracks, either remastered or different takes, are equally interesting and should be maintained, possibly with the indication of their differences. For the purpose of a TV broadcaster, the tracks are basically interchangeable since the average audience will never notice their differences.

Among the results of the first step we identified a number of far duplicates, that is song pairs that share a substantial part of the audio content but cannot be considered simple variants of the same audio source.

We considered two main typologies: mashups and montages. Examples of mashups are shown in Fig. 4, where in both cases the audio material contained in track l^1 is used to create l^2, possibly in combination with additional content taken from other tracks. This can easily be seen comparing the initial part of the top and bottom graphs. The best match m_j is quite low and corresponds to random time correspondences of p_j. When the mashup track starts using the audio material of the other track, the best match increases its value and the corresponding positions proceed aligned as in the case of near duplicates.

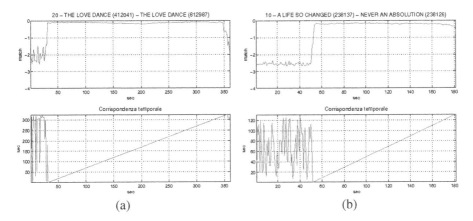

(a)   (b)

Fig. 4. Far duplicates: mashups with (a) short and (b) long songs not present in the collection that both precede the identified ones.

Examples of different montages are shown in Fig. 5. Here the two tracks share part or even all of the audio content, which is organized in different ways along time. This operation can be surprising if we consider normal pop songs, but it is not uncommon in instrumental music — especially when sound samples are used instead of real music instruments — where the author composes and performs independent parts and then combines them in different ways to create variants final track. For instance, Fig. 5(a) compares the opening and closing tracks of a TV program. The two tracks have basically the same beginning and almost the same ending while from 38 to 55 s of l^2 the diagonal lines show that different parts of l^1 have been used. Figure 5(b) shows that there is a very high value of the best match m_j along all l^2 but the corresponding elements of l^1 have been combined differently as shown by the discontinuities of p_j.

A particular case of far duplicates are loops. It may be argued that loops are more likely to be near duplicates, because one track uses and repeats many times the audio content of the other. This is shown in Fig. 6(a), where the longer track contains almost exact repetitions of the shorter one with the only instants with lower m_j values at the joints between repetition. Yet, the use of loops is common practice for hip-hop artists, who compose new songs directly from already published recordings. Although this is probably not the case of the comparison shown in Fig. 6(b) — the two songs have the same name — the trends of the two graphs show that the longer track is based on the repetition of the shorter plus additional instrumentation, which may be the typical situation where part of a song is looped and combined with additional material to create a new song.

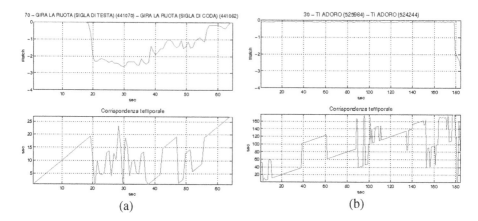

Fig. 5. Far duplicates: montages with the same audio material (a) with additional sources after an identical intro and (b) with pure permutations of the audio content.

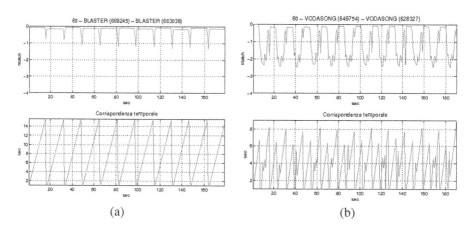

Fig. 6. Far duplicates: loops, with (a) simple juxtaposition and (b) additional edit of the original audio source.

Clearly, the simple approach of counting the common fingerprints of the first step can results also in false positives. Figure 7 shows two cases of false positives, where the percentage of common fingerprints may be explained by the use of the same audio samples probably taken from the same sound library. The trend of both bottom and top graphs are quite different from the ones shown in the previous figures, so the task of identifying false affinities does not present high complexity.

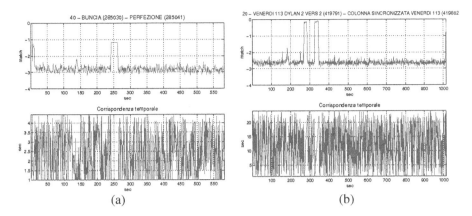

Fig. 7. False positives: the same libraries of audio samples have been used (a) once in the middle of both songs and (b) in two short parts of one song.

5 Discussion

Large multimedia digital collections are increasingly available on the Web, posing new challenges in organizing, storing and accessing the material. This paper focuses on a typical problem of music collections that is the presence of similar material with different levels of variations, which results in exact, near and far duplicates. We proposed the term *affinities* to refer to all these variations.

From the results of our initial experiments, it seems to be possible to efficiently search for affinities even in a large music collection and, furthermore, to describe the typology of affinity between two audio files with the aid of a pair of graphs representing the level of match between two parallel audio excepts and the alignment curve. The trend of the two graphs that can be interpreted in order to identify the kind of affinity. It is expected that visual identification would be faster and, in case of long audio excerpts, even more reliable than identification based on pure listening. Yet, the next step in the approach will be the automatic classification of affinities, which can be based on the statistical properties of the graphs and on the parallel analysis of the matching and the alignment curves.

Acknowledgments. The author wishfully thanks the company LaCosa s.r.l. for granting access to a large digital audio collection, which has been the basis for the tests, and for providing useful insights on how interpreting the results.

References

1. Casey, M., Slaney, M.: Fast recognition of remixed music audio. In: Proceedings of IEEE International Conference on Acoustics, Speech and Signal Processing, pp. IV:1425–IV:1428 (2007)

2. Datta, R., Joshi, D., Li, J., Wang, J.: Image retrieval: Ideas, influences, and trends of the new age. ACM Comput. Surv. **40**(2), 5:1–5:60 (2008)
3. Fetterly, D., Manasse, M., Najork, M.: On the evolution of clusters of near-duplicate web pages. J. Web Eng. **2**(4), 228–246 (2003)
4. Gracenote music solutions (2015). http://www.gracenote.com/music/recognition/. Accessed 31 Jan 2016
5. Haitsma, J., Kalker, T.: A highly robust audio fingerprinting system with an efficient search strategy. J. New Music Res. **32**(2), 211–221 (2003)
6. Imran, N.: Electronic media, creativity and plagiarism. ACM SIGCAS Comput. Soc. **40**(4), 25–44 (2010)
7. Ke, Y., Hoiem, D., Sukthankar, R.: Computer vision for music identification. In: Proceedings of IEEE Conference on Computer Vision and Pattern Recognition, pp. 597–604 (2005)
8. Lalinský, L.: How does Chromaprint work? (2011). https://oxygene.sk/2011/01/how-does-chromaprint-work/. Accessed 31 Jan 2016
9. Liu, J., Huang, Z., Cai, H., Shen, H., Ngo, C., Wang, W.: Near-duplicate video retrieval: Current research and future trends. ACM Comput. Surv. **45**(4), 44:1–44:23 (2013)
10. Liu, J., Huang, Z., Shen, H., Cui, B.: Correlation-based retrieval for heavily changed near-duplicate videos. ACM Trans. Inform. Syst. **29**(4), 21:1–21:25 (2011)
11. Montecchio, N., Di Buccio, E., Orio, N.: An efficient identification methodology for improved access to music heritage collections. J. Multimedia **7**(2), 145–158 (2012)
12. Nucci, M., Tagliasacchi, M., Tubaro, S.: A phylogenetic analysis of near-duplicate audio tracks. In: Proceedings of IEEE International Workshop on Multimedia Signal Processing, pp. 99–104 (2013)
13. Slaney, M., Casey, M.: Locality-sensitive hashing for finding nearest neighbors. IEEE Signal Process. Mag. **25**(2), 128–131 (2008)
14. Wang, A.: The Shazam music recognition service. Commun. ACM **49**(8), 44–48 (2006)

Searching and Exploring Data in a Software Architecture for Film-Induced Tourism

Sandro Savino and Nicola Orio(✉)

Department of Cultural Heritage, University of Padua, Padua, Italy
{sandro.savino,nicola.orio}@unipd.it

Abstract. Film induced tourism is a recent phenomenon, rising increasing interest in tourism management and promotion. A research project on this topic has been recently investigated at the Department of Cultural Heritage of the University of Padua, resulting in the development of a software architecture for the promotion of film-induced tourism, capable of storing and providing rich information about the movies produced in a selected geographic area. This paper presents the design and implementation of the solutions developed to search and explore the data stored in the software architecture.

Keywords: Film-induced tourism · Film annotation · User interfaces · Personalization

1 Introduction

Film-induced tourism has been defined by Sue Beeton as "visitation to sites where movies and TV programs have been filmed as well as to tour to production studios, including film-related theme parks" [1]. Film-induced tourism is an interesting asset that can be exploited in destination management and destination marketing: it attracts new visitors and also tourists who have already seen an area; it is largely independent from seasonal trends; it conveys tourists from overcrowded sites to new and less explored ones; and eventually can be suitable for a substantial re-branding of a certain area. The increasing interest in it is testified by the growing number of film-induced tourism related initiatives undertaken at international level by public and private bodies, which developed movie maps and movie tours or exploited the success of a particular movie as a tool for destination branding [2].

The Department of Cultural Heritage of the University of Padua recently investigated the topic of film-induced tourism in a project that brought together the expertise of film scholars and computer scientists; the goal of the project was to develop an information system that combines the data about a geographical area and the movies produced in it with the purpose of fostering film-induced tourism. The developed system is composed of two main components: a knowledge base storing all the relevant data about the movies shot in a given territory together with touristic information of the film locations, and an interface to query the knowledge base and retrieve the information.

© Springer International Publishing AG 2017
M. Agosti et al. (Eds.): IRCDL 2016, CCIS 701, pp. 71–81, 2017.
DOI: 10.1007/978-3-319-56300-8_7

A novel characteristic of the system resides in the idea to relate the information not to a movie as a whole (as it is instead commonly done in current systems) but to excerpts of the movie itself (called clips), leading to a database that has a very precise and fine-grained description of what appears in the movie; furthermore all these data are stored and organized in the system with the precise purpose to serve not only the tourist, but all the actors involved in film-induced tourism, as film-makers and destination managers.

The design and implementation of the model for this system can be found in [6]; this paper describes how the user interface has been developed and the techniques used to query the knowledge base to retrieve the information; the paper is organized as follows: the first part illustrates in more detail the context, the aim and the requirements of both the information system in general and of the interface to be developed; Sect. 3 reviews of the existing literature on these topics; in Sect. 4 we describe how we modeled the user experience and Sect. 5 details how the actual system was implemented; conclusion and future work are left in the final part of the paper.

2   Analysis of Requirements

The analysis of the requirements done at the beginning of the project led us to aim to a system capable of storing and retrieving rich and fine-grained data about movies and locations and to provide these data to different users. The intended users of the system were modeled in three main groups, based on their different interests:

- Tourists, interested in information to plan or enrich their visit;
- Agents of the touristic industry, interested in information to exploit and promote locations;
- Representatives of the movie industry, interested in information about locations and film-making related services.

In a previous work [6] we described how the system was modeled in order to store data that is informative for each of the different user groups; in particular, as a novel characteristic of the system, we decided that it should be able to store information at a fine-grained level, allowing to annotate portions of the movie. The idea is to record not only the places seen during the movie, but also other information like the actors on screen, any interesting objects on the scene, the emotions evoked, and to relate them to the specific portion of the movie they belong to. All these information can be then used to search and explore the data stored in the system, allowing the users to access and organize them in a manner that best suits their own needs. Figure 1 depicts an excerpt of the ER diagram, where the main entities and their relationships are represented. Each MOVIE is referenced by number of excerpts (ESTRATTO) selected by the film scholars according to their artistic relevance and by a number of moments-of-interest (MOI) that are short sequences selected according to their touristic interest. Both ESTRATTO and MOI have a relationship with one (the former) or many (the latter) points-of-interest (POI), that is georeferenced locations that are related to the MOVIE (setting, filming location). Each MOI shares a CLIP with one ESTRATTO. Searchable information is stored in full text descriptions (TESTO), information about involved persons (PERSONA) and keyword-based descriptions (TAG).

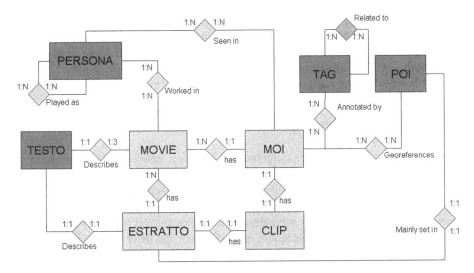

Fig. 1. ER diagram of the main entities and relations of the schema; entities in orange are used in the free text search; the relation in purple is computed using a lexical database. (Color figure online)

Once the model was finally implemented and we started to populate it, we had two big challenges to face: the first was how to enable the system to organize and relate the data and the second was how to present them to the different users. In particular we were interested in building a system that was attractive and informative to the tourists user group; true to our intent to promote tourism through cinema and also to promote cinema through tourism, we wanted our system to enable the user to explore both the geographic space and the cinematographic space, creating an engaging, culturally rich, experience.

In Sect. 5 we describe the solutions found to organize and explore the data; in particular we will describe how we implemented the search function, the user profiling and the recommendation system.

3   Related Work

While little or no works can be found in literature approaching the topic of film-induced tourism from the perspective of information systems and digital libraries, the proposed approach shares some common elements in the way user experience is modeled and in the way the search and recommendation functions have been developed.

The idea that users movements in a place, either the inner space of a museum or the open spaces of a city, can be classified according to user interest was first introduced in [7]. The user models (named after the behavior of four animals: ant, fish, grasshopper and butterfly) have been exploited in a number of approaches [8, 9]. More in general, the need to personalize multimedia access and to tailor it to different categories of users has been described by [10] as a relevant challenge in human centered multimedia.

In our system, touristically relevant movie excerpts are described also by semantic tags. The effectiveness of social tags for search and retrieval in an interactive context has been investigated in [11], we experienced similar results also in the case of tags created by a pool of experts. To partially overcome this approach, following the approach initially proposed in [12] we use WordNet in order to expand tag descriptions. The next section illustrate how we used some of the techniques above to develop our own solution.

4   Modeling the User Experience

As written above, our system has different intended users, divided in three user groups: tourists, agents of the tourism industry and professionals of the film industry. Each group has its own interests: tourist usually like to explore a place, both in a geographical, visual way and in a cultural sense; the second group is interested in materials for the touristic promotion of a location, such as texts, descriptions, pictures and video clips that can be used for instance to produce a brochure or an itinerary; the latter is more interested in finding information about filming, as a location for a new movie or a list of local professionals that can be hired for that purpose (Table 1).

Table 1. The users of our system, with different interests and ways to interact with the system.

User type	Interests	Interaction	Data presentation
Tourist	Discover new places, learn new things both on movies and the territory	Website, mobile app	Maps, itineraries, recommendations, video clips
Tour operator, destination manager	Tourism promotion, creation of tourist itineraries	DMS via RESTful API	Descriptions, video clips, search results
Film maker, location manager	Discover locations for new movies, see how the territory was read in previous movies	Website	Maps, video clips, data sheets, lists, search results

In order to provide data that could be useful for every user, we developed a system capable of storing a lot of information and we started to gather and produce these data, collecting them from archives, writing descriptions, geo-referencing and annotating movies.

To make this content accessible, we need also to develop an adequate interface, enabling all user groups to reach the information they wanted. In particular we took extra care in designing an interface that could appeal the tourist user group: they are usually the main target of film-induced tourism initiatives (and of our system as well) but, as in most cases where the same content is provide to professional and casual user, they are also the more "volatile" because they are not driven by any real necessity (on the contrary of the professionals using our system for work-related purposes); hence, in order to attract them, we wanted our system able to provide an engaging and rewarding user experience.

To achieve this, we developed an interface that lets the user explore our database as he would explore the touristic space, using what we call a "path". A path is a sequence of pieces of information extracted by our database, e.g. the general description of a movie, the profile of a director, a geo-referenced video clip of a movie; each step of a path is related to the subsequent one by some means as for example spatial proximity or content similitude. While populating the database, the content is created in such a way that all the data in the database is geo-referenced or it is related to a geo-referenced element (e.g. a director has a 1:N relation to the locations used in all his movies).

The user can follow a predefined path, whose content has been selected by film or tourism experts, and thanks to the geo-reference embedded in each part of the path, if the user is equipped with a mobile device, he can actually follow the path, using our system as a guide to explore the geographic space around him. Conversely, the user can explore the area and let the system enrich his visit by providing geo-localized information about the surrounding context; this way to explore the data can also be simulated by virtually navigating an online map and does not require the user to actually walk around. A search function enables the user to query the database for a specific text (e.g. name, place, keyword); each search result is a possible starting point of a path that the user can begin to follow to explore the database.

Most of the content in the database has more than one relation with other contents (e.g. a place or an actor appearing in different movies); on the one hand, this lets the user branch off a given path at any moment and start a different one; on the other hand, this often requires the system to filter the amount of choices offered to the user, to avoid overwhelming him/her. The filtering module tries to minimize the number of choices and, at the same time, to maximize their diversification, to encourage the user to explore new content; with respect to this, offering a loosely related option is not considered an error as it adds a sort of serendipity to the exploration of the data.

To make the experience more customized, some personalization has been implemented in the filtering: users are profiled depending on their previous searches and choices and the content suggested to them through recommendations is influenced by the profile associated to the user. The users belonging to the second group are less likely to need all these functionalities; for them we opted to offer a software interface instead of a graphical interface: by providing a list of APIs, tour operators and destination managers can access the data stored in the database with their DMS or other software. The APIs give access to some data that are not visible from the user interface described above because of scarce interest to the tourist (e.g. copyrights holders).

The requirements of the users in the third group are a mix between those of the first two: they can use some of the functionalities provided by the GUI (e.g. the geographical exploration, the visualization of clips) but they are also interested in some data that is not provided to the tourist (e.g. the list of professionals who worked in a production). To accommodate these needs, we decided to offer a signed-on access to the website: once logged in, this particular type of user is recognized and the GUI shows the extra information needed.

In the following section we will describe how we implemented the interfaces described above, with particular detail to the techniques used in the development of that for the first group of user.

5   Implementation of the Solutions

As highlighted above, the key features to make the system appealing to our intended users are to have a lot of data, to have them accessible and, possibly, related to each other. To achieve this we exploited a number of information retrieval techniques.

First of all, to make the data easily accessible, we implemented a free text search function, backed by a search engine that indexes most of the texts of our database (see Fig. 2 for the list of searchable fields). The search engine has been developed within the project and it handles single word searches and multi word searches separately. The first case is the simplest: the word is searched for an exact match in the indexed tables of the database, with the exception of the tables POI and PERSONA, where it is searched for an approximate match to account for the cases where the word is a part of the name of a place (e.g. "Piccadilly" in "Piccadilly Circus") or part of the name of an actor (e.g. "Loren" in "Sofia Loren"); if the word has a match with the name of an actor, the search is extended including all the characters associated to that actor. In the case of a multi word search string, the whole string is first searched for an exact match in the tables TAG and PERSONA and as an approximate match in POI, then the string is tokenized and a single word search is started on each token.

Fig. 2.   Attribute list used by the search engine.

The search is performed as case insensitive and a classical stop-list is used to remove parts of speech (pronouns, articles and prepositions) from the computation.

The output of a search is a list of clips to watch; if searching for a director's name, a link to a description and filmography of the director is added to the results.

To order the results a score is assigned to each of them: the exact matches have full score; approximate matches are scored by a custom function that measures the similarity between the word found and the word searched for; for matches in tables other than PERSONA, POI and TAG, a value combining *tf* and *idf* is computed. Tokens have a lower score (computed as a fraction), as they represent a partial match; however if different tokens point to the same element, their score is increased.

To rank the clips in the search result, the system takes also into account the scores assigned to them by the film experts (stored in the table MOI) and the ratings in the social media. In this way retrieved items are sorted also according to their quality (scores by scholars) and their popularity (ratings by the public).

The search function uses query expansion to widen the number of results found; query expansion is used only to search in the TAG table and was implemented using MultiWordNet [13], a free Italian version of WordNet. The search uses an auxiliary table containing each element of the TAG table plus the synsets related to it found iterating recursively on the lexical database. This table is populated automatically and it is updated every time the content of the database changes (e.g. a new movie is added); its contents however can be also manually checked and modified using a custom control panel that lets the administrator decide which synsets store in the table for a given tag.

To make the user experience more varied and to invite the user to explore our database and discover new things, we developed a recommendation system. Once the user has selected a first content object (e.g. clicking on a search result, or on one of the predefined path), the system generates a list of related content that is proposed to the user to continue his exploration. As with the search results, recommendations are mostly a link to another clip to watch. To produce this list the system searches which contents have the same tags of the present one; this relies on the same table used for the query expansion, containing all the tags and their related synsets. Given a clip currently being watched by the user, the recommendations might include clips shots in the same place or in the surroundings, clips with the same actor or from the same movie, clips conveying the same emotions or showing the same object. In a way similar to the search results, recommendations are ranked and ordered; however recommendations are also filtered and limited in numbers, with the filter trying to propose an heterogeneous list of different choices (e.g. different movies, different places).

Recommendations are ranked only on their scores and ratings; in the case the user is accessing the system from a mobile device and his location is known, they are also ordered by the geographical distance to the user.

To improve the recommendations, we also implemented some user customization. Customization is used to modify the list of recommendations in order to make them fit more the user's interests; as such it is triggered once the user has chosen a first content. Inspired by the paper [7] we decided to model our users in three profiles:

- Profile A: the user is more interested in the touristic aspect of his visit, i.e. he/she likes to explore the geographic space;
- Profile B: the user is more interested in the cinematographic aspect, i.e. he/she likes to explore a movie;
- Profile C: the user is in-between profile A and B, with no special preferences, he/she is simply attracted from what is good, interesting.

Whenever a user accesses the system, the software proposes a list of recommendations that is balanced, i.e. containing an equal number of clips that are set far from each other (profile A: exploring the territory), clips that belong to the same movie (profile B), clips that have high ratings (profile C); once the user starts to explore the recommendations, the system records which choices have been chosen and biases later recommendation lists to contain more options of the type the user seems more interested in. At present, the user cannot manually adjust his/her profile although this is an important aspect that will be taken into account in future development (Table 2).

Table 2. The profiles used to improve the recommendation system.

Profile	Moving around the territory	Following the same movie	Watching high rated contents
A	Yes	No	No
B	No	Yes	No
C	No	No	Yes

The system was developed and is currently deployed as a closed beta. The architecture consists of a database to store and query the data, a storage for the video contents, both the movies to annotate and the clips, a server with a backend interface to annotate the movies, insert data and manage the system, and a frontend interface to browse and explore the data, aimed mainly to the tourist user group.

The server was developed in PHP on a hosted Apache web server. The server contains an administration panel, to manage the system and a backend panel to populate the database; at the moment the database has been populated by a pool of experts in film studies using, where possible, controlled dictionaries for tags and places. The server also runs the code for searching and query expansion.

The web server exposes a list of RESTful APIs that enables other systems to interact with the system and query the database. This feature is aimed mainly to professionals (e.g. tour operator accessing the system using a Destination Management System -DMS) but resulted also very useful while developing the user interface.

The database was implemented in MySQL; this was almost a direct consequence of our choice to use Apache, as it can be hard to find a web host offering a different DBMS. Due to MySQL basic support of the SFA/SQL [SS12] standard, we developed a custom PHP library to complement the limited functionalities of the MySQL Spatial Extensions, implementing the missing spatial operations required to handle our geo-referenced data. The database was implemented following the model reported above (see Fig. 1) and populated using the backend web interface; some auxiliary tables have been added to the DBMS to speed up the search of keywords and to cache the results of the matching functions. The DBMS also contains the lexical database used to perform query expansion.

To store the video content, we needed a solution providing safety (as the contents are copyright protected materials) and, in perspective, performance, scalability and low maintenance costs. Our choice was to store the data in the cloud using Amazon Web Services (AWS); in particular we chose the Simple Storage Service (Amazon S3) due to its easy use and cheap pricing, compared to ad hoc video hosting solutions (e.g. Vimeo PRO). We converted all the video in a format supported by HTML5 (H264 video codec and AAC audio codec), and stored them as MP4 files, that are then streamed via http; to keep the location of the files secure, a PHP proxy is used to relay the video streams to the client device. The clips are automatically generated from the annotated source files; each clip, resized at 480p resolution and compressed, is less than 2 MB per 10 s, while a whole movie varies between 500 and 700 MB in size.

Fig. 3. Screen capture of the user interface.

The user interface is implemented as a website developed to be accessible by computers, tablets and mobile devices: this choice looked favorable to the development of specialized interfaces for these different platforms; the website uses Bootstrap to be responsive and jQuery to load contents progressively to reduce the amount of data sent to the user; we use Google Maps as the backdrop maps for the geographic contents, but the system can easily switch to other map services; the video contents are provided using the capabilities of HTML5, thus leaving to the users' clients the choice of the video player.

As a design choice, the user interface is completely isolated from the server, exchanging data with it only through the APIs; the website is implemented in PHP executed on a different Apache web server; this server also runs the code for user profiling and recommendation generation.

The website can be used both by logged and not logged users; logged users can access some specialized content (if enabled by the administrator); all users' activity is tracked and the choices made (i.e., which of the proposed contents is read first) are used to associate the user to one of the different user profiles described above.

Another important feature of the GUI is the integration with the social media. Users can comment, "share" and "like" most of the contents of the website; user contribution increase the engagement of the users in the system and enriches it; the "like" are also used to create a user-based ranking of the content.

Inspired by the theory of gamification, the GUI offers also a mini-game that asks the users to recognize a clip or to position on the map the location of a clip; the contents of the mini-game is automatically generated from the data available. We tested the effectiveness of a gamified approach by making available the system at a booth during the European Researchers' Night 2015. Users enjoyed to play with movies and their city and reported that it was a novel and fun way to discover new places. Additionally, participating to the game raised interest towards the movies themselves, because most participants were not aware that they were located in Padua.

6   Conclusions and Future Work

The system developed is currently under test. The user interface, with the functionalities of search, recommendation and personalization offers an easy access to the information of the database and also a simple way to discover new contents. A screenshot of the interface is shown in Fig. 3. Offering predefined paths, as well as the use of social media, are a good combination to invite the user of the group one to start exploring the system and all this together seems able to offer the engaging experience we were looking for.

Recommendations, that are mainly thought for the users of the group one, can also be useful for the users of the group three, as they can help them to discover similar places; furthermore, the use of controlled dictionaries in the annotation of some specific features of the movies, further improves the ability of our system to provide, through the search function, the data that this group of user may need.

The API developed allow to communicate with the system and they seem complete enough to cover the various needs to query the database that the user of the group two might have.

The use of a lexical database to perform query expansion proved to be more difficult than expected: the expansion (especially if iterated) may lead to unexpected results, and we had to develop a custom tool to let the administrator check which synsets are inserted in the database.

Future developments will regard a function to track the content already seen by the user, in order to avoid duplicate proposals, and a better integration with social media.

Acknowledgments. The work reported has been partially funded by the European Commission under the FSE (Fondo Sociale Europeo - European Social Fund) initiative. The authors thanks the colleagues in film study, Farah Polato and Giulia Lavarone, who collaborated to the system design and coordinated the population of the database.

References

1. Beeton, S.: Film-Induced Tourism, p. 11. Channel View Publications, Clevedon (UK) (2005)
2. Di Cesare, F., Rech, G.: Le produzioni cinematografiche, il turismo, il territorio, Carocci, Roma, pp. 45–88 (2007)
3. Provenzano, R.: Al cinema con la valigia. I film di viaggio e il cineturismo, FrancoAngeli, Milano, pp. 256–283 (2007)
4. Buhalis, D., Law, R.: Progress in information technology and tourism management: 20 years on and 10 years after the Internet—The state of eTourism research. Tour. Manag. **29**(4), 609–623 (2008)
5. Joliveau, T.: Connecting real and imaginary places through geospatial technologies: examples from set-jetting and art-oriented tourism. Cartographic J. **46**(1), 36–45 (2009)
6. Lavarone, G., Orio, N., Polato, F., Savino, S.: Modeling the concept of movie in a software architecture for film-induced tourism. In: Proceedings of the 11th Italian Research Conference on Digital Libraries (2015)
7. Veron, E., Levasseur, M.: Ethnographie de l'Exposition. Paris: Bibliothèque publique d'information: Centre Georges Pompidou (1989)
8. Chittaro, L., Ieronutti, L.: A visual tool for tracing users' behavior in Virtual Environments. In: Proceedings of the Working Conference on Advanced Visual Interfaces, pp. 40–47 (2004)
9. Antoniou, A., Lepouras, G.: Modeling visitors' profiles: a study to investigate adaptation aspects for museum learning technologies. J. Comput. Cult. Heritage **3**(2), 19 (2010). electronic publication
10. Elgammal, A.: Human-centered multimedia: representations and challenges. In: Proceedings of ACM Workshop on Human-Centered Multimedia, pp. 11–18 (2006)
11. Kim, Y.-M.: Social tags in text and image search. In: Proceedings of the Symposium on Information Interaction in Context, pp. 353–358 (2010)
12. Voorhees E.M.: Using WordNet to disambiguate word senses for text retrieval. In: Proceedings of ACM SIGIR Conference, pp. 171–180 (1993)
13. Pianta, E., Bentivogli, L., Girardi, C.: MultiWordNet: developing an aligned multilingual database. In: Proceedings of the First International Conference on Global WordNet, pp. 293–302 (2002)

Semantics

An Ontology to Make the DELOS Reference Model and the 5S Model Interoperable

Maristella Agosti, Nicola Ferro(✉), and Gianmaria Silvello

Department of Information Engineering, University of Padua, Padua, Italy
{agosti,ferro,silvello}@dei.unipd.it

Abstract. This paper is an extended abstract of the paper published in the Future Generation Computer System journal [2] which takes into account two of the foundational models defining what a digital library is and how it should work: the *DELOS Reference Model* and the *Streams, Structures, Spaces, Scenarios, Societies (5S)* model.

The aim of this work is to enable a high-level interoperability at the model level. To this end, we express these foundational models by means of ontologies which exploit the methods and technologies of Semantic Web and Linked Data. Moreover, we link the proposed ontologies for the foundational models to those currently used for publishing cultural heritage data in order to maximize interoperability.

1 Introduction

Digital Library (DL) have been steadily progressing since the early 1990s and they now determine how citizens and organizations study, learn, access and interact with their cultural heritage [3,12,17]. Despite their name, DL are not only the digital counter-part of traditional libraries but they are also concerned with other kinds of cultural heritage institutions, such as archives and museums, that is institutions typically referred to as *Libraries, Archives and Museums (LAM)*. In the context of LAM, unifying a variety of organizational settings and providing more integrated access to their contents are aspects of utmost importance.

These compelling integration and collaboration needs have propelled the evolution of *Digital Library System (DLS)* [1] as systems that permit us to design and implement the overlapping set of functions of LAM. This evolution has been favored by the development of two foundational models of what DL are: the *Streams, Structures, Spaces, Scenarios, Societies (5S)* model [9] and the *DELOS Reference Model* [4]. They made it clear what kind of entities should be involved in a DL, what their functionalities should be and how DLS components should behave, and fostered the design and development of operational DLS complying with them.

However, these two models are quite abstract and, still providing a unifying vision of what a DL is, they allow for very different choices when it comes to develop actual DLS. This has led to the growth of "ecosystems" where services and components may be able, at best, to interoperate together within the

M. Agosti et al. (Eds.): IRCDL 2016, CCIS 701, pp. 85–91, 2017.
DOI: 10.1007/978-3-319-56300-8_8

boundaries of DLS that have been inspired by just one of the two models for DL. However, there are no running examples of two DLS, one implementing the 5S model and the other the DELOS Reference Model, which are able to inter-operate. Therefore, interoperability still represents one of the biggest challenges in the DL field [1].

In [2], we addressed the open issue of making DL foundational models interoperable and in this work we outline the main results achieved by describing at an high-level the ontology making the DELOS Reference and the 5S Model interoperable.

The paper is organized as follows: Sect. 2 introduces the rationale behind this work; Sect. 3 outlines the main differences between the DELOS Reference Model and the 5S Model; Sect. 4 presents the general ontology allowing for the DELOS Reference Model and the 5S Model to interoperate; and Sect. 5 draws some final remarks.

2   Rationale

The current mainstream approach to bridge the interoperability gap between DLS and to provide comprehensive solutions able to embrace the full spectrum of LAM is to exploit semantic Web technologies and linked (open) data [11]. This allows for describing entities and information resources in a common way which enables their exchange, as for example happens in the case of library linked data.

This approach is both "external" and "bottom-up". It is "external" since it assumes that everything in a DL should be exposed on the Web rather than seeking direct interoperability among systems which may not necessarily be only Web-based. It is "bottom-up" because ontologies have been used only to describe the resources managed by a DLS and they are not used to represent the concepts themselves which constitute the DL model on which the DLS is based. Therefore, they allow for semantic interoperability and integration only at the data level, i.e. the lowest level possible in the architecture of a DLS.

What is needed is a deeper and more abstract interoperability based on a commonly shared semantic view of what a DL is rather than a lower level one where data is just wrapped in a commonly understandable format. The quite ambitious goal of this paper is to propose a solution to this open problem. The proposed solution is based on the representation of each foundational DL model through ontologies, leveraging semantic Web and linked data technologies in order to ease their linking to other already existing ontologies and to achieve maximum interoperability.

Therefore, the proposed approach will pave the way for a deeper interoperability among operational DLS and lower the barriers between LAM. It is also opening up more advanced possibilities for the automatic processing of resources, since, for example, DLS could automatically exploit the link between the models they are built upon in order to exchange resources, interoperate and integrate functionalities. To the best of our knowledge, there is no previous work in the field which attempted to achieve interoperability among DLS at a high level of abstraction through a semantic description and mapping of their foundational models. We can only mention our very preliminary work [7], where we started to explore this idea in the context of quality in DL.

3   Background

The 5S [8,9] is a formal model which draws upon the broad digital library literature to produce a comprehensive base of support. It was developed largely bottom up, starting with key definitions and elucidation of digital library concepts from a minimalist approach.

The DELOS Reference Model [4] is a high-level conceptual framework that aims at capturing significant entities and their relationships within the digital library universe with the goal of developing a more robust model of it.

The DELOS Reference Model and the 5S model address a similar problem with different approaches. The 5S is a formal model providing mathematical definitions of the digital library entities that can be used to prove properties, theorems and propositions. The DELOS Reference Model does not provide formal definitions, but it does provide a way to model and manage the resources of the digital library realm by using concept maps [13] because of their simplicity and immediacy.

4   Semantic Mapping Between DL Models

In Fig. 1 we present the *Resource Description Framework (RDF)* graph of the unifying data model relating the DELOS Reference Model to the 5S model by means of a mapping between their most relevant high-level concepts. The presented RDF graph is composed by classes represented as circles and properties represented as directed edges between the classes.

The main constituents of the DELOS Reference Model are: the digital universe divided into DL, DLS and *Digital Library Management System (DLMS)*, the concept of `Resource` and six high-level main domains: User, Functionality, Content, Quality, Policy and Architecture.

A DL, represented by the `Digital Library` class in Fig. 1, is supported by a `Digital Library System` which is extended and deployed by a `Digital Library Management System`. These three classes manage `Resource`s, where a `Resource` is any identifiable entity in the DL universe and resembles the concept of resource used in the Web [16]. A `Resource` represents the class of everything that exists in the DL universe and it is related to the `rdfs:Resource` class. In addition to this general concept, the `Resource` in the DELOS Reference Model has some additional features: it can be arranged or set out according to a resource format which, for example, allows a `Resource` to be composed of or linked to other `Resource`s.

All the DELOS domains are represented by key classes which are subclasses of `Resource`.

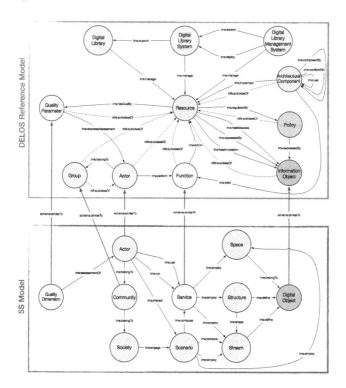

Fig. 1. Semantic mapping of the high level concepts in the 5S model and DELOS Reference Model and their relationships.

In the user domain these key classes are `Actor` and `Group`, where a `Group` may be a collection of actors and at the same time it is a subclass of `Actor` given that a group can be considered as a single actor itself. The user domain directly interacts with the functionality and the quality domains; indeed, an `Actor` may perform some `Functions` in the DL and may be assessed by some `Quality Parameter`.

The `Function` class always acts on a resource and the `Quality Parameter` is associated to a resource as happens in the case of `Actor`, which is related to `Quality Parameter`s by the `expressAssessment` property.

The main class of the content domain is `Information Object`, which represents any information managed by the DL and includes documents such as texts, images, videos, audio files, metadata and annotations.

The main class of the policy domain is `Policy`, which represents the single entity governing a resource with respect to a certain management point and it is connected to `Resource` by the `regulatedBy` property.

Lastly, the main class of the architecture domain is `Architectural Component`, which defines the organization or structure of the components of a given system or service; an architectural component may be `composedOf` other components or may `use` other components.

The RDF model of the 5S model is represented in the lower part of Fig. 1 where we can see five main classes representing the five S of the model: `Society`, `Scenario`, `Stream`, `Structure` and `Space`. A `Scenario` is engaged by a `Society` and employs or produces a `Stream` which is shaped by a `Structure`. The `Service` class is central to this model because it connects all of its fundamentals given that it employs a `Space`, a `Structure` and a `Stream`; furthermore, a `Service` is composed by one or more `Scenarios` which are related to a `Society`. A `Scenario` may employ a `Space`. The `Digital Object` class is defined by a set of streams and structures and employs some spaces.

The 5S RDF graph represents the user domain similarly to the DELOS Reference Model; indeed, the class `Actor` represents an agent (e.g. a human or a computer) which belongs to a `Community` belonging to a `Society`.

The mapping with DELOS is quite straightforward since `Actor` is mapped in the homonym class and the `Community` class is mapped into the `Group` class of DELOS. The central class of the quality domain in the 5S model is `Quality Dimension` which allows us to evaluate every major concept in a DL [10]; this class is mapped into the `Quality Parameter` of the DELOS Reference Model. The `Service` class is mapped into the `Function` class of the DELOS Reference Model and the `Digital Object` class is mapped into the `Information Object` class by the `schema:isSimilarTo` property.

As we can see, the 5S model has no explicit representation of the architecture and policy domain of the DELOS Reference Model.

5   Final Remarks

In [2] we proposed a common ontology which encompasses all the concepts considered by the two foundational models and creates explicit connections between their constituent domains.

In particular, we highlight the important role of *service* in the 5S Model which is a broad concept comprising both the concepts of *function* and *architectural component* in the DELOS Reference Model. The presented ontology explicitly points out the connection between these concepts enabling connections between the two models which were not easy to recognize and establish otherwise. Furthermore, we investigated how policies are modeled and used by the two models; we pointed out that in the 5S model, the idea of *policy* is encompassed by the concept of *Society* even though it is not explicitly treated. Starting from this consideration, the common ontology enables the possibility of using policies defined in the DELOS Reference Model to regulate services in the 5S.

Much work is still ahead of us, since the proposed ontology needs to be operationalized into actual DLS and, probably, it will need to be extended both to accomplish specific details that arise when you make actual systems interoperate and to address peculiar needs of specialised domains, which may depart from the common general view. As a concrete example, we have started to work on an extension of the Quality Domain to model the scientific data generated by the experimental evaluation of *Information Retrieval (IR)* systems and to link them with expert profiles and expertise topics [14]. This specialisation also constitutes the starting point for dealing with the more complex problem of reproducibility and data citation in IR evaluation [5,6,15].

References

1. Agosti, M.: Digital libraries. In: Melucci, M., Baeza-Yaetes, R.A. (eds.) Advanced Topics in Information Retrieval. The Information Retrieval Series, vol. 33, pp. 1–26. Springer, Heidelberg (2011)
2. Agosti, M., Ferro, N., Silvello, G.: Digital library interoperability at high level of abstraction. Future Gener. Comput. Syst. (FGCS) **55**, 129–146 (2016)
3. Borgman, C.L.: What are digital libraries? Competing visions. Inf. Process. Manag. **35**(3), 227–243 (1999)
4. Candela, L., Castelli, D., Ferro, N., Ioannidis, Y.E., Koutrika, G., Meghini, C., Pagano, P., Ross, S., Soergel, D., Agosti, M., Dobreva, M., Katifori, V., Schuldt, H.: The DELOS digital library reference model. Foundations for Digital Libraries. ISTI-CNR at Gruppo ALI, Pisa, Italy. http://delosw.isti.cnr.it/files/pdf/ReferenceModel/DELOS_DLReferenceModel_0.98.pdf
5. Ferro, N.: Reproducibility challenges in information retrieval evaluation. ACM J. Data Inf. Qual. (JDIQ) **8**(2), 8:1–8:4 (2017)
6. Ferro, N., Fuhr, N., Järvelin, K., Kando, N., Lippold, M., Zobel, J.: Increasing reproducibility in IR: Findings from the Dagstuhl seminar on "reproducibility of data-oriented experiments in e-science". SIGIR Forum **50**(1), 68–82 (2016)
7. Ferro, N., Silvello, G.: Towards a semantic web enabled representation of DL foundational models: the quality domain example. In: Calvanese, D., De Nart, D., Tasso, C. (eds.) IRCDL 2015. CCIS, vol. 612, pp. 24–35. Springer, Cham (2016). doi:10.1007/978-3-319-41938-1_3
8. Fox, E.A., Gonçalves, M.A., Shen, R.: Theoretical Foundations for Digital Libraries: The 5S (Societies, Scenarios, Spaces, Structures, Streams) Approach. Morgan & Claypool Publishers, San Rafael (2012)
9. Gonçalves, M.A., Fox, E.A., Watson, L.T., Kipp, N.A.: Streams, structures, spaces, scenarios, societies (5S): a formal model for digital libraries. ACM Trans. Inf. Syst. (TOIS) **22**(2), 270–312 (2004)
10. Gonçalves, M.A., Lagoeiro, B., Fox, E.A., Watson, L.T.: What is a good digital library? A quality model for digital libraries. Inf. Process. Manag. **43**(5), 1416–1437 (2007)
11. Heath, T., Bizer, C.: Linked Data: Evolving the Web into a Global Data Space. Morgan & Claypool Publishers, San Rafael (2011)
12. Lesk, M.: Practical Digital Libraries. Books Bytes & Bucks. Morgan Kaufmann Publishers, San Francisco (1997)
13. Novak, J.D.: Concept maps and Vee diagrams: two metacognitive tools to facilitate meaningful learning. Instr. Sci. **19**(1), 29–52 (1990)
14. Silvello, G., Bordea, G., Ferro, N., Buitelaar, P., Bogers, T.: Semantic representation and enrichment of information retrieval experimental data. Int. J. Dig. Libr. (IJDL) (2016)

15. Silvello, G., Ferro, N.: Data citation is coming. Introduction to the special issue on data citation. Bull. IEEE Tech. Comm. Dig. Libr. (IEEE-TCDL) **12**(1), 1–5 (2016)
16. W3C: Architecture of the world wide web, vol. 1 - W3C Recommendation, 15 December 2004. http://www.w3.org/TR/webarch/
17. Witten, I.H., Bainbridge, D.: How to Build a Digital Library. Morgan Kaufmann Publishers, San Francisco (2003)

Realizing a Scalable and History-Aware Literature Broker Service for OpenAIRE

Paolo Manghi, Claudio Atzori, Alessia Bardi[✉], Sandro La Bruzzo, and Michele Artini

Istituto di Scienza e Tecnologie dell'Informazione "A. Faedo", Consiglio Nazionale delle Ricerche, Pisa, Italy
`{paolo.manghi,claudio.atzori,alessia.bardi,sandro.labruzzo,`
`michele.artini}@isti.cnr.it`

Abstract. The OpenAIRE infrastructure is the point of reference for Open Science in Europe. Its services populate and provide access to a graph of objects relative to publications, datasets, people, organizations, projects, and funders aggregated from a variety of data sources, such as institutional repositories, data archives, journals, and CRIS systems. Not only, objects in the graph are harmonized to achieve semantic homogeneity, de-duplicated and merged, and enriched by inference with missing properties and/or relationships. The OpenAIRE Literature Broker Service is designed to offer subscription and notification functionalities for institutional repositories to: (i) learn about publication objects in OpenAIRE that do not appear in their collection but may be pertinent to it, and (ii) learn about extra properties or relationships relative to publication objects in their collection. Due to the high variability of the information space the following problems may arise: (i) subscriptions may vary over time to adapt to information space evolution, (ii) repository managers need to be able to quickly test their configurations before activating them, (iii) notifications may be redundant, and (iv) notifications may be very large over time. This paper presents the data model and software architecture of the OLBS, specifically designed to address these issues.

Keywords: Subscription and notification · Publications · Scholarly communication · e-Infrastructures

1 Introduction

The OpenAIRE initiative [5] is the point of reference for Open Access in Europe. Its mission is to foster an Open Science e-Infrastructure that links people, ideas and resources for the free flow, access, sharing, and re-use of research outcomes, services and processes for the advancement of research and the dissemination of scientific knowledge. OpenAIRE operates an open, participatory, service-oriented infrastructure that supports:

© Springer International Publishing AG 2017
M. Agosti et al. (Eds.): IRCDL 2016, CCIS 701, pp. 92–103, 2017.
DOI: 10.1007/978-3-319-56300-8_9

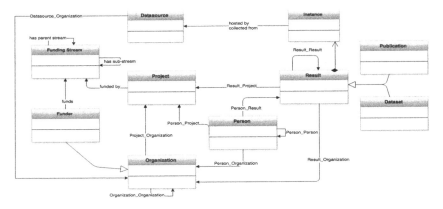

Fig. 1. The OpenAIRE data model

- The realization of a pan-European network for the definition, promotion and implementation of shared interoperability guidelines and best practices for managing, sharing, re-using, and preserving research outcomes of different typologies;
- The promotion of Open Science policies and practices at all stages of the research life-cycle and across research communities belonging to different application domains and geographical areas;
- The discovery of and access to research outcomes via a centralized entry point, where research outcomes are enriched with contextual information via links to objects relevant to the research life-cycle;
- The measurements of the impact of Open Science and the return of investment of national and international funding agencies.

Its technological infrastructure provides services [7] that populate the so-called OpenAIRE Information Space, a graph-like information space aggregating information about publications, datasets, organizations, persons, projects and several funders (e.g. European Commission, Wellcome Trust, Fundação para a Ciência e a Tecnologia, Australian Research Council) collected from hundreds of online data sources (e.g. publication repositories, dataset repositories, CRIS systems, journals, publishers).

The OpenAIRE Information Space, whose data model [10] is shown in Fig. 1, is obtained via the combined effort of three infrastructure sub-systems, depicted in Fig. 2:

- *Harmonization* (aggregation sub-system): The OpenAIRE infrastructure collects metadata records from data sources and derives from them objects and relationships that form the information space graph[1]. For example a bibliographic metadata record describing a scientific article will yield one publication object and a set of person objects (one per author) with relationships between them. Objects of given entities are transformed from their native data models (e.g. physically represented as XML

records, HTML responses, CSV files) onto the OpenAIRE data model [10] in order
to build an homogenous information space;

- *Merge* (de-duplication subsystem): objects of the same entity type are de-duplicated
  in order to remove ambiguities that may compromise statistics and impact (e.g. the
  same publication may be collected from different repositories as supposedly different
  objects);
- *Enrichment* (information inference sub-system): publication full-texts are collected
  and processed by text mining services [12] capable of inferring new property values
  or new relationships between objects.

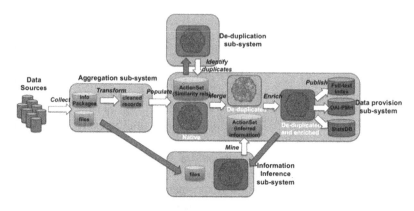

Fig. 2. OpenAIRE services high-level architecture

In order to give visibility to the contributing data sources, OpenAIRE keeps provenance information about each piece of aggregated information. Specifically, since de-
duplication merges objects collected from different sources and inference enriches such
objects, provenance information is kept at the granularity of the object itself, its properties, and its relationships. Object level provenance tells the origin of the object that is
the data sources from which its different manifestations were collected. Property and
relationship level provenance tells the origin of a specific property or relationship when
inference algorithms derive these, e.g. algorithm name and version. The OpenAIRE
Information Space is then made available for programmatic access via several APIs
(Search HTTP APIs, OAI-PMH, and soon Linked Open Data) [2] and for search, browse
and statistics consultation via the OpenAIRE portal[2].

Data sources providing content to OpenAIRE and interested in augmenting their
local collections may benefit in a number of ways from the OpenAIRE information
space. This is particularly true for institutional repositories, whose mission is that of
growing a complete collection of the scientific publications produced by the authors
affiliated to the institution they serve. Repository managers' goal is twofold: bringing

---

[1] Typologies and numbers of data sources currently included in OpenAIRE are available from
https://www.openaire.eu/search/data-providers.

[2] www.openaire.eu.

in the collection all articles produced by such authors and making sure the metadata is as complete and up-to-date as possible. To this aim, the infrastructure is currently being equipped with the OpenAIRE Literature Broker Service (OLBS) whose general principles and ideas are described in [16]. The OLBS implements a subscription and notification mechanism supporting repository managers at enhancing the content of their repository taking advantage of the OpenAIRE information space. As reported in [16], a number of initiatives started working on "brokering" approaches favoring single-deposition of publication metadata with subsequent automated delivery to other repositories. Some focused on techniques for automatic deposition into a repository (SWORD project [4]), while others focused on the complementary aspects of how to broker publication information from publishers to relevant/interested repositories. SHARE [3] and JISC/EDINA [9] are two of such initiatives, based respectively in the U.S. and U.K. The OpenAIRE Literature Broker Service (OLB Service) offers to repository managers the possibility to subscribe to special "addition" or "enrichment" events, in order to be respectively notified about: *(i)* publication objects in OpenAIRE that do not appear in their collection but may be pertinent to it, or *(ii)* properties or relationships relative to publication objects in their collection that do not appear in their local metadata. Due to the high variability of the OpenAIRE information space, where new data sources are continuously added or removed, harmonization rules, mining, and deduplication algorithms are refined, following problems may arise: *(i)* subscriptions may vary over time to adapt to information space evolution, *(ii)* repository managers need to be able to quickly test their configurations before activating them, *(iii)* the same notifications may be sent more than once, and *(iv)* notifications may be very large in number over time. This paper presents the OLBS data model and software architecture, specifically designed to address these issues.

2   OLBS Functional Requirements

The OLBS operates on top of the OpenAIRE information graph and supports repository managers with a Web Dashboard from which they can subscribe to (potential) "enrichment" and (potential) "addition" events occurring to the graph and of interest to their repository. Figure 3 shows how the OLBS integrates with the existing OpenAIRE infrastructure. Data sources are aggregated, de-duplicated and enriched by mining techniques so as to populate the OpenAIRE Information space graph. Whenever a new information space is generated, the OLBS explores the graph to detect if any of the active subscriptions finds a match and in such case notifications are generated, delivered, and archived.

2.1   Subscriptions

Repository managers will be able to subscribe to two main classes of subscriptions: "enrichment" and "addition".

Enrichment. The first class refers to notifications about publications that (i) were collected from the repository by OpenAIRE and (ii) have been enriched with properties

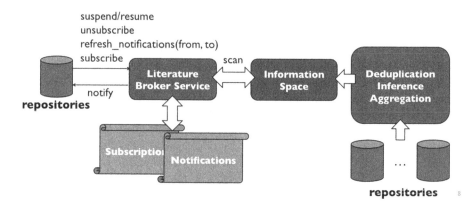

Fig. 3. The OLBS in the OpenAIRE infrastructure

or relationships to other objects by OpenAIRE inference algorithms (e.g. relationships to projects and datasets, citation lists, document classification properties) or by the side effect of being merged with richer publication objects (e.g. DOI of a publication, Open Access version of the publication). The identification of these events is straightforward as it is based on provenance of collection (i.e. selects publication objects collected from the given repository) and of enrichment (i.e. further selects objects of the given repository involved into a merge or enriched by inference algorithms). Repository managers will be able to fine-tune their subscriptions based on the bibliographic fields they would like to be notified about; e.g. "return the fields DOIs and Funding Project relative to my records".

Addition. The second class refers to notifications relative to publications that are "relevant to" the repository at hand, but are not present in the repository. The identification of these events requires the navigation of the Information Space graph, in an attempt to identify relationships between the subscribing institutional repositories (which are a specific OpenAIRE data source type) and publications that have not been collected from the given repository but are "relevant to" it. Three relationships have been identified, according to which a publication is relevant to a repository if one of the following chains of relationships exist in the OpenAIRE information graph:

- *Affiliation repository: publication-author-organization-repository*: the publication has an author whose organization (affiliation) has a given institutional repository of reference; the affiliation relationship *publication-author-organization* is extracted by inference and has a level of trust $T:[0.1]$, which represents the level of confidence of the inference algorithm for that specific statement; the relationship *organization-repository* is instead provided by an authoritative OpenAIRE data source, namely OpenDOAR[3], which maintains the directory of repositories and related responsible organizations;

- *Reference repository: publication-author-repository*: the publication has an author with a given institutional repository of reference; the relationship *author-repository* is inferred by mining the graph and identifying the correlations between authors, their co-authored publications and the repositories from which these publications were collected; each author can be associated to a repository with a weight of "repository reference-ness", obtained as the percentage of author publications occurring in the repository ("deposition rate"), and the repository with the highest percentage corresponds to the repository of reference for the author; the information space contains a relationship between authors and their inferred repository of reference, with a degree of trust $T:[0.1]$ that depends on the "dominance" of the repository over other repositories (variables are total of author publications and total of related repositories).

- *Funder repository: publication-project-organization-repository*: the publication has been funded by a project whose participants (organizations beneficiaries of the grant) have a given institutional repository of reference; the relationship *publication-project* is either collected from the data sources or inferred by mining and has therefore a level of trust $T:[0..1]$; the relationship *organization-repository* is instead provided, as in the first case, by the OpenDOAR data source; with a degree of approximation, the repositories reached by such relationship may be interested in the given publication.

Given a publication, if one of such relationships exists in the graph (collected or inferred) the OLBS may notify the subscribing repositories of the publication. Since the relationships are generally not authoritative (not collected from data sources), but inferred by OpenAIRE services, subscribing repository managers can also fine-tune the minimal threshold of trust T_m for their subscriptions.

2.2 Notifications

If a repository manager activates several subscriptions or modifies over time the parameters of existing subscriptions, the same record may meet the criteria of different subscriptions and be notified several times to the repository. Repositories should therefore not be notified more than once of each relevant publication, unless explicitly requested. As a consequence, the OLBS should keep the history of all past notifications to allow repository managers to consult them and avoid their re-sending to the repositories. As described in [16], two different notification strategies are under evaluation in order to meet diverse requirements of subscribers:

- **Mail postcards.** Subscribers may opt to be notified by email at given interval of times (e.g. daily, weekly, monthly) and with given granularity (individual records, digests, URL to a web user interface).

---

[3] The Directory of Open Access Repositories, http://www.opendoar.org.

- **Programmatic access.** *Pull mode*: APIs will be provided to retrieve notifications by status (e.g. read/unread), subscription typology, and filters (e.g. criteria on the meta-data fields). *Push mode:* the SWORD [4] protocol for automatic ingestion of records into repositories will be evaluated.

2.3 Web Dashboard

Repository managers are supported with the OLBS Web Dashboard, from where they can activate and configure subscriptions of the available types, how publications of these categories should be notified, and also explore the history of notifications they have so far received (e.g. searching and browsing notifications by type, publication title, authors publication date, notification date). Repository managers can fine-tune their subscriptions and test the quality of the notifications they would collect before they actually submit the subscription.

3   Data Model and Architecture

This section presents the data model specification, the high level architecture of the OLBS, and the proposed implementation aiming at satisfying the functional requirements described in Sect. 2.

3.1   Data Model

The data model is illustrated in Fig. 4 and includes the classes: *repository, subscription, potential notification,* and *notification.* The model relies on a "topic tree"[4] that encodes the typologies of subscriptions supported by the OLBS, which are of two main classes *addition* and *enrichment*:

- *addition <subclass>* : the values of *<subclass>* encode the three approaches for the identification of publications "relevant to" a repository, namely: *byAffiliation, byReference*, and *byFunder*.
- *enrichment <subclass>* : the values of *<subclass>* encode the six publication enrichment notification use-cases: *open_access_version, project_link, dataset_link, subject classifications, DOI, author_PID.*

  Repository. Institutional repository registered to the OLBS.
  Subscription. Subscriptions are associated to a *repository* and are characterized by the following configuration parameters:

- *trustThreshold*: the minimum value of trust in the interval [0..1] that a *potential notification* must satisfy to be included in the *notifications* of this subscription;
- *criteria:* CQL query identifying a further criteria to be respected by the set of publication fields included in *potential notification*;

---

[4] OASIS Standard WS-Topics specification 1.3 (2006), http://docs.oasis-open.org/wsn/wsn-ws_topics-1.3-spec-os.pdf.

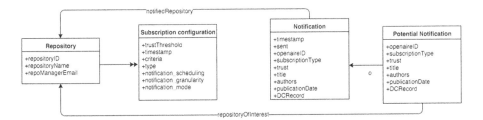

Fig. 4. Data model

- *type*: path in subscription tree identifying the *potential notifications* of interest;
- *notification_scheduling:* how often the notifications for this subscription must be generated and sent (daily, weekly, monthly);
- *notification_granularity*: what must be included in each notification (full Dublin Core of all publications, digest, or a URL to the web dashboard)
- *notification_mode:* possible options will depend on the OLBS functionalities, examples are email and SWORD protocol.

Potential Notification. Potential Notifications are generated by analyzing the Open-AIRE graph information space to identify the whole range of repository-publication pairs that may be of interest to repositories in OpenAIRE, i.e. independently from the existence of an active *subscription*. Each potential notification is associated to a *repository* and is characterized by the following properties:

- *openaireId*: the unique identifier of the publication in the information space;
- *title*, *authors*, *publicationDate* of the publication, to enable search and browse;
- *DCRecord*: the Dublin Core record of the publication;
- *subscriptionType*: path in the topic tree;
- *trust*: level of trust of publication-*repository* association w.r.t. subscription type;

Notification. When a *potential notification* matches a *subscription*, a corresponding notification is created and the *repository* is alerted, respecting *scheduling* and *mode* of the relative *notification configuration*. A notification must be persisted as the evidence that a publication has been notified to a repository. As such, it is a copy of the relative *potential notification*, which, due to the variability of the information space, may not necessarily persist as long as the notifications it has generated (publications in Open-AIRE may disappear). A notification includes all properties of the corresponding potential notification plus the *timeOfCreation* of the notification.

3.2 Architecture Overview

The OpenAIRE information space is stored in an HBASE cluster (8 worker nodes, each of them with 8 CPUs and 24 GB RAM) in order to support performance and scalability. Metadata records collected from data sources are harmonised and transformed into objects compliant to the OpenAIRE data model. The objects are then stored into HBASE, where each object is converted into one HBASE row. In December 2015, OpenAIRE collected more than 15,7 M publication metadata records, corresponding to more than 30 millions OpenAIRE objects (and therefore HBASE rows). Once populated, the HBASE table is ready to be processed by inference and de-duplication algorithms for enrichment:

- The inference subsystem analyzes the OpenAIRE information space, supported by the available full-texts of publications to generate properties and relationships, including the *relationships publication-XXX-repository* needed by the three subscription methods mentioned in Sect. 2.1. In December 2015, the inference subsystem enriched more than 1,2 M publications (8% of the total publications) with relationships and properties.
- The de-duplication subsystem runs Mapreduce jobs on the HBASE table that implement heuristics for the detection of duplicates of publications, organisations and persons [17]. Groups of duplicate objects are then merged into one disambiguated object. Depending on the configuration settings, the deduplication process for 15 M publications takes 2–3 h, identifying 4,1 M of duplicates and merging them into 1,7 M of disambiguated objects.

The enriched HBASE table is then processed for publishing via the OpenAIRE portal and standard APIs [2]. The OLBS will have to further process the OpenAIRE information space stored on HBASE to identify addition and enrichment events to be notified to subscribers. Figure 5 illustrates the OLBS integration in the OpenAIRE infrastructure, which consists of a three-phase data workflow.

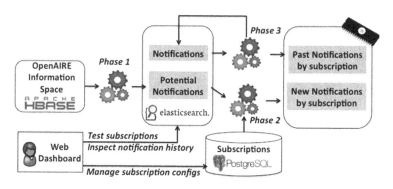

Fig. 5. OLB data flow

Phase 1: Generation of Potential Notifications. Whenever the OpenAIRE infrastructure generates a new version of the information space (i.e. hamornisation, deduplication, enrichment steps are performed), the OLBS will run MapReduce jobs on the HBASE table to identify the current *potential notifications*. These jobs produce tuples of the form: openaireID, SubscriptionType, repositoryId, trust, title, authors, PublicationDate, DCRecord. For each publication-repository pair such that: *(i)* the publication was collected from the repository but is richer in properties or relationships in OpenAIRE (*trust* corresponds to the level of *trust* of the OpenAIRE enrichment), or *(ii)* there exist a chains of relationships *addition.affiliation, addition.reference,* or *addition.funder* between the two (*trust* corresponds to a combination of the inferred relationship *trust* level and other parameters, see Sect. 2.1; the formulae will be refined over time).

Scalability challenges Potential notifications are at the core of the system, since they need to be often updated and searched for matching with subscriptions, and may reach very large numbers, which can be estimated as follows:

- Additions: institutional repositories aim at collecting all publications of authors of reference, hence the assumption that repositories miss an average of 20% of their publications makes a reasonable worst-case scenario. Since OpenAIRE counts around 400 institutional repositories with an average of 13,000 publications, the estimate of missing publications is around 1 M in the worst case.
- Enrichments: the number of institutional repository publications subject to de-duplication and therefore possibly affected by enrichment is around 1,4 M; inference is applied to publications with a PDF, which are today around 3 M. In summary, the worst-case envisages 4,4 M multiplied by the 6 potential "enrichment" notifications, for a total of around 27 M.

Hence, in the optimistic assumption that OpenAIRE would aggregate and elaborate all missing publications and all possible enrichments, the order of magnitude of potential notifications is overall around 28 M. In order to make them searchable (phase 2 and 3 below) the OLBS must build on a scalable back-end, efficient on dropping and feeding entries, and also capable of supporting efficient queries. The current implementation plan finds in Elasticsearch[5] full-text index the best fitting candidate among the Open Source search engines due to its capability of scaling up horizontally and the expressivity of its data model and query language.

Phase 2: Subscription Matching Subscriptions, managed by repository managers via the Web Dashboard, are stored on a relational database (PostgreSql[6]). Based on the *notification_schedule* property of the available subscriptions, the OLBS searches potential notifications matching the criteria of the existing subscriptions: repository, subscription type, criteria, and minimal level of trust. The resulting potential notifications are temporarily kept in memory, ready to be used in the following phase.

Phase 3: Find New Notifications The Elasticsearch index contains another collection of *notifications*, which tracks all *potential notifications* that matched a subscription and have been sent to the relative repositories. Notifications are entries of the form: timestamp, openaireID, Subscription Type, repositoryId, trust, title, Authors, Publication Date, DCRecord; where timestamp is the notification date (the same for all notifications identified and sent in the same Phase 2 session). Starting from the potential notifications identified in Phase 2, currently kept in memory, in Phase 3 the OLBS searches the *notifications* collection in order select which *potential notifications* are eligible to become new *notifications*, thereby avoiding multiple delivery of the same notifications

---

[5] Elasticsearch https://www.elastic.co.
[6] PostgreSql http://www.postgresql.org.

to the same repositories. Only new notifications will be fed to the index and be sent to the repositories according to the requested notification strategy.

4   Conclusions

The first BETA instantiation of the OLBS will be available by June 2016. The next steps are the generalization of the core of the OLBS to become a general-purpose Literature Broker Service, ready to support the same functionalities independently of the context. To this aim, the data model and internal representations of the OLBS, together with the acquired experience in operating the service, will inspire the definition of standard exchange formats and APIs to achieve interoperability across a network of similar services world-wide (collaborations are active with JISC-UK and SHARE-US). Concepts such as notification broker services, literature subscriptions/notifications descriptions, subscription/notification APIs should be agreed on, conform to existing standards[7], and shared across the community and become a common way to share objects across repositories.

Acknowledgement. This work is partially funded by the EC H2020 project OpenAIRE2020 (Grant agreement: 643410, Call: H2020-EINFRA-2014-1).

References

1. The OpenAIRE guidelines. https://guidelines.openaire.eu. Accessed 10 July 2015
2. The OpenAIRE API. https://api.openaire.eu. Accessed 10 July 2015
3. Walters, T., Ruttenberg, J.: Shared access research ecosystem. Educause Rev. **49**(2), 56–57 (2014). http://www.educause.edu/ero/article/shared-access-research-ecosystem. Accessed 10 July 2015
4. Lewis, S., de Castro, P., Jones, R.: SWORD: facilitating deposit scenarios. D-Lib Mag. **18**(1), 4 (2012). doi:10.1045/january2012-lewis
5. Manghi, P., Bolikowski, L., Manold, N., Schirrwagen, J., Smith, T.: Openaireplus: the European scholarly communication data infrastructure. D-Lib Mag. **18**(9), 1 (2012). doi: 10.1045/september2012-manghi
6. What is the open research data pilot? https://www.openaire.eu/ordp/ordp/pilot. Accessed 12 July 2015
7. Manghi, P., Artini, M., Atzori, C., Bardi, A., Mannocci, A., La Bruzzo, S., Candela, L., Castelli, D., Pagano, P.: The D-NET software toolkit: a framework for the realization, maintenance, and operation of aggregative infrastructures. Program Electr. Libr. Inf. Syst. **48**(4), 322–354 (2014). doi:10.1108/PROG-08-2013-0045
8. COAR: Confederation of Open Access Repositories. https://www.coar-repositories.org/. Accessed: 12 July 2015
9. The JISC website. https://jisc.ac.uk/. Accessed: 12 July 2015

---

[7] OASIS Web Services Notification (WSN), https://www.oasis-open.org/committees/tc_home.php?wg_abbrev=wsn (26/01/2016).

10. Manghi, P., Houssos, N., Mikulicic, M., Jörg, B.: The data model of the openaire scientific communication e-infrastructure. In: Dodero, J.M., Palomo-Duarte, M., Karampiperis, P. (eds.) Metadata and Semantics Research, vol. 343, pp. 168–180. Springer, Heidelberg (2012). doi:10.1007/978-3-642-35233-1_18

11. Houssos, N., Jörg, B., Dvořák, J., Príncipe, P., Rodrigues, E., Manghi, P., Elbæk, M.K.: OpenAIRE guidelines for CRIS managers: supporting interoperability of open research information through established standards. Procedia Comput. Sci. 33, 33–38 (2014). doi: 10.1016/j.procs.2014.06.006

12. Kobos, M., Bolikowski, Ł., Horst, M., Manghi, P., Manola, N., Schirrwagen, J.: Information inference in scholarly communication infrastructures: the OpenAIREplus project experience. Procedia Comput. Sci. 38, 92–99 (2014). doi:10.1016/j.procs.2014.10.016

13. DataCite web site. https://www.datacite.org. Accessed 12 July 2015

14. The CERIF data model. http://www.eurocris.org/cerif/main-features-cerif

15. Jisc Blog: Jisc publications router enters a new phase. http://tinyurl.com/h93ch9k

16. Artini, M., Atzori, C., Bardi, A., La Bruzzo, S., Manghi, P., Mannocci, A.: The OpenAIRE literature broker service for institutional repositories. D-Lib Mag. 21(11), 3 (2015)

17. Manghi, P., Mikulicic, M.: PACE: a general-purpose tool for authority control. In: García-Barriocanal, E., Cebeci, Z., Okur, M.C., Öztürk, A. (eds.) Metadata and Semantic Research, vol. 240, pp. 80–92. Springer, Heidelberg (2011)

Stratifying Semantic Data for Citation and Trust: An Introduction to RDFDF

Dario De Nart, Dante Degl'Innocenti, Marco Peressotti, and Carlo Tasso[✉]

Department of Mathematics and Computer Science, University of Udine, Udine, Italy
{dario.denart,marco.peressotti,carlo.tasso}@uniud.it,
deglinnocenti.dante@spes.uniud.it

Abstract. In this paper we analyse the functional requirements of linked data citation and identify a minimal set of operations and primitives needed to realise such task. Citing linked data implies solving a series of data provenance issues and finding a way to identify data subsets. Those two tasks can be handled defining a simple type system inside data and verifying it with a type checker, which is significantly less complex than interpreting reified RDF statements and can be implemented in a non data invasive way. Finally we suggest that data citation should be handled outside of the data, and propose a simple language to describe RDF documents where separation between data and metainformation is explicitly specified.

Keywords: RDF · Semantic web · Data citation · Theory · Data trust · Semantic publishing

Over the last years data has become a more and more critical asset both in research and in application. While there is a general agreement on the need for data citation to ensure research reproducibility and to facilitate data reuse, the research community is still debating how to concretely realize it. Citing data is not a trivial task since it has a few notable differences from citing literature: data evolve over time, data availability might change over time, only a subset of data might be relevant, and on top of that the authorship of data is not always clear since it may be the result of an automated process (e.g. sensor data), involve a large number of contributors (e.g. crowdsourcing), or even be built on the top of other data (e.g. inferring a taxonomy from a document corpus). Leveraging on the insights provided by [2,3,13,15] we outline the following Data Citation functional requirements:

- *Identification and Access*: Data Citation should provide a persistent, machine readable, and globally unique identifier for data; Moreover a reference to a persistent repository should also be provided to facilitate data access.
- *Credit and Attribution*: Data citation should facilitate giving credit and legal attribution to all contributors to the data. Such contributors might be humans as well as automated processes such as reasoners;

M. Agosti et al. (Eds.): IRCDL 2016, CCIS 701, pp. 104–111, 2017.
DOI: 10.1007/978-3-319-56300-8_10

– *Evolution*: Data Citation should provide a reference to the exact version of the cited data, since data might change over time. This is a fundamental requirement for research reproducibility purposes.

An additional, non functional requirement, is efficiency: the data citation should lead to the data in practical time, which means fast enough for the purposes of data consumer applications. For instance a database query allows to access the data in practical time, while solving a complex set of logical clauses probably does not. In the last years Linked Data has rapidly emerged as the preferred format for publishing and sharing structured data, creating a vast network of interlinked datasets [9]. However the open nature of the format makes data provenance hard to track, moreover the RDF Recommendation does not provide a clear mechanism for expressing metainformation about RDF documents. Semantic Web technologies such as OWL, RDF, and RDFS leverage upon description logic and first order logic and it is well known that an incautious usage of their primitives may lead to non decidable sets of conditions [10]. With respect to the requirements of a good data citation expressed above, the Semantic Web community has proposed a number of solutions to the data provenance problem which addresses the problem of assessing the authorship of data. Methods for partitioning RDF graphs have been proposed as well and also version identification and storage of RDF data have already been discussed. However most of those solutions imply the embedding of metainformation inside RDF data. This practice tends to make data cumbersome and the usage of reification [8] to realize tasks such as generating data subsets may lead to a combinatorial explosion of triples. In this paper we discuss a simple framework to satisfy data citation requirements leveraging on the stratification of linked data, which basically means providing a separation between proper data and metainformation. Such separation can be effectively guaranteed with the usage of a simple type system allowing programs such as reasoners to discriminate in an efficient way. We'd also like to show that the fact that Linked Data technologies such as RDF and OWL are powerful enough to let you seamlessly represent and embed metainformation inside the data does not mean that you really *should*.

1   Related Work

Data citation has already been explored by the Semantic Web community and it significantly overlaps with the problem of assessing data provenance since determining the authorship of data is vital for citation purposes and both tasks need metainformation over data. Provenance has already been widely discussed by the Semantic Web community leveraging on the insights provided by the Database community [5]. Provenance information can be represented exploiting two approaches: the annotation approach and the inversion approach [12]. In the first approach all metainformation is explicitly stated, while in the latter is computed when needed in a lazy fashion which requires external resources containing the information upon which provenance is entailed to be constantly available. The annotation approach is favored since it provides richer information and allows data to be self-contained; several vocabularies have been proposed to describe metainformation over linked data such as *VoID* (Vocabulary of Inter-linked Datasets) [1], that offers a rich language for describing Semantic Web resources built on top of well known and widely used ontologies such as foaf[1] and Dublincore[2], and *PROV Ontology* (PROV-O)[3], which is the lightweight ontology for provenance data standardized by the W3C Provenance Working Group. Regardless of the vocabulary used, adopting the annotation approach will result in producing a lot of metainformation which might exceed the actual data in size: provenance data in particular increases exponentially with respect to its depth [14]. For more information about the problem of data provenance, we reference the curious reader to [4]. The state of the art technique for embedding metainformation in RDF, is reification [15] which consists in assigning a URI to a RDF triple by expressing it as an *rdf:Statement* object. Recently the RDF 1.1 Recommendation [11] introduced the so called "RDF Quad Semantic" which consists in adding a fourth element to RDF statements which should refer to the name of the graph which the triple belongs to. The actual semantic of the fourth element however is only hinted, leaving room for interpretation and therefore allowing semantics tailored to fit application needs. In [13] is presented a methodology for citing linked data exploiting the quad semantics: the fourth element is used as identifier for RDF predicates allowing the definition of data subsets. Other usages of the fourth element include specification of a time frame, uncertainty marker, and provenance information container [6]. Finally, the idea of using a type system to ease the fruition of semantic resources is not new to the Semantic Web community: the authors of [7] propose a type system to facilitate programmatic access to RDF resources.

2 Well Stratified Linked Data

To introduce the concept of stratification of data we need to define a formal representation of metainformation in linked data that abstracts over the actual representation of such information (e.g. reification). Let us assume all the vocabulary of a collection of RDF data to be included in a set of labels named V and all the IRIs to be in U, subset of V. Given those definitions, associating labels to RDF graphs -thus creating named graphs- can be described by a partial function $n : u \mapsto (v, u', v')$ mapping each $u \in U$ to at most one triple $(v, u', v') \in V \times U \times V$. This function, that we will refer to herein as *naming function* maps identifiers to non void RDF graphs. Intuitively, assigning an IRI to a triple puts that IRI in the rôle of *metainformation* with respect to that triple whence thought as *information*. Note that the separation between information and metainformation is not absolute but *relative* to the context i.e. the level at which the reasoning happens. For a concrete example, consider the following RDF snipped:

---

[1] http://xmlns.com/foaf/spec/.

[2] http://dublincore.org/documents/dcmi-terms/.

[3] http://www.w3.org/TR/prov-o/.

```
x type       statement
x subject    y
x predicate  b
x object     c
y type       statement
y subject    a
y predicate  b
y object     c
```

Accordingly to the reification semantics, here x is assigned to triple (y, b, c) and y to the triple (a, b, c) hence, the naming function over the considered data includes the following associations:

$$x \mapsto (y, b, c) \qquad \text{and} \qquad y \mapsto (a, b, c).$$

Clearly, y plays the rôle of metainformation with respect to the triple (a, b, c) and x plays the rôle of metainforamtion about (y, b, c) whence (a, b, c). From now on we will refer to a vocabulary with an associated naming function as a *Named Graph Family* (herein NG family), moving along the lines of [6].

We consider a particular class of NG families called *well-stratified* with the fundamental property of stratifying metainformation over information in a way that prevents any infinite chain of "downward" references where the direction is interpreted as crossing the boundary between metainformation and information. Since practical NG families (hence triple stores) contain only a finite amount of explicit information, absence of such chains corresponds to the absence of cycles of references like, for instance, in the NG family:

$$x \mapsto (y, b, c) \sqcup y \mapsto (x, b, c).$$

In more formal terms, a relation R on a set X is *well-founded* whenever every non-empty subset S of X has a minimal element i.e. there exists $m \in S$ that is not related by $s \, R \, m$ for $s \in S$. This means that we can intuitively walk along R going from right to left for finitely many steps i.e we have to stop, eventually. This implies that R does not contain infinite descending chains (i.e. an infinite sequence $x_0, x_1, x_2, \ldots$ such that $x_{n+1} \, R \, x_n$). We call a NG family *well-stratified* whenever it comes equipped with a well-founded relation $\prec$ on its vocabulary such that the naming function n descends along $\prec$ i.e.:

$$n(u) = (a, b, c) \implies u \succ a \wedge u \succ b \wedge u \succ c.$$

The relation $\prec$ is called *witness* for n. It is intuitive that identifying what serves as metainformation and information is easily computable over well-stratified NG families, while non well-founded NG families include cycles wherein it is impossible to separate information from metainformation.

We now introduce the concept of *abstract reasoner* as anything that might alter data either by simply adding new triples (monotonic reasoners) or by deleting and replacing existing triples (non-monotonic reasoners). With abstract reasoners we represent both automated reasoning (and other data managing tasks) and human annotation. Abstract reasoners may easily break well-stratification. Intuitively most reasoning tasks and well-engineered human annotation processes should preserve stratification, however breaking the well-stratification of data is subtle and can be achieved even with monotonic reasoning. For instance, consider a set of triples where there exists a triple $(y, \texttt{type}, \texttt{statement})$ labelled with some IRI x and an abstract reasoner γ that adds a new triple $(x, \texttt{type}, \texttt{statement})$ labelled as y. This insertion is totally legit if we are using reification but introduces a circularity in the chain of meta data since the family now contains the following assignments:

$$x \mapsto (a, \texttt{type}, \texttt{statement}) \qquad a \mapsto (x, \texttt{type}, \texttt{statement})$$

and hence is no more well-stratified. We are interested in a class of abstract reasoners, called *coherent*, that preserve the well-stratification property of named graph families they operate on. Intuitively, reasoners for provenance, subsetting and versioning are coherent as they cross the boundary between information and meta information only in one direction: descent. However in order to let such reasoners terminate the well-stratification of data must be guaranteed, therefore, every abstract reasoner that interacts with data prior to the resolution of a data citation must be coherent as well. Wrapping up these considerations, data citation can happen if data is well stratified and data can be well stratified if all the abstract reasoners that built, expanded, and verified it are coherent. It is therefore needed a practical solution to assess the coherence of abstract reasoners.

3   Resource Description Framework Description Framework

In this section we propose a possible specification of a simple language called *RDFDF* whose main purpose is to guarantee the well stratification of data, hence the coherence of reasoning. RDFDF can be considered an extension to regular RDF, however it introduce some new top level concepts making it a new language built on the top of RDF rather than its extension (like OWL and RDFS). By design, RDFDF is a superset of RDF, thus every well formed RDF document is a well formed RDFDF document as well. RDFDF makes explicit the so-called fourth element introduced by the RDF 1.1 recommendation [11] and the basic unit of the RDFDF language is the quadruple (s, p, o, i) where s, p, and o are the subject, predicate, and object of regular RDF triples, and i is the optional *identifier* labelling the RDF triple. With this fourth element the naming function described in Sect. 2 can be easily represented since $x \mapsto (s, p, o)$ can be conveniently written as (s, p, o, x). IRIs that appear as fourth object are implicitly of type *meta-resource*, a sibling class to *rdfs:resource* which now is a subclass of a broader class called *data* which includes both information and metainformation. Resource and meta-resource are not disjoint, indeed an IRI that is used as identifier and as subject, object or predicate of another triple belongs to both of them. The rationale behind this choice is that identifiers can be described using resources such as data provenance ontologies, therefore interoperability between resources and meta-resources is needed, and there can exist multiple levels of meta-information such that the meta-information of a certain level serves as information for the upper one. In Fig. 1 we show a practical example of a case where an IRI, in this case U, belongs to both *meta-resource* and *rdfs:resource* since it is used as identifier for the triple (A, B, C) and as subject of $(U, author, foaf : x)$.

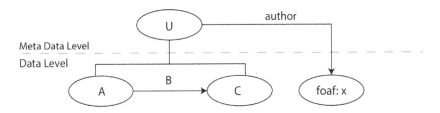

Fig. 1. An example of metainformation stratification in RDFDF.

At the semantics level, however, the most notable difference is the introduction of a basic *type system*: while the *rdf:type* property still indicates class membership, RDFDF introduces types at the data set level to check the well-stratification of data. In this context each IRI belongs to a specific level of information: the first one is information, the second meta-information, the third meta-meta-information, and so on. The absence of loops between such layers can be checked with a simple *type system*, similar to the ones used in programming language, to ensure the well-stratification of RDFDF documents. RDFDF introduces a simple type system whose only type ✓ is inhabited by exactly well-stratified data. Judgements are of the form

$$\Gamma \vdash n : \checkmark$$

where $n \colon U \rightharpoonup V \times U \times V$ is a data set (which corresponds to a family of named graphs) and the stage Γ is a partial function from the vocabulary V to a well-founded structure. For instance, could map V to the set of natural numbers under the successor relation: $\Gamma \colon V \rightharpoonup \mathbb{N}$. The proposed type system is composed by three typing rules:

$$\frac{}{\Gamma \vdash \varnothing : \checkmark}$$

$$\frac{\Gamma(x) > \Gamma(a) \quad \Gamma(x) > \Gamma(b) \quad \Gamma(x) > \Gamma(c)}{\Gamma \vdash x \mapsto (a, b, c) : \checkmark}$$

$$\frac{\Gamma_1 \vdash n_1 : \checkmark \quad \Gamma_2 \vdash n_2 : \checkmark \quad \Gamma = \Gamma_1 \sqcup \Gamma_2 \quad n = n_1 \sqcup n_2}{\Gamma \vdash n : \checkmark}$$

The first captures the fact that an empty document is always well-stratified. The second ensures that Γ describes relations on V such that the assignment

$x \mapsto (a, b, c)$ is well-stratified. Finally, the third rule allows to break n and Γ reducing the problem to smaller objects which can then be checked separately (clearly, applying this rule with either n_1 or n_2 being $\varnothing$ is pointless). We do not need to "guess" Γ. This function can be obtained by applying the above typing judgements while considering Γ as an unknown collecting all the hypotheses on it (e.g. $\Gamma(x) > \Gamma(a)$ from the second rule) in a set of constraints. Any partial function satisfying these constraints can be used as Γ to derive $\Gamma \vdash n : \checkmark$. Computing such solutions can be done pretty efficiently and the choice of the algorithm to be used is left to the implementer, anyway, RDFDF allows to provide explicit typing annotations as separate meta-data with the *level* property, as in the following snippet.

```
a, rdf:type, b, x
x, rdfdf:level, 1
```

The *level* property is defined as an *owl:AnnotationProperty* and therefore is ignored by OWL reasoners and is intended solely for type inference purposes. An explicitly typed document can be verified efficiently.

4 Conclusions and Future Works

In this paper we briefly introduced the concept of well stratification over linked data and highlighted how achieving well stratification over data is a fundamental requirement to realise data citation over RDF data. With respect to the problem of data citation, the expressive power of OWL and RDF is largely overabundant and might be harmful since a misuse of their primitives might break the stratification of information and metainformation, thus making resolving citations an undecidable problem. In our opinion, a more restricted language, designed specifically to grant the stratification of data, like RDFDF, should be taken into consideration to effectively enable problems such as data citation and provenance assessment to be resolved in practical time, allowing the creation of an effective data trust layer. Attaching RDFDF data or some other kind of well stratified metainformation to data published on the Web might be, in our opinion, Linked Open Data's sixth star, like publishing versioned code is a fundamental quality requirement for Open Source software. The similarity between data metainformation handling and source code versioning is striking since they address similar problems: tracking who and how edited something, identifying subsets of the managed items, and allowing external application or documents to refer to a specific revision. In our opinion this separation is also consistent with the present development of the Semantic Web stack: OWL itself, thought being a logical extension of RDFS, is not built on the top of RDFS but is rather a distinct language sharing concepts and primitives with RDFS. In a similar way a new language for data metainformation management could be built compatibly with RDF and the Linked Data philosophy without being RDF.

References

1. Alexander, K., Cyganiak, R., Hausenblas, M., Zhao, J.: Describing linked datasets with the void vocabulary (2011)
2. Altman, M., Borgman, C., Crosas, M., Matone, M.: An introduction to the joint principles for data citation. Bull. Am. Soc. Inform. Sci. Technol. **41**(3), 43–45 (2015)
3. Altman, M., Crosas, M.: The evolution of data citation: from principles to implementation. IASSIST Q. **63** (2013)
4. Anam, S., Kang, B.H., Kim, Y.S., Liu, Q.: Linked data provenance: state of the art and challenges. In: Proceedings of the 3rd Australasian Web Conference (AWC 2015), vol. 27, p. 30 (2015)
5. Buneman, P., Khanna, S., Wang-Chiew, T.: Why and where: a characterization of data provenance. In: Bussche, J., Vianu, V. (eds.) ICDT 2001. LNCS, vol. 1973, pp. 316–330. Springer, Heidelberg (2001). doi:10.1007/3-540-44503-X_20
6. Carroll, J.J., Bizer, C., Hayes, P., Stickler, P.: Named graphs, provenance and trust. In: Proceedings of the 14th International Conference on World Wide Web, pp. 613–622. ACM (2005)
7. Ciobanu, G., Horne, R., Sassone, V.: Minimal type inference for linked data consumers. J. Logical Algebraic Methods Program. (2014)
8. Hayes, P., McBride, B.: RDF semantics (2004)
9. Heath, T., Bizer, C.: Linked data: evolving the web into a global data space. In: Synthesis Lectures on the Semantic Web: Theory and Technology, vol. 1, no. 1, pp. 1–136 (2011)
10. Horrocks, I., Patel-Schneider, P.F., Van Harmelen, F.: From SHIQ and RDF to OWL: the making of a web ontology language. Web Semant. Sci. Serv. Agents World Wide Web **1**(1), 7–26 (2003)
11. Klyne, G., Carrol, J.J., Mc Bride, B.: RDF 1.1 concepts and abstract syntax (2014)
12. Omitola, T., Gibbins, N., Shadbolt, N.: Provenance in linked data integration (2010)
13. Silvello, G.: A methodology for citing linked open data subsets. D-Lib Magazine **21**(1), 6 (2015)
14. Simmhan, Y.L., Plale, B., Gannon, D.: A survey of data provenance techniques. Computer Science Department, Indiana University, Bloomington IN 47405 (2005)
15. Zhao, J., Bizer, C., Gil, Y., Missier, P., Sahoo, S.: Provenance requirements for the next version of RDF. Citeseer

Formal Components of Narratives

Valentina Bartalesi$^{(\boxtimes)}$ and Carlo Meghini

Istituto di Scienza e Tecnologie dell'Informazione "Alessandro Faedo" – CNR Pisa,
via Moruzzi 1, 56124 Pisa, Italy
{valentina.bartalesi,carlo.meghini}@isti.cnr.it

Abstract. One of the main problems of the current Digital Libraries
(DLs) is the limitation of the informative services offered to the users,
who express their queries in natural language. Indeed, DLs provide simple search functionalities that return a list of the information objects
contained in them. No semantic relation among the returned objects is
usually reported, which could help the user in obtaining a more complete
knowledge on the subject of the search. The introduction of the Semantic
Web, and in particular of the Linked Data, has the potential of improving
the search functionalities of DLs. In this context, our final aim is to introduce the *narrative* as new first-class search functionality. As output of a
query, the new search functionality does not only return a list of objects
but it also presents a *narrative*, composed of events that are linked to
the objects of the library and endowed with a set of semantic relations
connecting these events into a meaningful semantic network. This paper
presents a study of the Artificial Intelligence literature, especially of the
Event Calculus theory, in order to identify the formal components of
narratives. Furthermore, the mapping between these components and
the standard ontology CIDOC CRM is presented, in order to evaluate
if it could be taken as reference vocabulary to create an ontology for
narratives. On the top of this ontology, we will develop the new search
functionality for DLs.

Keywords: Digital libraries · Formal components of narratives ·
Narratives · Ontologies · Storytelling

1 Introduction

Digital libraries (DLs) are information systems that offer services over large
sets of digital objects [23]. The traditional search functionalities of DLs, such
as Europeana[1], consider that users express their information need through a
natural language query, and the digital library returns a ranked list of digital
objects. This approach works well on the Web, which may be intended as a
very large DL where the objects of the search are pages rich in textual contents,
images, video and interlinked each other. On the other hand, this type of traditional search functionality runs poorly on most DLs. The reason is that the

---

[1] http://www.europeana.eu/portal/.

© Springer International Publishing AG 2017
M. Agosti et al. (Eds.): IRCDL 2016, CCIS 701, pp. 112–121, 2017.
DOI: 10.1007/978-3-319-56300-8_11

digital objects contained in them (e.g. representations of books, manuscripts, photographs, videos) are not meant to be read and navigated on the fly like Web pages and the search is based only on the metadata associated to objects that are semantically poor. As a result, the response to a web-like query on a digital library is typically a ranked list of metadata descriptors. In our study, we aim at overcoming the limitations of the search functionality of current DLs by introducing a new first class search functionality: the *narrative*. The vision is that a user searching e.g. for Dante Alighieri – the major Italian poet of the late Middle Ages – in Europeana would obtain in response not the ranked list of objects concerning Dante Alighieri but rather a *narrative* about Dante, made up of a list of events that compose his biography, linked to the relevant objects of the digital library that contextualizes them.

First of all, in order to introduce this new search functionality and to develop an ontology for representing narratives, we studied the Artificial Intelligence (AI) literature, and in particular the Event Calculus theory, to identify the logical components of narratives (e.g. events, actions, fluents, physical object, agents), and give their formal definitions. Then, we mapped these logic components with the terms of the CIDOC CRM ontology [8] to evaluate if it would be possible to take it as reference vocabulary. In this paper we report the result of the study of the AI literature and the result of the mapping activity.

The paper is structured as follows: Sect. 2 reports an overview of the related works, in Sect. 3 the analysis of the AI literature in order to identify the formal components of narratives is presented. In Sect. 4, a mapping between the formal components of narratives and the CIDOC CRM is reported, in order to evaluate if it could be a reference ontology for representing narratives. Section 5 presents a brief discussion of the results of the mapping activity. Finally, Finally, we report our Sect. 6.

2   Related Works

In literary theory, narratology is a discipline devoted to the study of the narrative structure and the logic, principles, and practices of its representation. Computational Narratology studies narratives from a computational perspective. In particular, it focuses on "'the algorithmic processes involved in creating and interpreting narratives, modelling narrative structure in terms of formal computable representations"' [10]. The term "Computational Narratology" (CN) can assume different meanings according to the research context. In particular, in the context of Humanities, computational narratology is defined as a methodological instrument for constructing narratological theories, extending narratological models to larger bodies of text, providing precise and consistent explication of concepts [24]. From a cognitive computing point of view, this term refers to narrative texts, computer games, and more in general, software developed using semiotic, sociolinguistic and cognitive linguistic theories [12]. In the Artificial Intelligence field, computational narratology refers to the story generation systems, i.e. any computer application that creates a written, spoken, or visual presentation of a story. Storytelling systems aim at reproducing a human-like narrative behaviour or at creating interfaces or game environments using narrative as interactive method. Some of the early storytelling systems are TALE-SPIN [22], UNIVERSE [17], GESTER [29] and JOSEPH [15] that changes the story grammars to create new stories. Other storytelling systems are MINSTREL [40], MEXICA [30] and BRUTUS [3]. These are hybrid systems that implement a computer model of creativity in writing. Recently, ontologies were used to generate narratives. For example, MAKE-BELIEVE [18] uses common-sense knowledge, selected from the ontology of the Open Mind Commonsense Knowledge Base [39], to generate short stories from an initial one given by the user. ProtoPropp [11] uses an ontology of explicitly relevant knowledge and the Case-Based Reasoning method over a defined set of tales. In FABULIST [33] the user supplies a description of an initial state of the world and a specific goal, and the system identifies the best sequence of actions to reach the goal.

The concept of *event* is a core element of the narratology theory and of the narratives. People conventionally refer to an *event* as an occurrence taking place at a certain time in a specific location. Various models have been developed for representing events on the Semantic Web, e.g. Event Ontology [32], Linking Open Descriptions of Events (LODE) [37], the F-Model [36]. More general models for semantic data organization are the CIDOC CRM [8] and the Europeana Data Model [7]. Narratives have been recently proposed to enhance the information contents and functionalities of DLs, with special emphasis on information discovery and exploration. For example, in the CultureSampo project [13] an application to explore Finnish cultural heritage contents on the Web, based on Semantic Web technologies, was developed. This system uses an event-based model and makes links among events and digital objects. However, it does not allow visualizing the event and the related digital objects as a semantic network provided with the semantic relations that connect events and objects. Another example is Bletchley Park Text [28], a semantic application helping users to explore collections of museums. Visitors express their interests on some specific topics using SMS messages containing keywords. The semantic description of the resources is used to organize a collection into a personalized web site based on the chosen topics. In the PATHS project [9] a system that acts as an interactive personalized tour guide through existing digital library collections was created. In this system the events are linked by inherence relations. Similar to the approach of PATHS project, within the CULTURA project [1] a tool to enrich the cultural heritage collections with guided paths in the form of short lessons called *narratives* was developed. The Storyspace system [42] allows describing stories based on events that span museum objects. The system is focused on the creation of curatorial narratives from an exhibition. Each digital object has a linked creation event in its associated heritage object story.

The OntoMedia ontology [16] allows annotating the narrative content of heterogeneous media through description of the semantic content of that media (e.g. literary texts, TV program). The representation may be limited to the description of some or all of the elements contained within the source or may include information regarding the narrative relationship that these elements have both to the media and to each other. Another example is the tool developed within the Cadmos project [19], which adopts a computer-supported semantic annotation of narrative media objects (video, text, audio, etc.) and integrates a large commonsense ontological knowledge. A narrative ontological model has been developed also by the Labyrinth Project [5]. The Labyrinth system allows users exploring digital cultural heritage archives and is based on narrative relations among knowledge resources.

3   Logic Definitions of the Components of Narratives

In this Section we report the formal logic definitions of the components of narratives as defined in the Event Calculus theory, with a brief mention to the Situation Calculus as related background.

The Situation Calculus (SC) is a logic language for representing and reasoning about dynamical domains [20,21]. In dynamical domains the scenarios change because of the actions performed by the agents. A dynamic world is modelled as a series of situations resulting from actions performed in the world. SC represents changing scenarios as a set of first-order formulae, sometimes enriched with some second-order features [41]. The basic elements of the calculus are:

- Situations. A situation represents a sequence of actions. The situation is a state resulting from these actions. Sequences of actions are represented using the function symbol *do*, so that *do(a, s)* represents the new situation after that the action *a* is performed in situation *s*.
- Fluents. Fluents are functions and predicates that vary over situations (e.g. location of the agent). Fluents are situation-dependent components used to describe the effects of actions. The fluents can be distinguished in: relational fluents and functional fluents. The former has only two values: true or false, while the latter can take a range of values. As a convention, the situation is the last argument of a fluent [21], e.g. *Holding(G1, S0)* where *S0* is the situation.
- Actions. Actions are changes performed by agents from a situation to another in a dynamic world. Each action can be described in the simplest version of Situation Calculus using two axioms: (i) the Possibility Axiom that specifies when an action can be performed; (ii) the Effect Axiom that defines the consequences of an executed action.

SC works well when there is a single agent performing instantaneous, discrete actions. When actions have duration and can overlap with each other the alternative formalism is the Event Calculus (EC) [14,26,27], which is used for reasoning on actions and changes and it is based on points rather than on situations. EC allows reasoning over intervals of time and fluents are time-dependent rather than situation-dependent. EC axioms define a fluent true at a point in time if "the fluent was initiated by an event at some time in the past and was not terminated by an intervening event" [34].

Davidson [6] defines *actions* as a sub class of *events*. In Davidson's opinion, the distinct sign between general events and actions is the intentionality of actions, e.g. when an agent performs an action for a reason.

Like SC, Event Calculus has actions. However, the Davidson's distinction between events and actions is not present. In the EC actions are events. In the following list we reported the logical definitions of the components of narratives of some interest for our representation.

- *Generalized events.* In the context where actions and objects are aspects of a physical universe with a spatial and temporal dimension, a generalized event is a space-time chunk. This abstraction allows thinking to generalized event concepts like actions, locations, times, fluents and physical objects.
- *Mental events and mental objects.* The relations between an agent and "mental objects" like *believes, knows* and *wants*, are called propositional attitudes, because they identify attitudes that agents can have towards a proposition [34]. Using the reification method, it is possible to turn a proposition into an object that could become an argument of a sentence (because only terms and not sentences can be arguments of predicates).
- *Narrative.* As reported in [41], a narrative is a possibly incomplete specification of a set of actual event occurrences [25,35]. The EC is narrative-based, unlike the standard SC in which an exact sequence of hypothetical actions is represented.

Following the narratology theory [31,38], we envisage a *narrative* as consisting of two main elements: the *fabula* and one or more *narrations* of the fabula. The fabula is built on top of basic events (including actions), endowed with:

- a *mereological* relation, relating events to the sub-events that compose them.
- a *temporal occurrence* relation, associating each event with a time interval during which the event occurs; an event occurs before (or during, or after) another event just in case the period of occurrence of the former event is before (or during, or after) the period of occurrence of the latter event.
- a *causality* relation, relating events that in normal discourse are predicated to have a *cause-effect* relation.

4   CRM Ontology Mapping

In order to develop a semantic model to represent narratives, on top of which developing the new search functionality for DLs, we evaluate to use the CIDOC Conceptual Reference Model (CRM) as reference ontology. The CIDOC CRM (CRM for short) is a high-level ontology and an ISO standard[2] that allows the information integration of the data relating to the cultural heritage domain and their correlation with the knowledge stored in libraries and archives [8]. The CRM promotes a shared understanding of cultural heritage information through a semantic framework that any cultural heritage organization can use to map

---

[2] http://www.iso.org/iso/catalogue_detail?csnumber=34424.

its cultural objects. The evaluation was based on the mapping between the logic components of narratives and the definitions of the terms included in the CRM. The result of the mapping is reported below. The definitions are extracted from the CRM official documentation[3].

- *Event.* In the CRM, the class *E5 Event* corresponds to the definition of *event* in the EC theory. This class "comprises changes of states in cultural, social or physical systems, regardless of scale, brought about by a series or group of coherent physical, cultural, technological or legal phenomena. Such changes of state will affect instances of *E77 Persistent Item* or its subclasses".
- *Action.* Actions identified by Davidson correspond to the class *E7 Activity* in the CRM. "This class comprises actions intentionally carried out by an actor that result in changes of state in the cultural, social, or physical systems documented. This notion includes complex, composite and long-lasting actions such as the building of a settlement or a war, as well as simple, short-lived actions such as the opening of a door".

In order to refine our mapping, we analysed the single types of generalized events that are useful to represent the "factual" components of events and we mapped them with the classes of CRM.

- *Agent.* The CRM uses the class *E39 Actor* to represent people, either individually or in groups, who have the potential to perform intentional actions.
- *Location.* This concept is represented in the CRM through the class *E53 Place*. "This class comprises extents in space, in particular on the surface of the earth, in the pure sense of physics: independent from temporal phenomena and matter".
- *Time.* CRM uses the class *E52 Time-Span* to represent this concept. "This class comprises abstract temporal extents, in the sense of Galilean physics, having a beginning, an end and a duration. Time Span has no other semantic connotations".
- *Physical Objects.* In the CRM the class *E18 Physical Thing* describes "all persistent physical items with a relatively stable form, man-made or natural. Depending on the existence of natural boundaries of such things, the CRM distinguishes the instances of Physical Object from instances of Physical Feature, such as holes, rivers, pieces of land etc".
- *Mental Objects.* In the CRM the class *E28 Conceptual Object* comprises "nonmaterial products of our minds and other human produced data that have become objects of a discourse about their identity, circumstances of creation or historical implication. The production of such information may have been supported by the use of technical devices such as cameras or computers".

The relations defined on the events (and actions) of the fabula, are expressed by the following CRM properties:

---

[3] http://www.cidoc-crm.org/docs/cidoc_crm_version_6.2.pdf.

– *Mereological Relation.* The mereological relation is represented using the property *P9 consists of (forms part of)*, which associates an instance of *E4 Period* with another instance of *E4 Period* that is defined by a subset of the phenomena that define the former. Note that *E5 Event* is a sub-class of *E4 Period*, therefore *P9* can be used also as an event mereology.
– *Event Occurrence Relation and Temporal Relation.* The event occurrence relation is represented by the CRM property *P4 has time-span (is time span of)*, which describes the temporal confinement of an instance of an *E2 Temporal Entity* and therefore of an event. Because the period of occurrence of an event may not be known, the CRM allows to directly relate events based on their occurrence time. To this end, it introduces seven properties (*P114* to *P120*) mirroring the temporal relations formalized by Allen's temporal logic [2].
– *Causality Relation.* The causality relation is represented by the CRM property *O13 triggers (is triggered by)*, which is actually part of an extension of CRM, the CRMSci[4]. O13 associates an instance of *E5 Event* that triggers another instance of *E5 Event* with the latter (. . .); in that sense it is interpreted as the cause.

5   Discussion

As result of the mapping, the identified logic components of narratives can be defined using classes and properties of the CRM. Furthermore, the CRM provides several sub classes of *E5 Event* which recognize types of event (e.g. *E63 Beginning of Existence, E64 End of Existence, E65 Creation*). These sub classes are useful to establish a first categorization of events. Furthermore, another advantage of the use of the CRM is the existence of CRMinf, an extension of the CRM, which we are evaluating for the description of the inference processes of the narrator. Indeed, we additionally considered to represent the inferential process of a narrator who reconstructs the events composing a narrative starting from the study of the primary sources, e.g. a scholar who studied Dante Alighieri's biography analyses primary sources and on the basis of them s/he identifies and justifies that a particular event has to be included in Dante's life. Our model aims at describing the *knowledge provenance*, i.e. the process of tracing the origins of knowledge [4]. Reconstructing the inference process is important to evaluate the trustworthiness of the knowledge. Using this information, users can determine the quality of the knowledge based on its derivations. CRMinf is a formal ontology supporting the explicit representation of contextual information about data. In particular, it aims at representing data attribution, scientific concepts of observation, inferences and beliefs. Generally speaking, CRMinf represents "integrating metadata about argumentation and inference making in descriptive and empirical sciences[5], such as biodiversity, geology, geography, archaeol-

---

[4] www.ics.forth.gr/isl/CRMext/CRMsci/docs/CRMsci1.2.2.pdf.
[5] Empirical sciences aim to explain the observed phenomena and to draw hypothetical conclusions about their behaviour and their relationships under given circumstances. On the contrary, descriptive sciences collect, observe and describe phenomena and their correlations.

ogy, cultural heritage, conservation, research IT environments and research data libraries"[6].

The components of narratives defined in the previous Sections could be intended as a first conceptualization of an ontology for representing narratives. For this reason, we have started the validation of these components by partially expressing them in the CRM and by using them to formally represent some of the main events that compose the biography of Dante Alighieri, selected as case study. Our representation of the events of Dante's life is derived from a biography of the poet written by an authoritative Italian biographer of Dante.

6   Conclusions and Future Work

In this paper we have described a study of the Artificial Intelligent literature, especially of the Event Calculus theory, in order to identify the formal components of narratives. Then, we have mapped these components with the classes and properties of the standard ontology CIDOC CRM to evaluate if it could be taken as reference vocabulary to construct an ontology for representing narratives. On the top of this ontology for narratives, we aim at developing a new search functionality for DLs. Indeed, one of the main problems of the current DLs is the limitation of the informative services offered to the user. DLs provide simple search functionalities which return a list of information objects but no semantic relation among them is usually reported. Our aim is to allow the DLs to return a *narrative* instead of a simple list of objects. This *narrative* is based on the events that compose it linked to the correlated objects of the DL and endowed with a set of semantic relations that connect these events into a semantic network meaningful to the user. After this first study to identify the formal components of narratives and the mapping with the CIDOC CRM, we are currently working on creating an ontology for narratives.

References

1. Agosti, M., Manfioletti, M., Orio, N., Ponchia, C.: Enhancing end user access to cultural heritage systems: tailored narratives and human-centered computing. In: Petrosino, A., Maddalena, L., Pala, P. (eds.) ICIAP 2013. LNCS, vol. 8158, pp. 278–287. Springer, Heidelberg (2013). doi:10.1007/978-3-642-41190-8_30
2. Allen, J.F.: Maintaining knowledge about temporal intervals. Commun. ACM **26**(11), 832–843 (1983)
3. Bringsjord, S., Ferrucci, D.: Artificial Intelligence and Literary Creativity: Inside the Mind of Brutus, a Storytelling Machine. Psychology Press, UK (1999)
4. Committee, P.E., et al.: Premis data dictionary for preservation metadata, version 2.0 (2008). Accessed 22 May 2010
5. Damiano, R., Lieto, A.: Ontological representations of narratives: a case study on stories and actions. In: OASIcs-OpenAccess Series in Informatics, vol. 32. Schloss Dagstuhl-Leibniz-Zentrum fuer Informatik (2013)

---

[6] http://www.ics.forth.gr/isl/CRMext/CRMinf/docs/CRMinf-0.7.pdf.

6. Davidson, D.: Essays on Actions and Events: Philosophical Essays, vol. 1. Oxford University Press, Oxford (2001)
7. Doerr, M., Gradmann, S., Hennicke, S., Isaac, A., Meghini, C., van de Sompel, H.: The Europeana data model (EDM). In: World Library and Information Congress: 76th IFLA general conference and assembly, pp. 10–15 (2010)
8. Doerr, M., Ore, C.E., Stead, S.: The CIDOC conceptual reference model: a new standard for knowledge sharing. In: Tutorials, Posters, Panels and Industrial Contributions at the 26th International Conference on Conceptual Modeling, vol. 83, pp. 51–56. Australian Computer Society, Inc. (2007)
9. Fernie, K., Griffiths, J., Archer, P., Chandrinos, K., de Polo, A., Stevenson, M., Clough, P., Goodale, P., Hall, M., Agirre, E., et al.: Paths: personalising access to cultural heritage spaces. In: 2012 18th International Conference on Virtual Systems and Multimedia (VSMM), pp. 469–474. IEEE (2012)
10. Finlayson, M.A.: Inderjeet Mani. Computational Modeling of Narrative. Synthesis Lectures on Human Language Technologies, no. 18. Morgan & Claypool publishers, Seattle, WA (2013). ISBN 978-1-60845-981-0 (paperback: 40); ISBN 978-1-60845-982-7 (e-book: 30). xvii+ 124 p. (2014). doi:10.2200/s00459ed1v01y201212hlt018. Natural Language Engineering 20(02), 289–292
11. Gervás, P., Díaz-Agudo, B., Peinado, F., Hervás, R.: Story plot generation based on CBR. Knowl.-Based Syst. **18**(4), 235–242 (2005)
12. Harrell, D.A.: Theory and technology for computational narrative: an approach to generative and interactive narrative with bases in algebraic semiotics and cognitive linguistics (2007)
13. Hyvönen, E., Takala, J., Alm, O., Ruotsalo, T., Mäkelä, E.: Semantic kalevala-accessing cultural contents through semantically annotated stories. In: Proceedings of the Cultural Heritage on the Semantic Web Workshop at the 6th International SemanticWeb Conference (ISWC 2007), Busan, Korea. Citeseer (2007)
14. Kowalski, R., Sergot, M.: A logic-based calculus of events. In: Schmidt, J.W., Thanos, C. (eds.) Foundations of Knowledge Base Management, pp. 23–55. Springer, Heidelberg (1989)
15. Lang, R.R.: A formal model for simple narratives (1997)
16. Lawrence, K.F., Jewell, M.O., Prugel-Bennett, A., et al.: Annotation of heterogeneous media using ontomedia (2006)
17. Lebowitz, M.: Story-telling as planning and learning. Poetics **14**(6), 483–502 (1985)
18. Liu, H., Singh, P.: Makebelieve: using commonsense knowledge to generate stories. In: AAAI/IAAI, pp. 957–958 (2002)
19. Lombardo, V., Damiano, R.: Semantic annotation of narrative media objects. Multimedia Tools Appl. **59**(2), 407–439 (2012)
20. McCarthy, J.: A basis for a mathematical theory of computation. Comput. Program. Formal Syst. **354**, 225–238 (1963)
21. McCarthy, J., Hayes, P.J.: Some philosophical problems from the standpoint of artificial intelligence. Readings Artif. Intell., 431–450 (1969)
22. Meehan, J.R.: Tale-spin, an interactive program that writes stories. IJCAI **77**, 91–98 (1977)
23. Meghini, C., Spyratos, N., Sugibuchi, T., Yang, J.: A model for digital libraries and its translation to RDF. J. Data Semant. **3**(2), 107–139 (2014)
24. Meister, J.C.: Computing Action: A Narratological Approach, vol. 2. Walter de Gruyter, New York (2003)
25. Miller, R., Shanahan, M.: Narratives in the situation calculus. J. Logic Comput. **4**(5), 513–530 (1994)

26. Miller, R., Shanahan, M.: Some alternative formulations of the event calculus. In: Kakas, A.C., Sadri, F. (eds.) Computational Logic: Logic Programming and Beyond. LNCS (LNAI), vol. 2408, pp. 452–490. Springer, Heidelberg (2002). doi:10.1007/3-540-45632-5_17

27. Mueller, E.T.: Commonsense Reasoning: An Event Calculus Based Approach. Morgan Kaufmann, San Francisco (2014)

28. Mulholland, P., Collins, T.: Using digital narratives to support the collaborative learning and exploration of cultural heritage. In: Proceedings of 13th International Workshop on Database and Expert Systems Applications, pp. 527–531. IEEE (2002)

29. Pemberton, L.: A modular approach to story generation. In: Proceedings of the Fourth Conference on European Chapter of the Association for Computational Linguistics, pp. 217–224. Association for Computational Linguistics (1989)

30. PÉrez, R.P.Ý., Sharples, M.: Mexica: a computer model of a cognitive account of creative writing. J. Exp. Theor. Artif. Intell. **13**(2), 119–139 (2001)

31. Propp, V.: Morphology of the Folktale, vol. 9. University of Texas Press, Austin (1973)

32. Raimond, Y., Abdallah, S.: The event ontology. Technical report (2007). http://motools.sourceforge.net/event

33. Riedl, M.O., Young, R.M.: Narrative planning: balancing plot and character. J. Artif. Intell. Res. **39**(1), 217–268 (2010)

34. Russell, S., Norvig, P.: Artificial Intelligence: A Modern Approach. Prentice-Hall, Egnlewood Cliffs, 25, 27 (1995)

35. Sandewall, E.: Filter preferential entailment for the logic of action in almost continuous worlds. Universitetet i Linköping/Tekniska Högskolan i Linköping, Institutionen för Datavetenskap (1989)

36. Scherp, A., Franz, T., Saathoff, C., Staab, S.: F-A model of events based on the foundational ontology dolce+DnS ultralight. In: Proceedings of the Fifth International Conference on Knowledge Capture, pp. 137–144. ACM (2009)

37. Shaw, R., Troncy, R., Hardman, L.: LODE: linking open descriptions of events. In: Gómez-Pérez, A., Yu, Y., Ding, Y. (eds.) ASWC 2009. LNCS, vol. 5926, pp. 153–167. Springer, Heidelberg (2009). doi:10.1007/978-3-642-10871-6_11

38. Shklovsky, V.: Art as technique Russian formalist criticism: four essays. In: Lemon, L.T., Reis, M.J. (eds.) University of Nebraska Press, Lincoln (1965)

39. Singh, P., et al.: The public acquisition of commonsense knowledge. In: Proceedings of AAAI Spring Symposium: Acquiring (and Using) Linguistic (and World) Knowledge for Information Access (2002)

40. Turner, S.R.: The Creative Process: A Computer Model of Storytelling and Creativity. Psychology Press, New York (1994)

41. Van Harmelen, F., Lifschitz, V., Porter, B.: Handbook of Knowledge Representation, vol. 1. Elsevier, Amsterdam (2008)

42. Wolff, A., Mulholland, P., Collins, T.: Storyspace: a story-driven approach for creating museum narratives. In: Proceedings of the 23rd ACM Conference on Hypertext and Social Media, pp. 89–98. ACM (2012)

Evaluation

Proposal for an Evaluation Framework for Compliance Checkers for Long-Term Digital Preservation

Nicola Ferro[✉]

Department of Information Engineering,
University of Padua, Padua, Italy
ferro@dei.unipd.it

Abstract. In this paper, we discuss the problem of how to model and evaluate tools that allow memory institutions to check the conformance of documents with respect to their reference standards in order to ensure their appropriateness for long-term preservation. In particular, we propose to model the conformance checking problem as a classification task and to evaluate it as a multi-classification problem using a Cranfield-like approach.

1 Introduction

The *PREservation FORMAts for culture information/e-archives (PREF-ORMA)*[1] project is a *Pre-Commercial Procurement (PCP)* project focused on conformity checking of ingested files for the long-term preservation [8]. The main objective of the project is the development and deployment of an open source software licensed reference implementation for file format standards aimed at any memory institution (or other organisation with a preservation task) wishing to check conformance with a specific standard. This reference implementation, called the *conformance checker*, will consist of a set of modular tools which will be validated against specific implementations of specifications of standards relevant to the PREFORMA project and used by the European memory institutions for preserving their different kind of data objects.

A conformance checker:

- verifies whether a file has been produced according to the specifications of a standard file format, and hence,
- verifies whether a file matches the acceptance criteria for long-term preservation by the memory institution,
- reports in human and machine readable format which properties deviate from the standard specification and acceptance criteria, and
- performs automated fixes for simple deviations in the metadata of the preservation file.

---

[1] http://www.preforma-project.eu/.

© Springer International Publishing AG 2017
M. Agosti et al. (Eds.): IRCDL 2016, CCIS 701, pp. 125–136, 2017.
DOI: 10.1007/978-3-319-56300-8_12

The conformance checker software developed by PREFORMA is intended for use within the *Open Archival Information System (OAIS)* Reference Framework [23] and development is guided by the user requirements provided by the memory institutions that are part of the PREFORMA consortium.

The media types addressed by PREFORMA are: (i) *electronic documents* for establishing a reference implementation for PDF/A [24–26]; (ii) *images* for establishing a reference implementation for uncompressed TIFF [21,22]; and, (iii) *audio-video* for establishing a reference implementation for an audiovisual preservation file, using FFV1[2] for encoding video or moving images, uncompressed LPCM [19] for encoding sound and MKV[3] for wrapping audio- and video-streams in one file.

Evaluation and validation of the developed conformance checkers is a primary concern in PREFORMA and this paper describes the overall approach and framework we are going to apply to assess the performances of the developed tools.

The paper is organized as follows: Section 2 presents some related works in the digital preservation area; Section 3 explains how we frame the conformance checking process as a classification task; Section 4 discusses how we evaluate the performances of the developed conformance checkers; finally, Sect. 5 draws some conclusions and presents an outlook for future work.

2   Related Work

"Digital preservation is about more than keeping the bits [...] It is about maintaining the semantic meaning of the digital object and its content, about maintaining its provenance and authenticity, about retaining its interrelatedness, and about securing information about the context of its creation and use" [29, p. 45]. Since preservation aims at capturing the very essence of digital objects it is often associated with life cycles [27], preservation actions, and overall preservation frameworks and there is often the need to evaluate them and choose among them [6,7,20].

When it comes to preservation frameworks and their evaluation, this paper focuses on a specific step of a more general preservation framework, namely the checking for conformance of document with respect to their reference standards at ingestion time. In particular, the focus of the paper is on how to evaluate tools for carrying out this step, i.e. conformance checkers, and how to create a benchmark for this purpose.

The idea of benchmarking tools for preservation is gaining more and more traction recently [9] and we share a similar approach with [12], who identify the main components of a digital preservation benchmark as:

– *motivating comparison* defines the comparison to be done and the benefits that comparison will bring in terms of the future research agenda;

---

[2] http://www.ffmpeg.org/~michael/ffv1.html.
[3] http://www.matroska.org/.

- *task sample* is a list of tests that the subject, to which a benchmark is applied, is expected to solve;
- *performance measures* are qualitative or quantitative measurements taken by a human or a machine to calculate how fit the subject is for the task.

3   Conformance Checking as a Classification Task

The goal of the PREFORMA conformance checkers is to validate documents against their respective standards. This turns into determining, for each document, whether it is compliant, it suffers from issue 1, issue 2, and so on.

Therefore, we can model the conformance checking process as a classification task [2], where you label documents according to their characteristics and each label (compliant, issue 1, issue 2, ...) is a class C_i, representing the conformance of or an issue with a document.

In general, classes may intersect, since a document may suffer from multiple issues at the same time, but the compliant class must be a separate one, since you cannot have documents that are compliant and not compliant at the same time, as it is shown in Fig. 1.

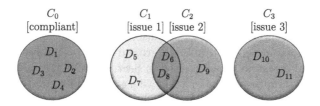

Fig. 1. Conformance checking as a classification task.

One of the challenges we have to face is how to determine the list of classes for each the media types targeted by PREFORMA. Domain experts – both from memory institutions and with technical skills on each specific media type – play a central role in this respect, since they can point out known validation issues, potential validation issues, preservation issues also related to policies of memory institutions, and so on.

One critical aspect in determining such classes is related to their cardinality and granularity. Producing hundreds and hundreds of classes for each media type may be tempting, if you consider this as an indicator of exhaustiveness, but it risks to be harmful in practice, since you may simply ask too much to a conformance checker and you may focus on too tiny or almost irrelevant compliance violations. Therefore, the class creation process must be conducted in an iterative way and domain experts need to work in panels, where they revise and refine each other proposals trying to find the right balance between exhaustiveness and usefulness.

In order to provide an additional degree of flexibility to conformance checking, and its evaluation, we plan to also attach a *severity* to each class since some issues are errors, some others are warnings, some others are mis-conformances to policies and best practices, as it is also shown by the different classes color in Fig. 1. If further analysis and requirements will support it, this could even be turned into a full *meta-classification* of the identified classes, in order to allow us to group them on the basis of their semantics and relationships and, for example, to express progressive levels of conformance, like core, intermediate and full.

4   Evaluating Conformance Checkers for Digital Preservation

In order to evaluate conformance checkers, we will rely on the Cranfield paradigm [10], which makes use of experimental collections $\mathcal{C} = (D, T, GT)$, where D is a collection of documents of interest, T is a set of topics and GT is the ground-truth which, for each document $d \in D$ and topic $t \in D$, determines the relevance of document d to topic t. In the classification context, this paradigm is instantiated considering the classes C_i as topics and the ground-truth is given by the correct labels assigned to each document d [31].

In terms of the approach proposed by [12], we have that: the *motivating comparison* is given by the need of assessing conformance checkers; the *task sample* is defined by the identified classes C_i, as discussed in Sect. 3, the gathered documents, as described in Sect. 4.1, and the ground-truth, as presented in Sect. 4.2; the *performance measures* are described in Sect. 4.3.

The proposed approach also enables a basic level of reproducibility [16,18] of the conducted experiments in the long-term, which we deem essential when it comes to evaluation compliance checkers for long-term preservation.

4.1   Document Collections

The preparation of the collection of documents to be used for assessing the performances of a conformance checker is a critical task that needs to be driven by domain experts. We need to gather a huge sample (ten thousands) for each media type (text, image, audio) from the memory institutions participating in PREFORMA, from the suppliers which are developing the conformance checker tools, and from the open source community at large, which is being built around the PREFORMA effort.

Documents must be representative of the different classes C_i we need to evaluate conformance checkers against. In particular, we cannot have empty classes, i.e. classes for which there is no document in the experimental collection, and the cardinality of each class, i.e. the number of documents in the collection belonging to that class, should make sense from two points of view. Firstly, it should have a size, relative to the other classes, which is proportional to the frequency of the issue represented by the class in real world settings; in other terms, there are issues that happen more frequently and there are issues which are more rare and

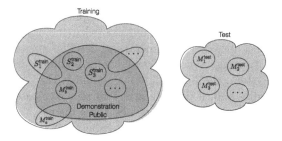

Fig. 2. PREFORMA document collections.

this should be reflected in the cardinality of the corresponding classes, in order to confront conformance checkers with realistic settings. Secondly, we should pay attention to not introduce any bias in the evaluation measurement and process due to an uncontrolled and excessive discrepancy in the cardinality of the classes.

Figure 2 shows the main data set which will be used and made available during the lifetime of the project [13]. The main distinction is between: *training dataset*: aimed at driving and facilitating the design and development of supplier systems, i.e. conformance checkers, as well as show casing their functionalities; *test dataset*: aimed at evaluating and testing the supplier systems in order to score and subsequently select the best of them.

Test and training datasets are kept as two distinct datasets, i.e. there is no intersection, in order to avoid overfitting supplier system on datasets and to ensure fair and unbiased assessment of them.

Both training and test dataset will be associated with ground-truth specifying the correct labels for the documents in the dataset but the ground-truth associated with the test data set will not be shared ahead, because it is needed for carrying out the final testing phase in an unbiased way.

More in detail, the test dataset is constituted by representative test data M_j^{test} provided by memory institutions that can be either partners of the PREFORMA consortium or members of the PREFORMA network of memory institutions. During the execution of the PREFORMA project, this dataset is private and it will be shared only within the consortium to test the supplier systems. After the end of the PREFORMA project, memory institutions may decide to make (part of) it public to favour the PREFORMA ecosystem and open source community.

The training dataset is constituted by: (i) representative training data M_k^{train} provided by memory institutions that can be either partners of the PREFORMA consortium or members of the PREFORMA network of memory institutions; (ii) representative training data S_k^{train} provided by the suppliers participating in the project.

The training dataset is constituted by two parts: a *demonstration* one, which is public and serves the purpose of show casing the suppliers systems both to the other suppliers and to the memory institutions; a *private* part, which is used internally by each supplier for designing, developing, and testing its own system.

Data provided by memory institutions and suppliers which are in the demonstration dataset are accessible and shared also with the other suppliers participating in the project, besides the general public. The purpose of the demonstration dataset is to trigger and facilitate the growth and development of the PREFORMA ecosystem, the open source community, the communication with standardization bodies and, if properly fed, will represent also a strategic asset for suppliers in order to sustain their own business plans.

An orthogonal distinction on the datasets is between *synthetic* and *real* data. The former are data created with the specific purpose of pinpointing some specific compliance problem or critical issue for a given preservation format, as proposed also by [5]. The latter are data actually managed by memory institutions for their preservation duties. It is intended that both the training and the test datasets will be comprised by both synthetic and real data.

4.2 Ground-Truth

As it is well known [30], ground-truth creation is an extremely demanding activity since it requires a great amount of human effort to be conducted. For this reason, a lot of research concentrated on how to reduce the burden of ground-truth creation ranging from the utopian attempt to eliminate assessments at all [33] to crowdsourcing [1,28].

Unfortunately, in the context of PREFORMA, crowdsourcing it is not a viable option since real domain experts are needed to carefully judge the compliance of a document to its reference standard.

Two interesting questions will arise during ground-truth creation in PREFORMA. The first issue is that, to assess the compliance of a document, domain experts will probably also use some of the already existing tools and this may introduce circularity and bias. The second issue is to understand the problem of inter-assessor agreement and see whether on this highly specialised task it will have similar ratios as those for ad-hoc retrieval [35], i.e. in the range 30%–50%, or whether discrepancies from previously known tasks will arise.

The above issues apply in the case of the *real* data while *synthetic* data help mitigating the burden of ground-truth creation, because each synthetic document is purposefully created for testing one or more issues in complying to a standard and it is therefore automatically labeled since its creation.

4.3 Measures

Evaluating conformance checkers is not a binary process, i.e. it is not like going through a long check-list and if any of the items in the list is missing or incorrect, the conformance checker is rejected. The evaluation we foresee is more flexible and we aim at quantifying the extent a conformance checker is able to spot deviations from its reference standard.

Considering that we frame conformance checking as a classification task, it becomes natural to evaluate it according to the confusion matrix [34] shown in Fig. 3.

Class C_i		Ground-Truth Positive	Ground-Truth Negative
Conformance Checker	Positive	True Positive (TP_i)	False Positive (FP_i)
	Negative	False Negative (FN_i)	True Negative (TN_i)

Fig. 3. Confusion matrix for the evaluation of conformance checkers for each class C_i.

Recall from Sect. 3 and Fig. 1 that each class C_i represents a possible misconformance with respect to a reference standard with the exception of the class C_0 which represents documents fully conforming to the standard.

In the confusion matrix: *True Positve (TP)*: it is the set of documents that a conformance checker has correctly labeled as belonging to class C_i; *True Negative (TN)*: it is the set of documents that a conformance checker has correctly labeled as not belonging to class C_i; *False Positive (FP)*: it is the set of documents that a conformance checker has incorrectly labeled as belonging to class C_i; *False Negative (FN)*: it is the set of documents that a conformance checker has incorrectly labeled as not belonging to class C_i.

Note that what we mean by the confusion matrix of Fig. 3 changes if we are considering C_0, i.e. the class representing a compliant document, or a generic C_i, $i \neq 0$, i.e. a class representing an issue within a document.

In the case of C_0, TP_0 is the set of compliant documents correctly identified as compliant; TN_0 is the set of not compliant documents correctly identified as not compliant; FP_0 is the set of not compliant documents incorrectly identified as compliant; and, FN_0 is the set of compliant documents incorrectly identified as not compliant.

In the case of C_i, $i \neq 0$, TP_i is the set of not compliant documents because of issue i correctly identified as suffering from issue i; TN_i is the set of documents correctly identified as not suffering from issue i; FP_i is the set of documents incorrectly identified as suffering from issue i; FN_i is the set of not compliant documents because of issue i but incorrectly identified as not suffering from issue i.

Note that the impact of FP and FN is different in the case we are considering C_0 or a generic C_i, $i \neq 0$. In the case of C_0, FPs are the worst error for a conformance checker, since they are not conforming documents marked as compliant and thus allowed to proceed in the preservation chain, possibly causing issues in the long term; on the other hand, FNs are a less sever error, since they are compliant documents marked as not compliant which will require some additional work for further checks and fixes (actually not necessary) but, eventually, they will have a chance to go ahead in the preservation chain. In the case of C_i, $i \neq 0$, FNs are the worst error for a conformance checker, since they are undetected not compliant documents thus allowed to proceed in the preservation chain, possibly causing issues in the long term; on the other hand FPs are just a kind of "false alarm", which will require some additional work for further checks and fixes (actually not necessary) but, eventually, they will have a chance to go ahead in the preservation chain.

This duality between the harshness of FNs and FPs resembles a similar duality between spam and ham misclassification [11], where spam misclassification annoys the user and may cause the user to overlook important messages while ham misclassification inconveniences the user and risks loss of important messages.

Therefore, we will rely on evaluation measures able both to give a general account of conformance checkers performances and to deal with this duality between FNs and FPs:

– *accuracy*: measures the overall effectiveness [34] of a conformance checker as

$$\text{Accuracy}_i = \frac{|TP_i| + |TN_i|}{|TP_i| + |TN_i| + |FP_i| + |FN_i|} \tag{1}$$

– *area under the curve (AUC)*: measures the ability of a conformance checker to avoid false classification [14,34] as

$$\text{AUC}_i = \frac{1}{2}\left(\frac{|TP_i|}{|TP_i| + |FN_i|} + \frac{|TN_i|}{|TN_i| + |FP_i|}\right) \tag{2}$$

– *logistic average misclassification rate (LAM)*: is the geometric mean of the *odds* of compliance and not-compliance misclassification, converted back to a proportion [11,32]. This measure imposes no a priori relative importance on compliance and not-compliance misclassification, and rewards equally a fixed-factor improvement in the odds of either.

$$\text{LAM}_i = \text{logit}^{-1}\left(\frac{\text{logit}\ (fpr) + \text{logit}\ (fnr)}{2}\right) \tag{3}$$

where $fpr = \frac{|FP_i|}{|FP_i| + |TN_i|}$ is the *false-positive rate*, $fnr = \frac{|FN_i|}{|FN_i| + |TP_i|}$ is the *false-negative rate*, and the logit transformations are given by $\text{logit}(x) = \ln\frac{x}{1-x}$ and $\text{logit}^{-1}(x) = \frac{e^x}{1+e^x}$.

In order to obtain a single score for each conformance checker across all the categories C_i, we will use a *macro-averaging* approach [31], which computes the arithmetic mean of the above measures over all the categories C_i.

Moreover, as explained in Sect. 3, since a document cannot be compliant and not compliant at the same time, the class C_0 of the compliant documents must be separate from any other class C_i representing a possible issue of a document, i.e. $C_0 \cap C_i = \emptyset\ \forall i,\ i \neq 0$. As a consequence, assuming perfect classification, i.e. no FP or FN happen, it should be $TP_0 \cap TP_i = \emptyset\ \forall i,\ i \neq 0$, i.e. there must be no intersection between the TP documents attributed to C_0 and those attributed to other classes C_i. Since classification is typically not perfect, it should hold that $(TP_0 \cup FP_0) \cap (TP_i \cup FP_i) = \emptyset\ \forall i,\ i \neq 0$, i.e. the documents that a conformance checker correctly or incorrectly attributes to C_0 should have no intersection with

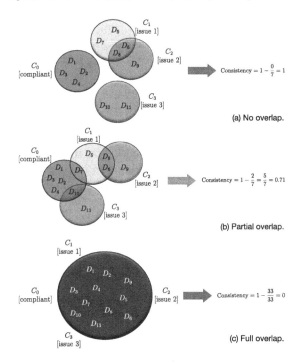

Fig. 4. Different cases for consistency: (a) no overlap between C_0 and the other classes; (b) partial overlap between C_0 and the other classes; (c) complete overlap between C_0 and the other classes.

the documents it correctly or incorrectly attributes to other classes C_i. Another consequence is that $TN_0 \cup FN_0 = \bigcup_{i=1}^{N} (TP_i \cup FP_i)$, i.e. the documents correctly or incorrectly marked as not compliant by a conformance checkers must have been attributed to some other class C_i by the same conformance checker.

Therefore, we can introduce an additional overall performance measure, called *consistency*, which assesses the ability of a conformance checker to adhere to the above constraint of separation of C_0 from the other classes:

$$
\begin{aligned}
\text{Consistency} &= 1 - \frac{\sum_{i=1}^{N} |(TP_0 \cup FP_0) \cap (TP_i \cup FP_i)|}{\sum_{i=1}^{N} |(TP_i \cup FP_i)|} \\
&= 1 - \frac{\sum_{i=1}^{N} |C_0 \cap C_i|}{\sum_{i=1}^{N} |C_i|}
\end{aligned} \tag{4}
$$

where N is the total number of classes, excluded C_0. Note that consistency is different from the evaluation measures typically used in classification [15,31,34] or clustering [3,4] and serves the specific purpose of assessing the degree of separation between the compliant and not-compliant classes.

Figure 4 shows some relevant cases for consistency: when there is no inter-section between C_0 and the other classes then Consistency $= 1$ (Fig. 4a);

on the other hand, in the extreme case of complete overall between C_0 and the other classes, i.e. when all the documents are assigned to all the classes, Consistency $= 0$ (Fig. 4c); in the other cases, when some overlap exists, consistency is in the range $(0, 1)$ (Fig. 4b).

5 Conclusions and Future Work

In this paper we discussed how to model the process of conformance checking for long-term digital preservation and, consequently how to evaluate it. In particular, we proposed to consider conformance checking as a multi-classification problem, with the constraint that C_0, the class of compliant documents, is separated from the others. We then discussed how to instantiate the Cranfield paradigm for the specific purpose of evaluating conformance checkers, we selected the existing measures – accuracy, AUC, and LAM – that best fit this peculiar applicative context and we proposed a new measure – consistency – that assess the extent to which conformance checkers are able to keep the C_0 class separated from the other classes.

Future work will concern the application of the proposed framework in the context of the PREFORMA project, with real memory institutions, domain experts and the suppliers which are actually developing the conformance checkers for the different media types targeted by PREFORMA. In particular, we see this as an iterative process, where we will go through repeated cycles to collect larger and larger datasets, to train memory institutions and suppliers on this evaluation methodology, and to refine it. An initial account of the defined classes can be found in [17].

Acknowledgements. The reported work has been partially supported by the PREFORMA project(http://www.preforma-project.eu/), as part of the Seventh Framework Programme of the European Commission, grant agreement no. 619568.

References

1. Alonso, O.: Implementing crowdsourcing-based relevance experimentation: an industrial perspective. Inf. Retrieval **16**(2), 101–120 (2013)
2. Alpaydin, E.: Introduction to Machine Learning. The MIT Press, Cambridge (2014)
3. Amigó, E., Gonzalo, J., Artiles, J., Verdejo, M.F.: A comparison of extrinsic clustering evaluation metrics based on formal constraints. Inf. Retrieval **12**(4), 461–486 (2009)
4. Amigó, E., Gonzalo, J., Verdejo, M.F.: A general evaluation measure for document organization tasks. In: Jones, G.J.F., Sheridan, P., Kelly, D., de Rijke, M., Sakai, T. (eds.) Proceeding 36th Annual International ACM SIGIR Conference on Research and Development in Information Retrieval (SIGIR 2013), pp. 643–652. ACM Press, New York (2013)
5. Becker, C., Duretec, K.: Free benchmark corpora for preservation experiments: using model-driven engineering to generate data sets. In: Downie, J.S., McDonald, R.H., Cole, T.W., Sanderson, R., Shipman, F. (eds.) Proceeding 13th ACM/IEEE-CS Joint Conference on Digital Libraries (JCDL 2013), pp. 349–358. ACM Press, New York (2013)

6. Becker, C., Duretec, K., Rauber, A.: The Challenge of Test Data Quality in Data Processing. ACM J. Data Inf. Qual. (JDIQ) **8**(2) (2016)
7. Becker, C., Rauber, A.: Decision criteria in digital preservation: what to measure and how. J. Am. Soc. Inform. Sci. Technol. (JASIST) **62**(6), 1009–1028 (2011)
8. Cappellato, L., Ferro, N., Fresa, A., Geber, M., Justrell, B., Lemmens, B., Prandoni, C., Silvello, G.: The PREFORMA project: federating memory institutions for better compliance of preservation formats. In: Calvanese, D., De Nart, D., Tasso, C. (eds.) IRCDL 2015. CCIS, vol. 612, pp. 86–91. Springer, Cham (2016). doi:10. 1007/978-3-319-41938-1_10
9. Chanod, J.P., Dobreva, M., Rauber, A., Ross, S., Casarosa, V.: Issues in digital preservation: towards a new research agenda. In: Chanod, J.P., Dobreva, M., Rauber, A., Ross, S. (eds.) Report from Dagstuhl Seminar 10291: Automation in Digital Preservation, pp. 1–14. Dagstuhl Reports, Schloss Dagstuhl-Leibniz-Zentrum für Informatik, Germany (2010)
10. Cleverdon, C.W.: The Cranfield tests on index languages devices. In: Spärck Jones, K., Willett, P. (eds.) Readings in Information Retrieval, pp. 47–60. Morgan Kaufmann Publisher Inc., San Francisco (1997)
11. Cormack, G., Lynam, T.: TREC 2005 spam track overview. In: Voorhees, E.M., Buckland, L.P. (eds.) The Fourteenth Text REtrieval Conference Proceedings (TREC 2005). National Institute of Standards and Technology (NIST), Special Publication 500–266, Washington, USA (2005)
12. Duretec, K., Kulmukhametov, A., Rauber, A., Becker, C.: Benchmarks for digital preservation tools. In: Proceeding of 11th International Conference on Preservation of Digital Objects (iPRES 2015) (2015)
13. Elfner, P., Justrell, B.: Deliverable D2.1 - Overall Roadmap. PREFORMA PCP Project, EU 7FP, Contract N. 619568, June 2014. http://www.digitalmeetsculture. net/wp-content/uploads/2014/05/PREFORMA_D2.1_Overall-Roadmap_v2.5.pdf
14. Fawcett, T.: An introduction to ROC analysis. Pattern Recogn. Lett. **27**(8), 861–874 (2006)
15. Ferri, C., Hernández-Orallo, J., Modroiu, R.: An experimental comparison of performance measures for classification. Pattern Recogn. Lett. **30**(1), 27–38 (2009)
16. Ferro, N.: Reproducibility challenges in information retrieval evaluation. ACM J. Data Inf. Qual. (JDIQ) **8**(2), 8:1–8:4 (2017)
17. Ferro, N., Buelinckx, E., Doubrov, B., Jadeglans, K., Lemmens, B., Martinez, J., Muñoz, V., Prandoni, C., Rice, D., Rohde-Enslin, S., Tarres, X., Verbruggen, E., Yousefi, B., Wilson, C.: Deliverable D8.1R2 - Competitive Evaluation Strategy. PREFORMA PCP Project, EU 7FP, Contract N. 619568, October 2016
18. Ferro, N., Fuhr, N., Järvelin, K., Kando, N., Lippold, M., Zobel, J.: Increasing reproducibility in IR: findings from the Dagstuhl Seminar on "Reproducibility of Data-Oriented Experiments in e-Science". SIGIR Forum **50**(1), 68–82 (2016)
19. IEC 60958: Digital audio interface - Part 1: General. Standard IEC 60958–1 Ed. 3.1 b:2014 (2014)
20. Innocenti, P., Ross, S., Maceviciute, E., Wilson, T., Ludwig, J., Pempe, W.: Assessing digital preservation frameworks: the approach of the SHAMAN project. In: Spyratos, N., Kapetanios, E., Traina, A. (eds.) Proceeding of ACM International Conference on Management of Emergent Digital EcoSystems (MEDES 2009), pp. 412–416. ACM Press, New York (2009)
21. ISO 12234–2: Electronic still-picture imaging - Removable memory - Part 2: TIFF/EP image data format. Recommendation ISO 12234–2:2001 (2001)
22. ISO 12639: Graphic technology - Prepress digital data exchange - Tag image file format for image technology (TIFF/IT). Recommendation ISO 12639:2004 (2004)

23. ISO 14721: Space data and information transfer systems - Open archival information system (OAIS) - Reference model. Recommendation ISO 14721:2012 (2012)
24. ISO 19005-1: Document management - Electronic document file format for long-term preservation - Part 1: Use of PDF 1.4 (PDF/A-1). Recommendation ISO 19005-1:2005 (2005)
25. ISO 19005-2: Document management - Electronic document file format for long-term preservation - Part 2: Use of ISO 32000-1 (PDF/A-2). Recommendation ISO 19005-2:2011 (2011)
26. ISO 19005-3: Document management - Electronic document file format for long-term preservation - Part 3: Use of ISO 32000-1 with support for embedded files (PDF/A-3). Recommendation ISO 19005-3:2012 (2012)
27. Kowalczyk, S.T.: Before the repository: defining the preservation threats to research data in the lab. In: Logasa Bogen II, P., Allard, S., Mercer, H., Beck, M. (eds.) Proceeding of 15th ACM/IEEE-CS Joint Conference on Digital Libraries (JCDL 2015), pp. 215–222. ACM Press, New York (2015)
28. Lease, M., Yilmaz, E.: Crowdsourcing for information retrieval: introduction to the special issue. Inf. Retrieval **16**(2), 91–100 (2013)
29. Ross, S.: Digital preservation, archival science and methodological foundations for digital libraries. New Rev. Inf. Networking **17**(1), 43–68 (2012)
30. Sanderson, M.: Test collection based evaluation of information retrieval systems. Found. Trends Inf. Retrieval (FnTIR) **4**(4), 247–375 (2010)
31. Sebastiani, F.: Machine learning in automated text categorization. ACM Comput. Surv. (CSUR) **34**(1), 1–47 (2002)
32. Smucker, M.D., Kazai, G., Lease, M.: Overview of the TREC 2012 crowdsourcing track. In: Voorhees, E.M., Buckland, L.P. (eds.) The Twenty-First Text REtrieval Conference Proceedings (TREC 2012). National Institute of Standards and Technology (NIST), Special Publication 500–298, Washington, USA (2013)
33. Soboroff, I., Nicholas, C., Cahan, P.: Ranking retrieval systems without relevance judgments. In: Kraft, D.H., Croft, W.B., Harper, D.J., Zobel, J. (eds.) Proceeding of 24th Annual International ACM SIGIR Conference on Research and Development in Information Retrieval (SIGIR 2001), pp. 66–73. ACM Press, New York (2001)
34. Sokolova, M., Lapalme, G.: A systematic analysis of performance measures for classification tasks. Inf. Process. Manage. **45**(4), 427–437 (2009)
35. Voorhees, E.M.: Variations in relevance judgments and the measurement of retrieval effectiveness. Inf. Process. Manage. **36**(5), 697–716 (2000)

Towards Sentiment and Emotion Analysis of User Feedback for Digital Libraries

Stefano Ferilli[1]([⊠]), Berardina De Carolis[1],
Domenico Redavid[2], and Floriana Esposito[1]

[1] Dipartimento di Informatica, Università di Bari, Bari, Italy
{stefano.ferilli,berardina.carolis,floriana.esposito}@uniba.it
[2] Artificial Brain S.r.l., Bari, Italy
redavid@abrain.it

Abstract. The possibility for people to leave comments in blogs and forums on the Internet allows to study their attitude (in terms of valence or even of specific feelings) on various topics. For some digital libraries this may be a precious opportunity to understand how their content is perceived by their users and, as a consequence, to suitably direct their future strategic choices. So, libraries might want to enrich their sites with the possibility, for their users, to provide feedback on the items they have consulted. Of course, manually analyzing all the available comments would be infeasible. Sentiment Analysis, Opinion Mining and Emotion Analysis denote the area of research in Computer Science aimed at automatically analyzing and classifying text documents based on the underlying opinions expressed by their authors.

Significant problems in building an automatic system for this purpose are given by the complexity of natural language, by the need of dealing with several languages, and by the choice of relevant features and of good approaches to building the models. Following the interesting results obtained for Italian by a system based on a Text Categorization approach, this paper proposes further experiments to check whether reliable predictions can be obtained, both for opinions and for feelings.

1 Introduction

For some digital libraries, knowing the attitude of their users toward their content may be very important to understand how it is perceived by their (actual or potential) audience and, as a consequence, to suitably direct their future strategic choices. They might be interested in just the valence of the attitude, or more specifically in the feelings that some items have raised in their users. This may be particularly true for libraries containing works of art (movies, music, leisure literature, etc.), but also for libraries more oriented toward scientific contents. So, libraries might want to enrich their sites with the possibility, for their users, to provide feedback on the items they have consulted, e.g. in the form of forums or blogs. Although they are not libraries technically speaking, most websites of online shops for buying items that might well end up in libraries already provide

© Springer International Publishing AG 2017
M. Agosti et al. (Eds.): IRCDL 2016, CCIS 701, pp. 137–149, 2017.
DOI: 10.1007/978-3-319-56300-8_13

this option (e.g., Amazon). By going through the users' messages, the library managers might gain precious information. Of course, manually analyzing all the available comments would be infeasible. Hence, the interest in automatic techniques to extract the users' attitude from their textual comments.

In fact, opinions play a fundamental role in our everyday life, directing or affecting our decisions in all contexts. People often look for the opinions of others before deciding about their own actions. Companies and politicians want to know what people thinks about their products or actions. So, obvious applications of SA have been to recommender systems, marketing, brand analysis, business and government intelligence, Web monitoring, terrorism prevention, etc. Market-oriented applications, in particular, may take great advantage from the availability of websites (such as epinions.com and rateitall.com), that collect feedback, opinions and reviews of users about all kinds of products and services. E.g., the possible correlations between the dominant sentiment in a film's reviews and its income was analyzed in [12].

Opinion Mining was originally aimed at "process[ing] a set of search results for a given item, generating a list of product attributes (quality, features, etc.) and aggregating opinions about each of them (poor, mixed, good)" [7]. It is now considered as a synonym of *Sentiment Analysis* (SA), appeared in [6,18] (where the meaning was borrowed from economics) and in [14,15,20,25]. The area of interest of SA was subsequently extended to the study, analysis and classification of text documents based on the underlying opinions expressed by their authors (e.g., about a product, a service, an event, an organization, or a person). While early works in the field date back to 1979 [3] and 1984 [23], thorough research started only in the new millennium, thanks to the availability of huge amounts of data to be processed in the World Wide Web and, in particular, in Social Networks, where people exchange ideas and comments on any branch of human interests [6,13,18,20,21]. While SA is interested just in the polarity of the opinion (positive or negative, or maybe neutral), *Emotion Analysis* aims at classifying the specific kind of emotion expressed by the text.

Opinions are expressed as text. The text carrying an opinion is called an *opinionated text*, and the person or organization who expresses the opinion is called the *opinion holder*. The target of the opinion is called *object* or *entity*. The opinion may be about specific features of an object, rather than (or in addition to) the object as a whole. This is the domain of *Feature-Based Sentiment Analysis*, and requires suitable processing to extract the features about which opinions are expressed, and the associated portion of text. Somehow tricky are features implicitly expressed by some kinds of adjectives, adverbs or verbs (e.g., 'costly' implicitly identifies the feature 'price').

Classifying the polarity of a text based only on the terms that make it up is not easy [15], especially for machines. There are several reasons for this:

– Intrinsic complexity of natural language (a well-known example is Mark Twain's review of a book by Jane Austen: "Jane Austen's books madden me so that I can't conceal my frenzy from the reader. Everytime I read 'Pride and Prejudice' I want to dig her up and beat her over the skull with her own shin-bone.")

- Subjectivity of opinions. Even worse, some subjective sentences do not express any opinion (e.g., "I think I will go there"), while some objective sentence do (e.g., "the phone I bought stopped working in three days").
- The opinion holder might be different than the author of the message (e.g., in a quoted sentence).
- The context of an utterance may change the polarity of an opinion (e.g., "should never be missing" is positive if referred to an object, or negative if referred to a feature).
- Differently from normal Text Categorization, the order in which the terms appear in the text may be very relevant.
- While 'direct' opinions concern a single object and/or feature, 'comparative' ones highlight the similarities, differences or preferences between many objects.

To properly handle this complex landscape, a SA system must accomplish several sub-tasks, such as the identification of the object of the opinion (when many objects are compared), of the evaluated features, sometimes of the opinion holder and even of the moment in which the opinion is expressed.

This paper aims at evaluating whether useful indications about the opinion and feelings of users toward library items might be drawn from an analysis of their comments on such items, if available. In particular, we wanted to focus on the Italian language, whose grammar is more complex and for which less advanced pre-processing techniques are available with respect to English. The next section overviews related works. Then, the proposed approach is described in Sect. 3 and evaluated in Sect. 4. Finally, Sect. 5 draws some conclusions and outlines future work.

2   Background and Related Work

There are several sub-problems to be faced to carry out SA. First of all, some pre-processing steps may be needed to clean the input from formatting information (e.g., in Web pages). Also, it may be useful to filter out all sentences that do not carry opinions (a problem known as *subjectivity classification*) [21,22,26].

Given the plain text of opinionated sentences, full natural language is still out of reach for automatic procedures. The lexical level is often considered a fair trade-off between expressiveness and computational complexity. At this level, the items of interest are just tokens (words or other elements having an atomic meaning). To reach further simplification, tokens that are considered meaningless for the task at hand are removed, and inflected forms of words are normalized. Stemming reduces each term to its stem, with the risk of merging, as a side effect, terms having different meaning but the same stem. Lemmatization reduces a term to its base form, but requires additional linguistic knowledge to be able to do this. It is unclear whether exploiting phrases or *n*-grams (i.e., sequences of n terms in a text) brings a real advantage over just using single words [11].

Although the position of terms may be relevant for SA, the given corpus is usually represented as a *Vector Space*, i.e. as a matrix where rows are indexed with the filtered and normalized terms and columns represent the documents. Each cell expresses the relevance of a term to a document using a weighting scheme (e.g., TF*IDF) that is typically directly proportional to the number of occurrences of the term in that document and inversely proportional to its spread across the whole corpus. The vector space is often used for learning predictive models. So, each document can be seen as a vector, that identifies a point in a space whose dimensions are the terms in the vocabulary. Since the very large dimensionality may cause various problems, among which inefficiency and overfitting, dimensionality reduction may be obtained by eliminating some terms (as in [24]) or by considering a transposed space (as in Latent Semantic Indexing [8]).

Considering the Part-of-Speech (PoS) tag of terms, i.e. their lexical category, may be useful for some purposes. Indeed, it is a common feeling that nouns and verbs express objective concepts, while adjectives or adverbs may be more indicative of subjectivity. PoS tagging can nowadays be carried out automatically with satisfactory results. However, problems may arise due to ambiguous words (e.g., as in "We can can the can") or unknown ones. Also, using a large set of tags usually results in tags that have very close meaning, which makes it difficult to distinguish them using automatic taggers (or even human ones).

The presence of specific words may be very indicative for SA. Opinion words, i.e. words used to express opinions, are strictly related to PoS. There are also typical phrases that are commonly understood as expressing definite sentiments independently of their strict semantics. Sentiment shifters are phrases used to change the polarity of an opinion from positive to negative or *vice versa*. Negations are an outstanding example, but again the issue may be tricky (e.g., in the correlation 'not only ... but also').

Sentiment Polarity Classification consists in assigning the text to a category that represents a value in a given scale. In 'Binary Sentiment Classification' the scale includes just the two extremes (to be interpreted as positive/negative, or in favor/against, etc.). Document-level Sentiment Classification focuses on the assessment of the opinion of an opinion holder on a single entity in a whole opinionated document. The underlying assumption is that the document was written by a single author, and that the author expressed opinions on a single object. While product reviews usually fulfill this assumption, blog posts or forum discussions often do not. In these cases, one needs to preliminarily decompose the text in different pieces, each referred to a single object. If the pieces corresponds to sentences, one gets Sentence-Level Sentiment Classification.

Machine Learning-based techniques for sentiment classification can use supervised or unsupervised approaches. In the former case, a 'training set' of documents annotated with the correct sentiment is needed, and performance can be evaluated using a different 'test set'. Producing these sets manually can be very costly, but opinions on the Web are often associated with a numeric evaluation (e.g., in terms of 'stars') that can be used to derive the associated sentiment. In the unsupervised case, the system takes unlabeled data and tries to find meaningful correlations among them. Supervised learning is more interesting here, because it somehow constrains the systems to reproduce in the learned models the same behavior as the expert who labeled the data, which is very important in our case. In the supervised setting, [15] profitably used Naive Bayes (NB), Maximum Entropy (ME) and Support Vector Machines (SVM) to classify film reviews as positive or negative. As features they use term vectors obtained without stemming or stopword removal, and considered only single terms appearing at least 4 times in the corpus and bi-grams appearing at least 7 times. They also implemented a simple mechanism to recognize the presence of negations that invert the polarity. Different settings led to precision slightly above 80%, but the results of ME based only on adjectives reached just 77.7%.

Emotions and opinions are strictly related. The intensity of opinion is related to the intensity of some emotions, such as happiness and anger. Ekman [9] identified a set of 'primary' emotions that are universal (i.e., not determined by the culture or place where one lives): anger, disgust, sadness, joy, fear, and surprise. 'Secondary' emotions derive from them, but depend on the culture and are developed during growth. Emotions can be exploited to understand the behavior of people on social media, or of individuals (e.g., understanding suicides based on letters written before the event) [4]. Emotions are inherently multi-modal, involving text, sound and images. However, most works focused on text, due to its explicit encoding of information. Feeler [5], an emotion-based document classifier, exploits stopword removal (excluding emotional words), negations, question and exclamation marks (replaced by explicit labels) but no PoS information. The Vector Space Model-based classifier proved to be as effective as a Support Vector Machines-based one and a Naive Bayes approach on short sentences. It also emerged that the use of stemming improves accuracy.

3   Proposed Approach

In a previous work [10], we developed a system for Sentiment Analysis/Opinion Mining and Emotion Analysis that obtained interesting results on the task of determining the polarity of opinions concerning movies and expressed in Italian. This is especially relevant because Italian is a more complex language than English, and so many and so reliable linguistic resources and systems are not available for it as for English. This allows to hypothesize that good results can be obtained also for several other languages. To be general and context-independent, the system relies on supervised Machine Learning approaches. For the sake of flexibility, it allows to select different combinations of features to be used for learning the predictive models. In the following, we recall the system's technical features.

Our system casts the Sentiment Classification problem as a TC task, where the categories represent the polarity (or the emotions). However, several differences exist with respect to classical topic-based TC: topics are objective, while sentiments are subjective; there may be hundreds (or even thousands) of topics, but just a few sentiments (at the extreme, just two polarities, positive and negative); topics are usually application-dependent, while sentiment is general; topics may be independent from each other, while sentiments typically are not (e.g., in the evaluation of an object based on a number of 'stars' the categories are different degrees of a single scale).

Text Categorization (TC) is the activity aimed at mapping documents in natural language to a pre-defined set of categories. Formally, given a set of documents D and a set of categories C, a text *classifier* implements a function $\Phi : D \times C \to \{True, False\}$ that for each document-category pair says whether the document belongs to the category. The 'hard' categorization can be replaced by a degree of belonging ($\Phi_i : D \times C \to [0,1]$). Often, the target function Φ is unknown, and must be approximated by another function Φ' with the same pattern as Φ. Manually creating logic rules for each category, to be used to classify documents, is costly, difficult (both for creation and for update) and allows limited reuse of the rules in different domains. Supervised Machine Learning approaches learn Φ' inductively based on the observation of the features of a 'training set' of documents manually classified by experts as belonging ('positive examples') or not ('negative examples') to specific categories. The learned classifier can be applied on an additional 'test set' of documents whose category is known to check whether its predictions are correct.

To learn a classifier, one must first choose what features to consider to describe the documents, and what is the learning method to be exploited. An analysis of the state-of-the-art, as reported in previous sections, suggested that no single approach can be considered as the absolute winner, and that different approaches, based on different perspectives, may reach interesting results on different features. Assuming that these perspectives are sufficiently complementary to mutually provide strengths and support weaknesses, our proposal is to set up a subset of approaches and features to be brought to cooperation.

3.1   Features

As said, most NLP approaches and applications focus on the lexical/grammatical level as a good tradeoff for expressiveness and complexity, effectiveness and efficiency. Accordingly, we have decided to take into account the following kinds of descriptors:

- single, normalized words (ignoring dates, numbers and the like), that we believe convey most informational content in a text;
- abbreviations, acronyms, and colloquial expressions, especially those that are often found in informal texts such as blog posts on the Internet and phone messages;
- n-grams (groups of n consecutive terms) whose frequency of occurrence in the corpus is above a pre-defined threshold, that sometimes may be particularly meaningful;
- PoS tags, that are intuitively discriminant for subjectivity;
- expressive punctuation (dots, exclamation and question marks), that may be indicative of subjectivity and emotional involvement;
- emoticons, due to their direct and explicit relationship to emotions and moods.

For NLP pre-processing, we used the TreeTagger [17] for PoS-tagging and the Snowball suite [16] for stemming.

All the selected features are collectively represented in a single vector space based on the real-valued weighting scheme of Term Frequency - Inverse Document Frequency (TF-IDF):

$$tfidf(t_i, d_j) = \#(t_i, d_j) \cdot \log_2 \frac{|T|}{\#_T(t_i)}$$

where $\#(t_i, d_j)$ is the number of occurrences of term t_i in document d_j, and $\#_T(t_i)$ is the number of documents in the training set T that include term t_i. To have values into $[0, 1]$ we use cosine normalization:

$$w_{ij} = \frac{tfidf(t_i, d_j)}{\sqrt{\sum_{k=1}^{n} tfidf(t_k, d_j)^2}} \tag{1}$$

where n is the number of terms occurring at least once in the training set documents. To reduce the dimensionality of the vector space, Document Frequency (i.e., removing terms that do not pass a pre-defined frequency threshold) was used as a good tradeoff between simplicity and effectiveness.

3.2 Algorithms

To build the classification model we focused on two complementary approaches that have been proved effective in the literature: a similarity-based one (Rocchio) and a probabilistic one (Naive Bayes).

For each category $c_k \in C$, Rocchio's algorithm creates an explicit profile, reporting the weight of each term in the training set vocabulary, in the form of a 'prototype vector' $p_k = \langle p_{1k}, \ldots, p_{nk} \rangle$:

$$p_{ik} = \beta \cdot \sum_{d_j \in P_k} \frac{w_{ij}}{|P_k|} - \gamma \cdot \sum_{d_j \in N_k} \frac{w_{ij}}{|N_k|}$$

where w_{ij} is the weight reported in the vector space, in our case as defined in (1), P_k is the subset of documents in the training set that belong to category c_k, N_k is the subset of documents in the training set that do not belong to category c_k, and β, γ are parameters that allow to balance the importance of positive and negative instances on the classifier (e.g., taking $\beta = 1, \gamma = 0$ ignores negative examples and returns as a prototype the centroid of the positive ones). A new document is classified simply by comparing its associated vector to all prototype vectors, and taking the category associated to the most similar. Cosine similarity, measuring the angle between two vectors, can be used for this purpose:

$$sim(d_j, p_k) = \frac{\overline{d_j} \cdot \overline{p_k}}{|\overline{d_j}| \cdot |\overline{p_k}|} = \frac{\sum_{i=1}^{n} w_{ij} \cdot w_{ik}}{\sqrt{\sum_{i=1}^{n} w_{ij}^2 \cdot \sum_{i=1}^{n} w_{ik}^2}}$$

It has the advantage of being less affected by the dimensionality of the space and by the normalization applied to the TF*IDF value. Note that consistency in this approach a training example might be classified differently than its known label used for learning.

A Naive Bayes classifier allows to infer the posterior probability $p(c_k|d)$ of a document $d = \langle d_1, \ldots, d_n \rangle$ belonging to a category c_k based on the likelihood of its terms being found in documents that are known to be in that category:

$$p(c_k|d) \propto p(c_k) \cdot p(d|c_k) \approx \frac{|T_k|}{|T|} \cdot \prod_{j=1}^{n} \frac{n_{kj} + 1}{n_k + n}$$

$p(c_k)$ is the a priori likelihood of category c_k. Assuming that the categories are disjoint (i.e., each document may belong to only one category), it can be computed as $p(c_k) = \frac{|T_k|}{|T|}$, where T_k is the subset of the training set T that belongs to class c_k. Assuming that the terms in the document are statistically independent from each other (a clearly false assumption, but one that significantly reduces computational demands—whence the term 'naive'), one gets $p(d|c_k) = p(d_1 \wedge \cdots \wedge d_n|c_k)) = \prod_{j=1}^{n} p(d_j|c_k)$ where the posterior probability of terms can be computed as $p(d_j|c_k) = \frac{n_{ij}}{n_i}$, with n_{kj} the number of occurrences of term d_j in documents belonging to category c_k and n_k the sum of all occurrences of all terms in documents of category c_k. The Laplace correction to the relative frequency $p(d_j|c_k) \approx \frac{n_{kj}+1}{n_k+n}$ avoids that $p(t|c) = 0$ if a term t is not present in the documents of a category c, which would yield 0 for the whole product. The category of an unknown document d is computed as the one that maximizes the posterior probability:

$$\arg \max_{c_k \in C} p(c_k) \cdot \prod_{j=1}^{t} p(d_j|c_k)$$

where t is the number of terms that are present in d, and d_j is the j-th document in d.

Our system combines the above approaches in a committee, where each classifier $i = 1, 2$ plays the role of a different domain expert that assigns a score s_k^i to category c_k for each document to be classified. The final prediction is obtained as class $c = \arg \max_k S_k$, considering a function $S_k = f(s_k^1, s_k^2)$ [19]. This approach has the advantage of allowing easy extension with additional classifiers when needed. There is a wide range of options for function f. In our case we use a weighted sum, which requires that the values returned by the single approaches are comparable, i.e. they refer to the same scale. In fact, while the Naive Bayes approach returns probability values, Rocchio's classifier returns similarity values, both in $[0, 1]$.

4   Experiments

Experiments on Opinion Mining were run in [10] on a dataset of 2000 reviews in Italian language, concerning 558 movies, taken from http://filmup.leonardo.it/. The evaluation, expressed as a number of 'stars' (from 1 to 10), associated to reviews was used to distinguish positive (6 to 10 stars) from negative (1 to 5 stars) examples. The corpus included half positive reviews and half negative ones. On a quite mediocre platform (a PC endowed with an Intel Core 2 Duo E6750 working at 2.66 GHz and 2 GB RAM, running Windows 8), using different sets of features, runtime ranged between 3'25" (for 5892 features) and 13'08" (for 9001 features, of which 2784 n-grams). This should ensure applicability of our method even using very cheap resources. The use of n-grams significantly increases the number of features, and runtime as a consequence. Classification performance was evaluated on 17 different feature settings using a 5-fold cross-validation procedure. Equal weight was assigned to all classifiers in the committee. Overall accuracy reported in [10] was always above 81%, and always above 82% for the committee. These are very good results, compared to the state-of-the-art for English and especially for Italian. When Rocchio outperformed Naive Bayes, accuracy of the committee was greater than that of the components; in the other cases, corresponding to settings that used n-grams, Naive Bayes alone was the winner. Even if balanced between positive and negative cases, accuracy on the former was always better than that on the latter. This is somehow surprising, because it is commonly believed that negative emotions are stronger, and hence easier to recognize.

To further evaluate the proposed approach in the perspective of using it for digital libraries, we devised two experiments. One still concerned the Opinion Mining task, but involved the Evalita Sentipolc 2014 dataset. It consists of 4513 tweets, collected by harnessing Twitter messages in Italian with mainly a politic content, encoded as described in [2]. Compared with the previous dataset, it has two peculiarities. First, it is standard in the literature, and was used as a benchmark for state-of-the-art competitions. Second, it involves tweets, that are shorter than the movie reviews, so that it can check the performance of the system on a different ground. Since we were again interested in just distinguishing positive messages from negative ones, neutral items in the dataset were removed, yielding a reduced dataset made up of 2091 tweets (1412 negative and 679 positive ones). In this case we used only the system configuration that provided the best results in the previous experiments:

Normalization	PoS tags	Punct./Abbrev.	n-grams
lemmas	nouns, verbs, adjectives, adverbs, emoticons	Yes	–

We carried out a 10-fold cross validation whose results in terms of Precision (P), Recall (R) and F1-measure ($F1$) are as follows:

Positive			Negative			Average		
P	R	F1	P	R	F1	P	R	F1
0.752	0.498	0.599	0.750	0.901	0.819	0.751	0.700	0.724

In this case we used Precision (P), Recall (R), and F1-measure ($F1$), since the dataset was imbalanced toward negative examples. These are figures that compare well to the state-of-the-art best system in the competition [1]. Recall on positive cases is worse than on negative ones, possibly due to the difference in the number of examples in the two classes of the dataset. Anyway, this may be a useful outcome, because library managers (differently from e-business site holders) may be more interested in identifying and analyzing criticisms than on reading positive comments.

Analyzing the emotions expressed by the users' comments may also be of interest, since it may provide a more precise and detailed account about which sentiment the digital content (document, movie, song, etc.) triggered in the user. To this aim we trained the classifier on three classes, selected to represent the more standard and relevant emotions that items in a library might cause in a user. So, we included one positive emotion (happiness) and two negative ones (for the moment we focused on a lightly negative one, sadness, and a strongly negative one, anger). We used a dataset purposely collected for this experiment by taking 800 comments about movies from filmup and showing them randomly to 11 human raters. The raters were asked to evaluate whether the opinion about the movie expressed one of the three feelings of interest, and in such a case which one. A label was given to each comment according to the majority agreement criterion. Those comments for which majority was not reached were discarded. At the end of this process the dataset included 752 entries (namely: 406 for happiness, 175 for sadness, and 171 for anger). The features for this experiment involved an extended set of Pos tags:

Normalization	PoS tags	Punct./Abbrev.	n-grams
lemmas	nouns, verbs, adjectives, adverbs, articles, pronouns, emoticons	Yes	–

Then we ran a 10-fold cross validation whose results in terms of Precision (P), Recall (R) and F1-measure ($F1$) are as follows:

Anger			Happiness			Sadness			Average		
P	R	F1	P	R	F1	P	R	F1	P	R	F1
0.698	0.408	0.514	0.742	0.870	0.801	0.630	0.575	0.600	0.690	0.617	0.651

The emotion analyzer performs well on Happiness, while its performance is less accurate for the other two classes. This might be due to the fact that the dataset was imbalanced. However, positive emotions are typically harder to recognize than negative ones. This makes us confident that, in any case, combining our classifier with other state-of-the-art ones might improve the overall results.

5   Conclusions

The possibility for people to leave comments in blogs and forums on the Internet allows to study their attitude (in terms of valence or even of specific feelings) on various topics. For some digital libraries this may be a precious opportunity to understand how their content is perceived by their users and, as a consequence, to suitably direct their future strategic choices. So, libraries might want to enrich their sites with the possibility, for their users, to provide feedback on the items they have consulted. Of course, manually analyzing all the available comments would be infeasible. Sentiment Analysis, Opinion Mining and Emotion Analysis denote the area of research in Computer Science aimed at automatically analyzing and classifying text documents based on the underlying opinions expressed by their authors.

Significant problems in building an automatic system for this purpose are given by the complexity of natural language, by the need of dealing with several languages, and by the choice of relevant features and of good approaches to building the models. Following the interesting results obtained for Italian by a system based on a Text Categorization approach, this paper proposed further experiments to check whether reliable predictions can be obtained, both for opinions and for feelings. Experimental results compare well to state-of-the-art tools, suggesting that the proposed approach might be profitably exploited in the target application domain.

To test this hypothesis, future work will include experiments on use cases specifically concerning digital libraries dedicated to art, provided that the users comments are collected and made available by such libraries. We also plan to extend the set of emotions to be recognized, including at least all primary ones.

Acknowledgment. This work was partially funded by the Italian PON 2007–2013 project PON02_00563_3489339 'Puglia@Service'.

References

1. Basile, V., Nissim, M.: Sentiment analysis on Italian tweets. In: Proceeding of the 4th Workshop on Computational Approaches to Subjectivity, Sentiment and Social Media Analysis, pp. 100–107 (2013)
2. Basile, V., Bolioli, A., Nissim, M., Patti, V., Rosso, P.: Overview of the evalita 2014 sentiment polarity classification task. In: Proceedings of the 4th Evaluation Campaign of Natural Language Processing and Speech tools for Italian (EVALITA 2014), pp. 50–57. Pisa University Press (2014)
3. Carbonell, J.: Subjective Understanding: Computer Models of Belief Systems (1979)
4. Cherry, C., Mohammad, S.M., de Bruijn, B.: Binary classifiers and latent sequence models for emotion detection in suicide notes. **5**, 147–154 (2012)
5. Danisman, T., Alpkocak, A.: Feeler: emotion classification of text using vector space model. In: Proceedings of the AISB 2008 Convention, Communication, Interaction and Social Intelligence (2008)

6. Das, S., Chen, M.: Yahoo! for amazon: extracting market sentiment from stock message boards. In: Proceedings of the Asia Pacific Finance Association Annual Conference (APFA) (2001)
7. Dave, K., Lawrence, S., Pennock, D.M.: Mining the peanut gallery: opinion extraction and semantic classification of product reviews. In: Proceedings of WWW, pp. 519–528 (2003)
8. Deerwester, S., Dumais, S.T., Furnas, G.W., Landauer, T.K., Harshman, R.: Indexing by latent semantic indexing. J. Am. Soc. Inform. Sci. Technol. **41**, 391–407 (1990)
9. Ekman, P.: Sixteen enjoyable emotions. Emotion Researcher **18**, 6–7 (2003)
10. Ferilli, S., De Carolis, B., Esposito, F., Redavid, D.: Sentiment analysis as a text categorization task: a study on feature and algorithm selection for Italian language. In: IEEE International Conference on Data Science and Advanced Analytics (DSAA), 36678 2015, pp. 1–10 (2015)
11. Lewis, D.D.: An evaluation of phrasal and clustered representations on a text categorization task. In: Proceedings of SIGIR-92, 15th ACM International Conference on Research and Development in Information Retrieval, pp. 37–50 (1992)
12. Mishne, G., Glance, N.: Predicting movie sales from blogger sentiment. In: Proceedings of AAAI-CAAW-2006, the Spring Symposia on Computational Approaches to Analyzing Weblogs (2006)
13. Morinaga, S., Yamanishi, K., Tateishi, K., Fukushima, T.: Mining product reputations on the web. In: Proceedings of ACM SIGKDD International Conference on Knowledge Discovery and Data Mining (KDD-2002) (2002)
14. Nasukawa, T., Yi, J.: Sentiment analysis: capturing favorability using natural language processing. In: Proceedings of the Conference on Knowledge Capture (K-CAP) (2003)
15. Pang, B., Lee, L., Vaithyanathan, S.: Thumbs up? Sentiment classification using machine learning techniques. In: Proceedings of the Conference on Empirical Methods in Natural Language Processing (EMNLP), pp. 79–86 (2002)
16. Porter, M.F.: Snowball A language for stemming algorithms, October 2001
17. Schmid, H.: Probabilistic part-of-speech tagging using decision trees. In: Proceedings of International Conference on New Methods in Language Processing, pp. 44–49 (1994)
18. Tong, R.M.: An operational system for detecting and tracking opinions in on-line discussion. In: Proceedings of the SIGIR Workshop on Operational Text Classification (OTC) (2001)
19. Tulyakov, S., Jaeger, S., Govindaraju, V., Doermann, D.: Review of classifier combination methods. In: Marinai, S., Fujisawa, H. (eds.) Machine Learning in Document Analysis and Recognition. SCI, vol. 90, pp. 361–386. Springer, Heidelberg (2008)
20. Turney, P.: Thumbs up or thumbs down? Semantic orientation applied to unsupervised classification of reviews. In: Proceedings of the Association for Computational Linguistics (ACL), pp. 417–424 (2002)
21. Wiebe, J.M.: Learning subjective adjectives from corpora. In: Proceedings of National Conference on Artificial Intelligence (AAAI-2000) (2000)
22. Wiebe, J.M., Bruce, R.F., O'Hara, T.P.: Development and use of a gold-standard data set for subjectivity classifications. In: Proceedings of the Association for Computational Linguistics (ACL-1999) (1999)
23. Wilks, Y., Bien, J.: Beliefs, points of view and multiple environments. In: Proceedings of the International NATO Symposium on Artificial and Human Intelligence, pp. 147–171. Elsevier North-Holland Inc. (1984)

24. Yang, Y., Pedersen, J.O.: A comparative study on feature selection in text categorization. In: Proceedings of ICML-97, 14th International Conference on Machine Learning, pp. 412–420 (1997)
25. Yi, J., Nasukawa, T., Bunescu, R., Niblack, W.: Sentiment analyzer: extracting sentiments about a given topic using natural language processing techniques. In: Proceedings of the IEEE International Conference on Data Mining (ICDM) (2003)
26. Yu, H., Hatzivassiloglou, V.: Towards answering opinion questions: separating facts from opinions and identifying the polarity of opinion sentences. In: Proceedings of Conference on Empirical Methods in Natural Language Processing (EMNLP-2003) (2003)

Layout

Layout Analysis and Content Classification in Digitized Books

Andrea Corbelli, Lorenzo Baraldi$^{(\boxtimes)}$, Fabrizio Balducci, Costantino Grana, and Rita Cucchiara

Dipartimento di Ingegneria "Enzo Ferrari",
Università degli Studi di Modena e Reggio Emilia,
Via Vivarelli 10, 41125 Modena, MO, Italy
{andrea.corbelli,lorenzo.baraldi,fabrizio.balducci,
costantino.grana,rita.cucchiara}@unimore.it

Abstract. Automatic layout analysis has proven to be extremely important in the process of digitization of large amounts of documents. In this paper we present a mixed approach to layout analysis, introducing a SVM-aided layout segmentation process and a classification process based on local and geometrical features. The final output of the automatic analysis algorithm is a complete and structured annotation in JSON format, containing the digitalized text as well as all the references to the illustrations of the input page, and which can be used by visualization interfaces as well as annotation interfaces. We evaluate our algorithm on a large dataset built upon the first volume of the "Enciclopedia Treccani".

Keywords: Layout analysis · Content classification · SVM · Annotation interfaces

1 Introduction

Document digitization plays a key role in the preservation and diffusion of historical books: digital archives, indeed, protect fragile and valuable originals from handling, while still presenting their content to a vastly increased audience. Just like multimodal digital libraries need to be properly organized via computer vision and multimedia algorithms [4,5], the simple digital copy of an archive is often not sufficient to present its content in an effective and enjoyable way: beyond the application of Optical Character Recognition (OCR) methods, which are nowadays almost completely reliable, graphical elements, like tables, images and charts, should be automatically segmented and categorized.

Despite the recent advances in this field, layout and content analysis are still unsolved problems due to the high variability of the possible content. In this setting, we propose a novel pipeline for the analysis of structured documents, which includes a page layout analysis algorithm to segment the input document into coherent regions, and a content classification strategy to classify the actual content of each region. Our layout analysis builds upon the Recursive XY-Cut

© Springer International Publishing AG 2017
M. Agosti et al. (Eds.): IRCDL 2016, CCIS 701, pp. 153–165, 2017.
DOI: 10.1007/978-3-319-56300-8_14

algorithm, and extends it with an SVM-aided detector for graphical elements; then, tables are identified by means of the Hough transform, and supervised machine learning techniques are employed in conjuction with local features to classify other graphical elements, like images, charts and scores. The final output is a structured annotation in JSON format, which can be read and modified by an annotation interface, useful for correcting mistakes in the automatic analysis, and by a visualization interface.

The rest of this paper is structured as follows: Section 2 gives a brief discussion of the state of the art in layout analysis, Sect. 3 explains the main components of our pipeline, and Sect. 4 reports the performance evaluation and a comparison against the state of the art.

2   Related Work

Layout analysis has been an active area of research since the seventies. There are two main approaches to layout analysis, *bottom up* and *top down*.

Top-down methods, such as XY cuts [6,13] or methods that exploit white streams [2] or projection profiles [11] are usually fast but tend to fail when dealing with complex layouts. Bottom-up methods are instead more flexible and process the image page from the pixel level and subsequently aggregate into higher level regions but with an higher computational complexity.

These approaches are usually based on mathematical morphology, Connected Components (CCs), Voronoi diagrams [15] or run-length smearing [22]. Many other methods exist which do not fit exactly into either of these categories: the so called mixed or hybrid approaches try to combine the high speed of the top-down approaches with the robustness of the bottom-up ones. Chen *et al.* [7] propose a method based on whitespace rectangles extraction and grouping: initially the foreground CCs are extracted and linked into chains according to their horizontal adjacency relationship; whitespace rectangles are then extracted from the gap between horizontally adjacent CCs; CCs and whitespaces are progressively grouped and filtered to form text lines and afterward text blocks. Lazzara *et al.* [16] provide a chain of steps to first recognize text regions and successively non-text elements. Foreground CCs are extracted, then delimiters (such as lines, whitespaces and tab-stop) are detected with object alignment and morphological algorithms. Since text components are usually well aligned, have a uniform size and are close to each other, the authors propose to regroup CCs by looking for their neighbors. Filters can also be applied on a group of CCs to validate the link between two CCs. Another algorithm based on whitespace analysis has been proposed by Baird *et al.* [3]: the algorithm uses the white space in the page as a layout delimiter and tries to find the biggest background empty rectangles to extract connected regions.

Kaur *et al.* [14] and Zanibbi *et al.* [24] present surveys about the approaches applied to table recognition. Mandal *et al.* dealt with the detection and segmentation of tables and formulas [18,19], and proposed a detector with the heuristic that each table has distinct columns which implies that gaps between the fields are substantially larger than the gaps between the words in text lines; a similar approach was presented by Ferilli *et al.* in [9]. Liu *et al.* [17] deal with table boundary detection and content extraction considering the sparse-line property of table rows, while Bertrand and Lemaitre [8] focus on the recognition of tables and forms.

3   Our Proposal

3.1   Page Layout Segmentation

The first stage of our pipeline is the segmentation of the input page into coherent regions. Our layout analysis step builds upon the well known XY-Cut algorithm [13], and extends it to go beyond its limitations. XY-Cut is an iterative top-down page segmentation algorithm, which takes as input a Region of Interest (ROI) and segments it into rectangular regions which are separated by white spaces. In particular, the algorithm projects the pixels' values on the vertical and horizontal axes of the ROI, and then finds low density regions in the projection histograms, which corresponds to white spaces. If a low density point is found on at least one of the projections, the ROI is split into two subregions, which are then further analyzed (and possibly split) in the next iteration. The resulting segmentation is therefore composed by a set of rectangular regions, each of which is separated from the others by white space on all sides.

The XY-Cut algorithm works well with simple layouts, where elements are actually rectangular and separated by vertical or horizontal white spaces which span on all their sides. However, it often happens that illustrations have complex shapes, or are surrounded by text on more than one side, thus making the application of such a simple technique insufficient (see Fig. 1a for an example).

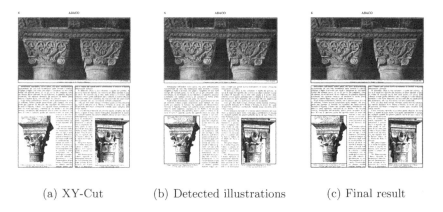

(a) XY-Cut   (b) Detected illustrations   (c) Final result

Fig. 1. The page layout segmentation pipeline. First the Recursive XY-Cut algorithm is applied to detect candidate regions inside the page; then, illustrations are detected using local autocorrelation features. A second application of the XY-Cut algorithm gives the final segmentation.

To complete the layout segmentation phase, we therefore apply an additional step whose aim is to detect illustrations (and their corresponding boundaries) inside the page, and which is inspired by the algorithm proposed in [12].

The core assumption of this step is that local autocorrelation statistics are sufficient to distinguish between text and illustration. The autocorrelation matrix of a region, indeed, is an effective feature for finding repeating patterns and is particularly suited in this case since textual textures have a pronounced orientation that heavily differs from that of illustrations. The original image is subdivided into square blocks of size $n \times n$, and for each block the autocorrelation matrix $C(k,l)$, with $k,l \in [-n/2, n/2]$, is computed. Then, the autocorrelation matrix is encoded into a directional histogram $w(\cdot)$, in which each bin contains the sum of the pixels along that direction. Formally,

$$w(\theta) = \sum_{r \in (0, n/2]} C(r \cos\theta, r \sin\theta) \tag{1}$$

We compute the directional histogram in the range $\theta \in [0, 180°]$, and quantize θ with a step of $1°$, and r with a step of 1 pixel. The histogram is then concatenated with the vertical and horizontal projections of the autocorrelation matrix, to enhance the repeating pattern of the text lines. The resulting descriptor is fed to a two-class SVM classifier with RBF kernel, trained to distinguish between blocks of text and blocks of illustrations.

Given a region segmented by XY-Cut, we classify each block inside the region as text or illustration, and identify the boundaries of illustrations by finding the connected components created by illustration blocks. Once illustrations have been detected, XY-Cut is again applied on a temporary image where illustrations are removed. The final result of the layout segmentation process is the union of the illustration regions and of the regions found by the second execution of XY-Cut. Figure 1 gives an example of the overall process.

3.2   Table Detection

We developed a simple yet effective method for table detection which is based on the Hough transform [10] and heuristic rules. The Hough transform allows to automatically detect lines in an image, and it is therefore appropriate to detect structures like tables which contain vertical and horizontal lines.

The Hough transform finds objects within a certain class of shapes using a voting procedure, which is carried out in a parameter space from which object candidates are obtained as local maxima, in a so-called accumulator space that is explicitly constructed by the algorithm (Fig. 2).

A straight line in the image space can be expressed as:

- $y = mx + b$ in the Cartesian coordinate system, with the associated point (m, b) in the parameter space
- $r = x \cos\theta + y \sin\theta$ in the Polar coordinate system with the associated point (r, θ), where r is the distance from the origin to the closest point on the

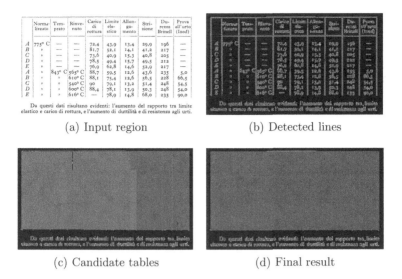

(a) Input region   (b) Detected lines

(c) Candidate tables   (d) Final result

Fig. 2. The table detection pipeline.

straight line, and θ is the angle between the x axis and the line connecting the origin with that closest point.

The Polar coordinate system permits to overcome the problem of vertical lines, which would rise unbounded values of the slope parameter m in the Cartesian one. Given a single point, the set of all straight lines passing through that point corresponds to a sinusoidal curve in the (r, θ) plane, which is unique to that point. A set of two or more points that form a straight line will produce sinusoids which cross at (r, θ) for that line. In general, a line can be detected by finding the number of intersections between curves: the more curves intersect, the more likely is that a line may be found with those parameters. A threshold can be defined on the minimum number of intersections needed to detect a line.

The proposed algorithm starts detecting all the lines of the image region, using the implementation proposed in [20], and selects the most promising ones using some heuristics; finally, recursively, it uses the detected lines to build a set of rectangles merging those that have an intersection. In this way, starting from small adjacent table pieces (often separated due to inaccuracies of the Hough Transform), the table area is detected.

The pseudo-code for the table detector is provided in Algorithm 1.

It should be noted that, even if the goal of the system is the attribution of meaning to a region which comes from the Recursive XY-Cut, the proposed algorithm is able to detect multiple table structures in a whole page, ensuring that each structure found is the largest (piece of) table which contains all other detected pieces of (the same) table.

Even though the results of the Hough Transform depend on its parameters values and on the properties of the original image, the implementation of the

---

Algorithm 1. Table detection

Lines ← HoughLines(parameters);
/* each line identified by two points (x_i, y_i) and (x_j, y_j) */
Horizontal_lines ← FindHorizontals(lines);
/* $x_i \neq x_j \wedge y_i = y_j$ */
Vertical_lines ← FindVerticals(lines);
/* $x_i = x_j \wedge y_i \neq y_j$ */

tables = { };
forall the $hl \in Horizontal\_lines$ **do**
  if $\exists\ vl \in Vertical\_lines : vl \cap hl \neq \emptyset \wedge length(vl) > lenght(l)\ \forall\ l \in \{l : l \in$
  $Vertical\_lines,\ l \cap hl \neq \emptyset\}$ **then**
   | rect ← BoundingRectangle(hl,vl)
  end
  while $\exists\ t \in tables : t \cap rect \neq \emptyset$ **do**
   | tables = tables-{ t };
   | rect ← merge(rect,t);
  end
  tables ← rect;
end

---

proposed algorithm is scalable and permits great customization: in particular, the method which finds the longest vertical line that intersects an horizontal one (candidate to be a side of the rectangle) permits to specify:

– the minimum number of vertical lines which must intersect an horizontal one for a candidate horizontal line to be considered
– the minimum length of the maximum vertical line which must intersect an horizontal one
– the offset (number of pixels) for considering an horizontal line intersecting a vertical one
– the offset (number of pixels) for considering a vertical line intersecting an horizontal one

3.3   Content Classification

The classification step is necessary to assign each region to a specific class. In particular, in addition to tables, we consider six different classes: text, images, charts and graphs, formulas, scores, and borderless tables. An example of each class is given in Fig. 3.

In order to classify each region, dense SIFT descriptors are computed using the Harris-Laplace detector. This step results in a variable number of 128-dimensional descriptors for each region. To obtain a representation for a region, with fixed size, we summarize SIFT descriptors using the Bag-of-Words technique. To include spatial information into the feature vector we also add the position, the dimensions and the aspect ratio of the image bounding box. A SVM classifier with RBF

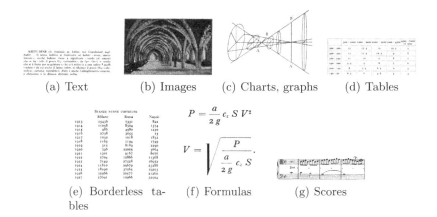

(a) Text   (b) Images   (c) Charts, graphs   (d) Tables

(e) Borderless ta-   (f) Formulas   (g) Scores
bles

Fig. 3. We consider seven different content categories: text, images, charts and graphs, tables, borderless tables, formulas, and scores.

kernel is then trained using the feature vectors described earlier. The output of this classifier is the class that will be assigned to the region.

3.4   JSON Description

The output of the overall pipeline is a structured JSON description. For each page, indeed, a JSON file is created with the corresponding OCR results for each text entry and with all the illustrations found inside the page. Moreover, the proposed JSON schema allows textual entries to be linked together. This can be particularly beneficial in the case of encyclopedias, in which each paragraph belongs to a lemma.

An example of the JSON description is reported in Listing 1.1. The `entries` element contains all the textual entries of the page. Each entry contains the body of the paragraph, the column the entry belongs to (in case of multi-column documents), a boolean `is_tabbed` that indicates whether the first line of the paragraph is tabbed or not, and a reference to the lemma. In case the considered text entry is a lemma, the `opening` element is used set a lemma identifier, which can in turn be used to reference other paragraphs, using the `lemma_ref` element. Each text entry also contains the location of the text region inside the page.

Graphical elements are instead grouped into the `graphics` element. Each of them is described by its own caption, position and size inside the page, and contain a reference to the lemma it belongs to. It also contains a `type` field which reports the category of the graphic element, obtained with the content classification pipeline.

3.5   Annotation and Visualization Interfaces

Two more tools have been developed, the first one is an annotation tool which allows a user to visualize the result of the analysis process and, if needed, allows

```json
{
    "filename":"0006_00_T_V01.K_scaled.png",
    "layout": {
        "entries": [
            {
                "body":"Sottilissimo nell'ordine ionico greco, era quivi ordinariamente...",
                "centered": false,
                "closing": {
                    "author":"",
                    "selected": false,
                    "sign":"",
                    "valid": false
                },
                "col": 0,
                "is_tabbed": true,
                "lemma_ref": {
                    "major":"ABACO",
                    "minor":"",
                    "pageNumber": 5,
                },
                "opening": {
                    "major":"",
                    "minor":"",
                },
                "par": {
                    "rect": {
                        "height": 137,
                        "width": 562,
                        "x": 125,
                        "y": 835
                    },
                },
            },
        ],
        "graphics": [
            {
                "caption": {
                    "rect": {
                        "height": 24,
                        "width": 347,
                        "x": 524,
                        "y": 788
                    },
                    "text":"CAPITELLI DELL'ATRIO DI S. MARCO A VENEZIA",
                },
                "type":'IMAGE',
                "hascaption": true,
                "image": {
                    "rect": {
                        "height": 639,
                        "width": 1162,
                        "x": 123,
                        "y": 150
                    },
                },
                "lemma_ref": {
                    "major":"",
                    "minor":"",
                    "pageNumber": 5,
                    "x": 0,
                    "y": 0
                },
            },
        ],
    }
}
```

Listing 1.1. JSON Description of a sample page with one text entry and one graphic element

for modifications to the segmentation results. This tool is useful for many reasons: it makes the creation of an annotated dataset possible for all the subsequent learning and evaluation processes and allows users to apply corrections to the processed data. A screenshot of the annotation tool is reported in Fig. 4.

The second tool is a visualization interface used to present and browse the content of the encyclopedia, making all the information easily accessible. This tool lets the users access the content at different levels and from different points of view, it's possible to browse the encyclopedia page by page, lemma by lemma

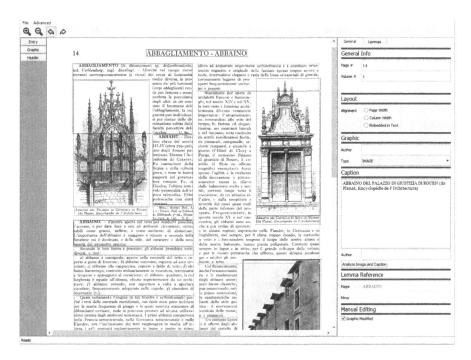

Fig. 4. The main view of the annotation tool. A processed page is visible on the left while on the right all the information relative to a particular page element are displayed

(a)   (b)

Fig. 5. Displaying a page in the visualization interface. The page content is highlighted in blue when the cursor hovers on it. (Color figure online)

and image by image in each volume. The full text is also accessible and readable in HTML format. Hovering the cursor over a page shows the underlying extracted content and double clicking on it takes the user to a different view which displays the digitized version of the document. The visualization tool is visible in Fig. 5.

4   Experimental Evaluation

The performance evaluation of layout analysis algorithms can be conducted using two different approaches, namely pixel-level and region-level. The first evaluates how each pixel has been classified in a single page comparing the class assigned to the pixel with the class assigned to the same pixel in the ground truth annotation, the accuracy for a single page is then calculated as the percentage of correctly classified pixels. A region-level approach tries instead to find the best matching between areas of a page that are semantically coherent, called regions, between the analyzed page and the ground truth annotation. Once the matching process is completed, the accuracy value for a single page is calculated with regard to the matching quality. In both cases a cumulative accuracy measure can be calculated as the mean accuracy over multiple pages.

Since we use a top-down page segmentation algorithm in our method and the final output of the page processing pipeline consists of polygons containing pixels of a page classified of the same type, we have chosen a region-level approach to performance evaluation. We used the matching method described by Phillips and Chhabra [21], which has also been used in the ICDAR 2003 page segmentation competition [1]. We used the suggested *acceptance threshold* and *rejection threshold*, respectively 0.85 and 0.05, and we used intersection over union as a similarity function to determine match scores. To evaluate the classification performances we compared the results against the ground truth annotations creating a confusion matrix and calculating accuracy values, one for each class and a cumulative one.

All our tests have been conducted on the first volume of the "Enciclopedia Treccani" (http://www.treccani.it), which was published in 1929 and is composed of 999 pages. The block size n was set to 64, and we used the Tesseract OCR [23]. Considering the Table detector algorithm, all the parameters, both for the Hough Transform and for the heuristic rules, have been set empirically performing several tests on the first 20 tables of the dataset.

Concerning the page segmentation algorithm step we have compared three different algorithms, the standard XY-Cut, the Whitespace Analysis algorithm, proposed by Baird in [3], and, finally our method. Results are shown in Table 1 and it is clear how our method performs largely better than the other two.

Classification results are shown in Tables 2 and 3.

Table 1. Page segmentation experimental results.

	XY-Cut	Whitespace analysis	Our method
Accuracy	61.8%	71.4%	93.8%

Table 2. Classification accuracies

Class	# Elements	Accuracy
Images	1102	0.71
Graphics	145	0.66
Formulas	535	0.77
Tables	91	0.99
Scores	132	0.08
Borderless tables	142	0.10
Text	13628	0.96
TOTAL	**15775**	**0.92**

Table 3. Confusion matrix for classification results of the SVM classifier.

			Truth			
	I	G	F	S	BT	Txt
I	74.8%	13.2%	5.2%	0.8%	0.8%	5.3%
G	6.6%	70.6%	11.0%	1.5%	1.5%	8.8%
F	3.2%	4.5%	77.4%	0%	2.1%	12.8%
S	16.0%	6.4%	62.4%	8.8%	1.6%	4.8%
BT	4.1%	7.4%	37.7%	0%	11.5%	39.3%
Txt	0.2%	0.3%	1.8%	0%	0.3%	97.3%

(Prediction, rows: I, G, F, S, BT, Txt)

5 Conclusion

We presented a complete pipeline for layout analysis and content classification in digitalized documents. The layout analysis algorithm is based on the Recursive XY-Cut and an SVM-aided illustration detection, while the content classification pipeline builds on the Hough transform for table classification and on local features for the classification of images, scores, formulas and charts. The final output is a JSON description, which can in turn be used by two tools, useful for the display and correction of analyzed data. Experimental results showed the effectiveness of our method when tested on the first volume of the "Enciclopedia Treccani".

References

1. Antonacopoulos, A., Gatos, B., Karatzas, D.: ICDAR 2003 page segmentation competition. In: ICDAR, p. 688. IEEE (2003)
2. Appiani, E., Cesarini, F., Colla, A.M., Diligenti, M., Gori, M., Marinai, S., Soda, G.: Automatic document classification and indexing in high-volume applications. Int. J. Doc. Anal. Recogn. 4(2), 69–83 (2001)
3. Baird, H., Jones, S., Fortune, S.: Image segmentation by shape-directed covers. In: International Conference on Pattern Recognition, vol. 1, pp. 820–825, June 1990

4. Baraldi, L., Grana, C., Cucchiara, R.: A deep siamese network for scene detection in broadcast videos. In: ACM International Conference on Multimedia, pp. 1199–1202. ACM (2015)
5. Bertini, M., Del Bimbo, A., Serra, G., Torniai, C., Cucchiara, R., Grana, C., Vezzani, R.: Dynamic pictorial ontologies for video digital libraries annotation. In: IEEE MultiMedia Magazine, pp. 42–51. ACM (2009)
6. Cesarini, F., Lastri, M., Marinai, S., Soda, G.: Encoding of modified XY trees for document classification. In: Proceedings of the Sixth International Conference on Document Analysis and Recognition, pp. 1131–1136. IEEE (2001)
7. Chen, K., Yin, F., Liu, C.L.: Hybrid page segmentation with efficient whitespace rectangles extraction and grouping. In: 12th International Conference on Document Analysis and Recognition (ICDAR), pp. 958–962. IEEE (2013)
8. Coüasnon, B., Lemaitre, A.: Recognition of tables and forms. In: Doermann, D., Tombre, K. (eds.) Handbook of Document Image Processing and Recognition, pp. 647–677. Springer, London (2014)
9. Mauro, N., Ferilli, S., Esposito, F.: Learning to Recognize Critical Cells in Document Tables. In: Agosti, M., Esposito, F., Ferilli, S., Ferro, N. (eds.) IRCDL 2012. CCIS, vol. 354, pp. 105–116. Springer, Heidelberg (2013). doi:10.1007/978-3-642-35834-0_12
10. Duda, R.O., Hart, P.E.: Use of the Hough transformation to detect lines and curves in pictures. Commun. ACM **15**(1), 11–15 (1972)
11. Esposito, F., Malerba, D., Lisi, F.A.: Machine learning for intelligent processing of printed documents. J. Intell. Inf. Syst. **14**(2–3), 175–198 (2000)
12. Grana, C., Serra, G., Manfredi, M., Coppi, D., Cucchiara, R.: Layout analysis and content enrichment of digitized books. Multimed. Tools Appl. **75**(7), 3879–3900 (2016)
13. Ha, J., Haralick, R.M., Phillips, I.T.: Recursive XY cut using bounding boxes of connected components. In: Proceedings of the Third International Conference on Document Analysis and Recognition, vol. 2, pp. 952–955. IEEE (1995)
14. Kaur, S., Sharma, D.V.: Table structure identification from document images: a survey. Int. J. Innov. Adv. Comput. Sci. **4**, 581–585 (2015)
15. Kise, K., Sato, A., Iwata, M.: Segmentation of page images using the area Voronoi diagram. Comput. Vis. Image Underst. **70**(3), 370–382 (1998)
16. Lazzara, G., Levillain, R., Géraud, T., Jacquelet, Y., Marquegnies, J., Crépin-Leblond, A.: The scribo module of the olena platform: a free software framework for document image analysis. In: 2011 International Conference on Document Analysis and Recognition (ICDAR), pp. 252–258. IEEE (2011)
17. Liu, Y., Mitra, P., Giles, C.L.: A fast preprocessing method for table boundary detection: narrowing down the sparse lines using solely coordinate information. In: The Eighth IAPR International Workshop on Document Analysis Systems, pp. 431–438. IEEE (2008)
18. Mandal, S., Chowdhury, S.P., Das, A.K., Chanda, B.: Detection and segmentation of tables and math-zones from document images. In: Proceedings of the 2006 ACM Symposium on Applied Computing. SAC 2006, pp. 841–846. ACM (2006)
19. Mandal, S., Chowdhury, S., Das, A., Chanda, B.: A simple and effective table detection system from document images. Int. J. Doc. Anal. Recogn. (IJDAR) **8**(2–3), 172–182 (2006)
20. Matas, J., Galambos, C., Kittler, J.: Robust detection of lines using the progressive probabilistic Hough transform. Comput. Vis. Image Underst. **78**(1), 119–137 (2000). http://dx.doi.org/10.1006/cviu.1999.0831

21. Phillips, I.T., Chhabra, A.K.: Empirical performance evaluation of graphics recognition systems. IEEE Trans. Pattern Anal. Mach. Intell. **21**(9), 849–870 (1999)
22. Sebastiani, F.: Machine learning in automated text categorization. ACM Comput. Surv. (CSUR) **34**(1), 1–47 (2002)
23. Smith, R.: An overview of the Tesseract OCR engine. In: International Conference on Document Analysis and Recognition, pp. 629–633. IEEE (2007)
24. Zanibbi, R., Blostein, D., Cordy, J.: A survey of table recognition. Doc. Anal. Recogn. **7**(1), 1–16 (2004)

A Study on the Classification
of Layout Components for Newspapers

Stefano Ferilli[1]([⊠]), Floriana Esposito[1], and Domenico Redavid[2]

[1] University of Bari, Bari, Italy
{stefano.ferilli,floriana.esposito}@uniba.it
[2] Artificial Brain S.r.l., Bari, Italy
redavid@abrain.it

Abstract. While nowadays most newspapers are born-digital (typeset directly in PDF), up to a few years ago they were only available in printed form. Digitizing the paper artifact to make it available in digital libraries yields a sequence of raster images of the pages that make up the documents. Such images consist of just matrices of pixels, and carry no explicit information about their organization into meaningful higher-level components. So, in the perspective of automatically extracting useful information from the newspapers and indexing them for future retrieval, a necessary preliminary task is to identify the layout components that are meaningful from a human interpretation viewpoint.

Unfortunately, approaches proposed in the literature for automatic layout analysis are often ineffective on newspapers, because of the much more complex layout of this kind of documents compared, e.g., to books and scientific papers. This work specifically focuses on the classification of layout blocks according to their content type. It investigates on the adaptation of an existing approach, that has been successfully applied to documents having standard layout, to the case of newspapers, working on the description features and set of classes. The modified approach was implemented and embedded in the DoMInUS system for document processing and management. Experimental results aimed at its evaluation are reported and commented.

Keywords: Layout analysis · Document representation · Document rendering

1 Introduction

In addition to book libraries, important information concerning our culture and history is preserved in newspaper and periodical libraries. As for the former, the current digital age is strongly interested in building digital versions of the latter, as well. This would significantly improve not just the availability and spread of the collected items, but first and most important might provide dramatic advantages in the retrieval of useful information, using suitably adapted versions of the search engine algorithms that have been developed in the recent decades.

© Springer International Publishing AG 2017
M. Agosti et al. (Eds.): IRCDL 2016, CCIS 701, pp. 166–178, 2017.
DOI: 10.1007/978-3-319-56300-8_15

Nowadays, most newspapers provide for a digital edition that typically consists in the PDF version of the paper artifact that is sold in newsstands. Actually, these documents are born-digital, and the printed version is just a consequence of the original PDF file that was typeset by the editors. For several aspects, this provides a very desirable input for the existing automatic indexing procedures. Up to a few decades ago, however, typesetting was not digital, and the only available source for legacy newspapers is their printed version, that is to be digitized. Of course, digitization returns a sequence of images of the pages that make up the documents, where the basic bricks are just pixels, and no explicit information is provided about their organization into meaningful higher-level components.

Hence, the strong interest of the community in effective and efficient ways to extract such components and then for classifying them, so that they can undergo different processing depending on their type. The former step is the task of *segmentation* techniques, while the latter requires the availability of suitable models that the system may automatically apply. Manually building such models is significantly complex and sometimes impossible, due to the huge semantic gap separating the pixel level from the human perception level. So, there is a need for automatic approaches that can learn predictive classification models.

While interesting results were obtained by researchers in the past decades for documents having a more standard layout, such as books and scientific papers, solving this problem in newspapers poses new and significant challenges, due to the very complex layout and kind of layout components that they involve. First of all, they often do not use Manhattan layout. Also, they use extremely different character sizes. They are made up of several 'patches', each made up of related content blocks, but completely unrelated to each other. Particularly some kinds of newspapers, such as sports newspapers, provide additional difficulties, such as titles or articles in reverse (white characters on colored background), images with irregular contours that overlap text, and the like. Figure 1 shows a sample newspaper page, where many of these challenging peculiarities are evident.

Existing solutions available in the literature, that proved effective in handling documents having standard layout, cannot be straightforwardly applied to this kind of documents, and require suitable adaptations. The aim of this work is investigating which adaptations to the these solutions may help in handling the following aspects:

1. use of colors;
2. text blocks written on background different than the main background;
3. frequent interleaving of very different text font sizes.

Specifically, extensions of both the description features and the set of classes are studied. The performance of the adapted approach on newspapers is checked for determining its strengths and weaknesses, and for drawing conclusions about how to further improve it. For this evaluation, the proposed approach was embedded in a wider system for document processing and management, DoMInUS, that provided tools to carry out several preliminary and subsequent layout analysis tasks.

Fig. 1. Sample newspaper page

The remainder of this document is organized as follows. In the next section, the background and relevant related work for this paper is presented. Then, Sects. 3 and 4 describe how the original approach to layout analysis and component classification was modified to deal with newspapers. Section 5 provides an evaluation of the proposed approach. Finally, Sect. 6 concludes the paper and outlines future work issues.

2   Background and Related Work

The full range of steps involved in document processing and management can be partitioned into two broad groups, yielding two macro-steps aimed at the following objectives: *Document Image Understanding* and *Document Understanding*. The following taxonomy reports the macro- or micro-steps that are specifically relevant to this work.

Document Image Understanding is concerned with determining the physical structure of the document, from both a syntactic and a semantic viewpoint (*layout structure* and *logical structure*, respectively). Among other tasks, it is in charge of identifying the document class (e.g., book, scientific paper, bill, newspaper, etc.) and the role of its components (e.g., title, author, abstract, etc. in a scientific paper). It involves the task of

Layout Analysis. Starting from the basic components that are present in the source document, it identifies the high-level geometrical structure of the document, made up of frames that may be semantically relevant to the reader. Among others, it includes the following two sub-tasks.

    Segmentation: Starting from the basic components that are present in the source document, it identifies the blocks having homogeneous and (hopefully) strictly related content.

    Component Classification: Labels each block returned by segmentation with the type of content it includes.

Document Understanding. Aims at understanding and managing the information content of the document. This includes identifying its topic, extracting relevant information from it, and indexing it for future retrieval.

Of course, Document Image Understanding is very relevant to Document Understanding, in that it provides the ground on which the latter works. So, the quality of the outcome of the former is extremely important, since it may determine the quality of the outcome of the latter, or even its feasibility. In turn, a fundamental task in layout analysis is *segmentation*, that is specifically concerned with document pages represented as images. Given the source (raster or vector) document page representation, it returns a partition of its area into portions of content representing significant pieces of the layout (*blocks*) that should be consistent and significant (and possibly meaningful enough to deserve further and specialized processing).

Several segmentation methods have been proposed in the literature. Here we are interested in algorithms that work on digitized images directly at the pixel-level, ignoring any possible structure of pixel aggregates. These strategies aim at obtaining directly high-level components, without first identifying intermediate pixel aggregates that can play a role in the document (e.g., single characters or straight lines). Some methods are based on *Run Length Smoothing*. Given a sequence of black and white pixels, a *run* is defined as a sequence of adjacent pixels of the same kind (usually foreground), delimited by pixels of the opposite kind (usually background). The run length is the number of pixels in a run, and 'smoothing' a run means changing the color of its pixels so that they become of the same color as the pixels delimiting the run. A classical and efficient segmentation technique of this kind is the *Run Length Smoothing Algorithm* (RLSA) [12]. RLSA identifies runs of background pixels in the document image and fills them with foreground pixels whenever they are shorter than a given threshold. Much work in the literature is based on RLSA, exploiting it or trying to improve its performance by modifying it [2,9,10]. RLSA has some shortcomings. First, the presence of thin black lines produced on the border of the image by scanning or photocopying, may cause the horizontal smoothing to cover most of the margin of the page. Another shortcoming of this technique lays in its inability to handle documents having non-Manhattan layout (i.e., a layout in which blocks are not always separated by perpendicular background rectangles). The assessment of suitable thresholds is a hot problem, directly affecting the overall effectiveness of the technique.

RLSO [5] is a variant of the RLSA, that works as follows:

1. horizontal smoothing of the image, carried out by rows with threshold t_h;
2. vertical smoothing of the image, carried out by columns with threshold t_v;
3. logical OR of the images obtained in steps 1 and 2.

Each connected component in the resulting image is considered a frame, and exploited as a mask to filter the original image through a logical AND operation in order to obtain the frame content. Compared to RLSA, RLSO is able to handle also non-Manhattan layouts. It involves one step less, and requires shorter thresholds (and hence fills less runs) to merge original connected components (e.g., characters) into larger ones (e.g., frames). Thus, it is more efficient than RLSA, and can be further sped up by avoiding the third step and applying vertical smoothing directly on the horizontally smoothed image obtained from the first step. This does not significantly affect, and may even improve, the quality of the result. However, the OR causes every merge of components to be irreversible, which can be a problem when logically different components are very close to each other and might be erroneously merged if the threshold is too high. Conversely, too low thresholds might result in an excessively fragmented layout. Thus, as for RLSA, the choice of proper horizontal/vertical thresholds is a very important issue for effectiveness.

The blocks singled out by segmentation may contain graphical or textual information. To properly submit them to further processing (e.g., text might be acquired using an Optical Character Recognition system, while graphical components could be input to an image processing system), their kind of content must be identified. Interesting results for this task, on A4 document images whose resolution was scaled down from 300 dpi to 75 dpi [1], were obtained by applying supervised Machine Learning techniques to distinguish text, horizontal or vertical lines, raster images and vector graphics based on several numeric features extracted from each block as suggested by [11].

Specifically, decision tree learning [8] was exploited. A *decision tree* is a branching structure in which the root is the starting point, each internal node corresponds to a test over an attribute, each branch represents a possible outcome (or set of outcomes) for the test, and the leaves bear class information. Given an observation (in this case, a content block) described according to the same attributes as the tree, starting from the root and routing the tree by repeatedly carrying out the tests in the nodes and following the branch labelled with the corresponding results, one gets the class to be assigned to the observation at hand (in this case, the type of content in the block). Machine Learning techniques for automatically building decision trees starting from a set of observations already tagged with the correct classes (called the *training set*) usually place in the nodes that are closer to the root the attributes that turn out to be more discriminative for partitioning the training set instances into different classes, according to the outcome of class-driven information measures applied to the training set.

DoMInUS (acronym for Document Management Intelligent Universal System) [3,4] is a framework for document processing and management that embeds several Artificial Intelligence techniques to automatize the whole document life-cycle spanning from its submission to a digital library up to its retrieval and fruition by end users. It provides a variety of tools for the various steps involved in these tasks. Here, we will focus on the Pre-processing and Layout Analysis steps, that are in charge of identifying the high-level geometrical structure of the document.

3 Layout Analysis

Given a color raster image representing a newspaper page, we devised the following procedure:

1. pre-processing:
   (a) binarization, used to filter out noise from the image (iterative global thresholding);
   (b) **chromatic component separation**, used to divide the image in its relevant color components;
   (c) skew correction, used to compensate for acquisition problems.
2. *classification of layout components* **in each color layer**:
   (a) text
   (b) lines
   (c) **non-standard background**
   (d) images
3. **text blocks identification**:
   (a) **removal of non-textual components**
   (b) **extraction of text from non-standard background**
   (c) *text blocks aggregation* using RLSO

Compared to the standard procedure provided by DoMInUS, steps in bold are those specifically introduced for dealing with newspapers, and steps in italics are those that were already present but were changed for dealing with newspapers.

Step 1b allows to deal with peculiarity #1 in the Introduction. The chromatic components of interest for our purposes are typically artificially colored parts of the page, where halftones are not relevant. For this reason, the existing procedure available in DoMInUS was modified so as to ignore the saturation component of colors. The result is a sequence of filtered versions of the page, such that: the first one contains the background (which in the following will be considered white); the second one contains the graylevel pixels; and the other contain portions with other colors. The reverse of the background layer corresponds to a color-independent binarization of the document page.

Step 2c allows to deal with peculiarity #2 in the Introduction. This is obtained by taking all connected components in a layer that were classified

Fig. 2. Partial processing steps of the sample newspaper page

as Images, reversing them and running again the classifier to see whether the reversed block is classified as Text.

Step 3a modifies the overall binarized image by removing all components classified as non-text in the various color layers. Then, step 3b adds the text found on non-standard background, obtained by turning the original non-standard background into standard background, and representing the text as standard foreground. At this point, the binarized image includes only textual components on standard background (see Fig. 2 on the left). Now, step 3c performs segmentation on this input to obtain aggregate text blocks. Due to the non-Manhattan layout used by newspapers, the RLSO approach was used for this purpose. Note that the segmentation step is exploited here in a very different way than on other documents: first, it is applied as a last step, while on standard documents it is applied before classifying the type of layout blocks; second, it is applied on a filtered image containing only text, instead of the overall binarized image; third, it is applied iteratively to obtain block aggregations that are compliant to peculiarity #3 in the Introduction (the detailed procedure for this step is outside the scope of this paper). The outcome for the sample document is shown in Fig. 2 on the right.

4   Component Type Classification

The decision trees learned in the approach to layout components classification proposed in [11] are based on the following features:

1. block height (h);
2. block width (w);

3. block area $(a = w \times h)$;
4. block eccentricity (w/h);
5. number of black pixels in the block (b);
6. number of black-white transitions in the block rows (t);
7. percentage of black pixels in the block (b/a);
8. average number of black pixels per black-white transition (b/t);
9. short run emphasis $(F1)$;
10. long run emphasis $(F2)$;
11. extra long run emphasis $(F3)$.

Measures F1, F2 and F3, in particular, are to be interpreted as follows: F1 gets large values for blocks containing many short runs, which happens when the text is made up of small-sized characters (e.g., in newspaper articles); F2 gets large values for blocks containing many runs having medium length, which happens when quite large characters are used (e.g., newspaper subtitles); finally, F3 gets large values for blocks containing few runs, all of which very long, which means that the characters used for writing the text have a very large size (this is typical in the main titles of newspaper pages). F3 requires to properly set two parameters, T_1 and T_2.

These features were used in both [1,11] to learn decision trees for classifying the kind of layout blocks found in documents, with the following set of classes:

Text a group of alphanumeric characters or symbols (even just one character or symbol).

Horizontal Line

Vertical Line

Graphic an artificial image (e.g., one that might have been produced using vector graphics tools).

Image a (possibly halftone) raster image.

Mixed a combination of text and image(s), but clearly disjoint (text within images would fall in the Image class).

Undefined none of the above (e.g., a portion of an image, or a particularly eroded line).

[1] worked on scientific papers, while [11] specifically addressed newspapers. However, the sample newspapers shown in [11] seem not to show the complexities that this work aims at addressing.

A first consequence of these challenging peculiarities reported in the Introduction is that it is quite difficult to set the segmentation algorithm so that the resulting blocks correspond to semantically relevant components from a human perspective. Indeed, setting too high a threshold would identify titles as single blocks, but would also merge pieces of several different articles. Setting too low a threshold, on the other hand, would return several separate blocks for a single semantic component (e.g., a block for each letter in a title). Also, they do not work well with reversed text, and are not always able to handle non-Manhattan layouts and images that overlap text or are interleaved with text.

In such cases, a cautious approach is advisable, that prefers returning an over-segmented set of blocks (i.e., one in which a single semantic component is split into several blocks) rather than returning and under-segmented one (i.e., one in which semantically unrelated components have been merged), leaving to a subsequent post-processing step the task of merging different related blocks.

This landscape suggested to extend the set of features, adding the following:

Spread measures the spatial distribution of black pixels in a pattern, according to the following formula [7]:

$$s = \frac{n}{b} \cdot \min(w, h)^2$$

which is inverse to the number of black pixels b (because raising the density reduces the distance among pixels), and proportional to the number of black runs n (because the more the runs, the more fragmented the black zones) and to the area of square sections, obtained as follows:

$$a \cdot sq = w \cdot h \cdot \frac{\min(w, h)}{\max(w, h)} = \min(w, h)^2$$

(where $sq = \frac{\min(w,h)}{\max(w,h)}$ expresses how 'square' the block is).

Number of components useful because we expect that blocks having large area and many components are of type text, while blocks having small area and 1 component are of type character.

Number of black-white transitions in the block columns that provides a complementary perspective with respect to feature #6.

Extra long run emphasis ($F3$) with parameters $T_1 = 30$ and $T_2 = 5$

Extra long run emphasis ($F3$) with parameters $T_1 = 5$ and $T_2 = 5$

The parameters for $F3$ were determined as the most appropriate for the peculiarities of newspapers, based on both the meaning of the parameter in the feature and the results of several tests with a range of different values.

We also tried to extend the set of classes of interest, by splitting the class Text into **Text**, **Character**, **Reverse Text** and **Reverse Character**. Indeed, it seemed likely that single characters are characterized by very different features than compound texts, and that the values characterizing reversed items are in some way complementary to those characterizing normal items.

5   Evaluation

To evaluate the modified approach, a baseline performance was obtained on a dataset including 30 images of newspapers' first pages, some in color and some in black and white, yielding 789 connected components of various kind, as reported in Table 1. There were no instances of graphic or diagonal line, but we think that these classes are meaningful and thus should be still taken into account in future investigations. A 10-fold cross-validation run on this dataset using the decision tree learner J48 provided by the WEKA suite [6] returned the results reported in Table 1 (the last row reports the weighted average for performance columns, and the total for the number of components). The figures show that the worst class for accuracy is Mixed, possibly because instances of this class have very subtle (and mostly semantic) differences compared to instances of class Image, especially when they include text. Indeed, some newspapers use text superimposed to images. Based on this classification performance, the layout analysis task on an additional set of 45 newspapers reached the following results:

Precision	Recall	F-measure	Accuracy
0.885	0.909	0.897	0.784

Then, we ran additional experiments aimed at investigating the effect of adding new features and classes to the learning problem, as discussed in the previous section. Due to unavailability of the previous dataset, we ran these experiments on a different set made up of 10 newspapers. Statistics on the number of connected components in the dataset, and experimental results, are reported in Tables 2 and 3. All experiments were run using the extended set of features, but changing the set of classes. We tried the same set of classes as the baseline (see Table 3), where class Text included both text and single characters, both normal and reversed. Then, we tried to add a separate class for reversed text only (see Table 2 bottom). Finally, we added specific classes for text and characters, either normal or reversed (see Table 2 top). Looking at the figures, we can see that the new settings are all much better than the baseline, and that different settings yield mixed performances for the different classes, in that some are better on some classes and some are better on others. However, the overall results in terms of weighted averaged F-measure clearly show that the original setting, with no specific classes for characters and reverse text, is significantly better than the others. This suggests that the really relevant change in setting was the extension to the set of features. Looking at the learned models, it is interesting to note that attribute 'extra long run emphasis' ($F3$) with thresholds $T_1 = 30$ and $T_2 = 5$ is never considered by the models.

Table 1. Baseline experimental results for component type classification

Class	TP rate	FP rate	Precision	Recall	F-measure	Instances
Text	0.757	0.172	0.748	0.757	0.752	317
Horizontal line	0.916	0.013	0.906	0.916	0.911	95
Vertical line	0.857	0.004	0.923	0.857	0.889	42
Image	0.655	0.112	0.607	0.655	0.63	165
Mixed	0.368	0.04	0.42	0.368	0.393	57
Undefined	0.646	0.047	0.695	0.646	0.67	113
Overall	0.716	0.104	0.715	0.716	0.715	789

Table 2. Experimental results with additional features and classes

Class	TP rate	FP rate	Precision	Recall	F-measure	Instances
Text	0.875	0.103	0.848	0.875	0.861	376
Horizontal line	0.958	0.004	0.968	0.958	0.963	96
Vertical line	0.974	0.001	0.974	0.974	0.974	39
Image	0.845	0.056	0.801	0.845	0.822	200
Mixed	0.238	0.014	0.278	0.238	0.256	21
Undefined	0.741	0.033	0.748	0.741	0.744	112
Reverse Text	0.432	0.022	0.487	0.432	0.458	44
Character	0.680	0.011	0.773	0.680	0.723	50
Reverse character	0.143	0.002	0.333	0.143	0.200	7
Overall	0.812	0.059	0.804	0.812	0.807	945
Class	TP rate	FP rate	Precision	Recall	F-measure	Instances
Text	0.862	0.130	0.844	0.862	0.852	426
Horizontal line	0.958	0.004	0.968	0.958	0.963	96
Vertical line	0.949	0.002	0.949	0.949	0.949	39
Image	0.850	0.066	0.776	0.850	0.811	200
Mixed	0.238	0.011	0.333	0.238	0.278	21
Undefined	0.714	0.024	0.800	0.714	0.755	112
Reverse text	0.333	0.031	0.387	0.333	0.354	51
Overall	0.810	0.078	0.802	0.810	0.805	945

Table 3. Experimental results with additional features only

Class	TP rate	FP rate	Precision	Recall	F-measure	Instances
Text	0.876	0.121	0.880	0.876	0.878	477
Horizontal line	0.948	0.004	0.968	0.948	0.958	96
Vertical line	0.974	0.006	0.884	0.974	0.927	39
Image	0.830	0.051	0.814	0.830	0.822	200
Mixed	0.286	0.015	0.300	0.286	0.293	21
Undefined	0.768	0.031	0.768	0.768	0.768	112
Overall	0.849	0.076	0.846	0.849	0.848	945

6   Discussion and Conclusions

While nowadays most newspapers are born-digital (typeset directly in PDF), up to a few decades ago they were only available in printed form. Digitizing the paper artifact to make it available in digital libraries yields a sequence of raster images of the pages that make up the documents. Such images consist of just matrices of pixels, and carry no explicit information about their organization into meaningful higher-level components. So, in the perspective of automatically extracting useful information from the newspapers and indexing them for future retrieval, a necessary preliminary task is to identify the layout components that are meaningful from a human interpretation viewpoint.

Unfortunately, even approaches specifically proposed in the literature for automatic layout analysis of newspapers, are often unable to handle particular features such as use of colors, text written on background different than the main background, and frequent interleaving of very different text font sizes. This work specifically focused on the classification of layout blocks according to their content type. It investigated on the adaptation of an existing approach, that was successfully applied to documents having standard layout, to the case of newspapers, working on the description features and set of classes. The modified approach was implemented and embedded in the DoMInUS system for document processing and management. Experimental results aimed at its evaluation were reported and commented.

Future work includes experimenting on a larger dataset, and testing the final effect that the improved block type classification approach has on the final layout analysis performance.

Acknowledgments. The authors would like to thank Vincenzo Raimondi for his help in implementing the prototype. This work was partially funded by the Italian PON 2007-2013 project PON02_00563_3489339 'Puglia@Service'.

References

1. Altamura, O., Esposito, F., Malerba, D.: Transforming paper documents into XML format with WISDOM++. Int. J. Doc. Anal. Recogn. **4**, 2–17 (2001)
2. Cao, H., Prasad, R., Natarajan, P., MacRostie, E.: Robust page segmentation based on smearing and error correction unifying top-down and bottom-up approaches. In: Proceedings of the 9th International Conference on Document Analysis and Recognition (ICDAR), vol. 1, pp. 392–396. IEEE Computer Society (2007)
3. Esposito, F., Ferilli, S., Basile, T.M.A., Di Mauro, N.: Machine learning for digital document processing: from layout analysis to metadata extraction. In: Marinai, S., Fujisawa, H. (eds.) Machine Learning in Document Analysis and Recognition. Studies in Computational Intelligence, vol. 90, pp. 105–138. Springer, Heidelberg (2008)
4. Ferilli, S.: Automatic Digital Document Processing and Management - Problems, Algorithms and Techniques. Springer, London (2011)
5. Ferilli, S., Biba, M., Esposito, F., Basile, T.M.A.: A distance-based technique for non-manhattan layout analysis. In: Proceedings of the 10th International Conference on Document Analysis Recognition (ICDAR), pp. 231–235 (2009)
6. Hall, M., Frank, E., Holmes, G., Pfahringer, B., Reutemann, P., Witten, I.H.: The weka data mining software: an update. SIGKDD Explor. Newsl. **11**(1), 10–18 (2009)
7. Mitchell, P.E., Yan, H.: Newspaper layout analysis incorporating connected component separation. Image Vis. Comput. **22**(4), 307–317 (2004)
8. Mitchell, T.M.: Machine Learning. McGraw-Hill, New York (1997)

9. Shih, F.Y., Chen, S.-S.: Adaptive document block segmentation and classification. IEEE Trans. Syst. Man Cybern. - Part B **26**(5), 797–802 (1996)
10. Sun, H.-M.: Page segmentation for Manhattan and non-manhattan layout documents via selective CRLA. In: Proceedings of the 8th International Conference on Document Analysis and Recognition (ICDAR), pp. 116–120. IEEE Computer Society (2005)
11. Wang, D., Srihari, S.N.: Classification of newspaper image blocks using texture analysis. Comput. Vis. Graph. Image Process. **47**, 327–352 (1989)
12. Wong, K.Y., Casey, R., Wahl, F.M.: Document analysis system. IBM J. Res. Dev. **26**, 647–656 (1982)

Author Index

Agosti, Maristella   85
Artini, Michele   92
Atzori, Claudio   92

Balducci, Fabrizio   153
Baraldi, Lorenzo   153
Bardi, Alessia   92
Bartalesi, Valentina   112
Braides, Orsola   3
Bressan, Federica   47

Canazza, Sergio   47
Corbelli, Andrea   153
Cucchiara, Rita   153

De Carolis, Berardina   137
De Nart, Dario   104
Degl'Innocenti, Dante   104

Esposito, Floriana   137, 166

Ferilli, Stefano   137, 166
Ferro, Nicola   85, 125

Grana, Costantino   153

La Bruzzo, Sandro   92
Leman, Marc   47

Manghi, Paolo   92
Meghini, Carlo   112
Micheletti, Andrea   20

Orio, Nicola   59, 71

Peressotti, Marco   104
Ponchia, Chiara   16

Redavid, Domenico   137, 166

Savino, Sandro   71
Sciarra, Elisabetta   3
Silvello, Gianmaria   85

Tammaro, Anna Maria   31
Tasso, Carlo   104

Vets, Tim   47

Printed in the United States
By Bookmasters